Luisa Focacci
Robert J. Mockler, PhD
Marc E. Gartenfeld

Application Service Providers in Business

Pre-publication
REVIEWS,
COMMENTARIES,
EVALUATIONS . . .

"The advent of ASPs is one of the most significant technology management developments of the past decade. This revolutionary approach will affect all organizations, large and small, in the coming years in ways we do not yet fully understand. Some firms will leverage these services for true performance and effectiveness gains while others will fail to capitalize on the opportunity. This book provides an authoritative yet readable guide to this important technology and the various factors that must be understood and considered by managers, developers, users, attorneys, and academic researchers in this field. It will prove to be a valuable resource for anyone seeking to manage an ASP implementation, to perform feasibility analyses on a potential ASP project, or to research ASPs further.

The book provides a clear introduction to all ASP categories and presents the experiences of many firms. The text focuses on understanding the various ASP models within the context of inter-firm relationships and discusses the challenges of adopting ASP services. Finally, the authors provide the reader with their vision of the future in this area, with analyses of vertical-market ASPs and ASP aggregators, for example.

The well-researched book is based on a solid evaluation of many industry reports and original sources coupled with personal experiences and interviews. The primary target readership is the technology or business manager who must learn about this important new reality; but researchers, policymakers, and others will also benefit from this required reading."

Merrill Warkentin, PhD
Professor of MIS,
Mississippi State University

More pre-publication
REVIEWS, COMMENTARIES, EVALUATIONS . . .

"This comprehensive and timely book provides a definitive guide for all those seeking to understand what application service providers (ASPs) can offer. By combining the latest detailed information with practical advice, the book enables the complexities and scope of the ASP marketplace to be properly understood.

This accessible book explains how ASPs manage delivery, integration, software support, and maintenance in a manner that fits within customers' own business contexts. A particular strength of the book lies in its combination of best practice advice and an honest and realistic view of the challenges facing ASPs. This book is an invaluable resource and a must-read item for ASPs seeking to improve their effectiveness and for customers wishing to evaluate the scope of offers and the suppliers behind them."

Sally Dibb, MSc, PhD
Reader in Marketing and Strategic Management, Warwick Business School, University of Warwick, United Kingdom

"This is a highly recommended book on application service providers (ASPs) that offers straightforward and practical how-to guidelines for decision makers on both sides of the customer/ provider relationship. ASP managers who read *Application Service Providers in Business* will benefit from hands-on advice on how to successfully manage

an ASP now and in the future. Decision makers of companies looking for a suitable ASP will also find detailed, clear-cut guidelines on how best to choose one.

The underlying business models and processes that lead to these guidelines are based on rigorous and thorough research of the ASP industry and its major players. Close attention is also paid to the very dynamic and quickly changing nature of this industry."

Dorothy G. Dologite, PhD
Professor of Computer Information Systems, Zicklin School of Business, Baruch College, City University of New York

"Wow, a book about technology that people can understand! This book is full of examples and profiles of real providers that small, medium, and large businesses can utilize to become a more lean, efficient business. We are a global market now and access to revolutionary software is no longer an exclusive right of the large firms. This book tells you the good, the bad, and the ugly about ASPs and how they can affect your business; but you have to get off the bench to take your business to the next level. Reading this book is a great start."

Jerold Hall
Business Development Manager, Amstaff Human Resources

Application Service Providers in Business

BEST BUSINESS BOOKS®
Robert E. Stevens, PhD
David L. Loudon, PhD
Editors in Chief

Marketing Research: Text and Cases by Bruce Wrenn, Robert Stevens, and David Loudon

Doing Business in Mexico: A Practical Guide by Gus Gordon and Thurmon Williams

Employee Assistance Programs in Mananged Care by Norman Winegar

Marketing Your Business: A Guide to Developing a Strategic Marketing Plan by Ronald A. Nykiel

Customer Advisory Boards: A Strategic Tool for Customer Relationship Building by Tony Carter

Fundamentals of Business Marketing Research by David A. Reid and Richard E. Plank

Marketing Management: Text and Cases by David L. Loudon, Robert E. Stevens, and Bruce Wrenn

Selling in the New World of Business by Bob Kimball and Jerold "Buck" Hall

Many Thin Companies: The Change in Customer Dealings and Managers Since September 11, 2001 by Tony Carter

The Book on Management by Bob Kimball

The Concise Encyclopedia of Advertising by Kenneth E. Clow and Donald Baack

Application Service Providers in Business by Luisa Focacci, Robert J. Mockler, and Marc E. Gartenfeld

The Concise Handbook of Management: A Practitioner's Approach by Jonathan T. Scott

The Marketing Research Guide, Second Edition by Robert E. Stevens, Bruce Wrenn, Philip K. Sherwood, and Morris E. Ruddick

Marketing Planning Guide, Third Edition by Robert E. Stevens, David L. Loudon, Bruce Wrenn, and Phylis Mansfield

Concise Encyclopedia of Church and Religious Organization Marketing by Robert E. Stevens, David L. Loudon, Bruce Wrenn, and Henry Cole

The Economies of Competition: The Race to Monopoly by George G. Djolov

Market Opportunity Analysis: Text and Cases by Robert E. Stevens, Philip K. Sherwood, J. Paul Dunn, and David L. Loudon

Application Service Providers in Business

Luisa Focacci
Robert J. Mockler, PhD
Marc E. Gartenfeld

Best Business Books®
An Imprint of The Haworth Press, Inc.
New York • London • Oxford

For more information on this book or to order, visit
http://www.haworthpress.com/store/product.asp?sku=5182

or call 1-800-HAWORTH (800-429-6784) in the United States and Canada
or (607) 722-5857 outside the United States and Canada

or contact orders@HaworthPress.com

Published by

Best Business Books®, an imprint of The Haworth Press, Inc., 10 Alice Street, Binghamton, NY 13904-1580.

Cover design by Kerry E. Mack.

Library of Congress Cataloging-in-Publication Data

Focacci, Luisa.
  Application service providers in business / Luisa Focacci, Robert J. Mockler, Marc E. Gartenfeld.
      p. cm.
  Includes bibliographical references and index.
  ISBN 0-7890-2480-2 (hard : alk. paper) — ISBN 0-7890-2481-0 (soft : alk. paper)
  1. Application service providers. 2. Electronic commerce. 3. Business enterprises — Computer networks. I. Mockler, Robert J. II. Gartenfeld, Marc E. III. Title.

HF5548.32.F62 2005
658.8'72—dc22

                                                                                    2004014858

CONTENTS

Preface

A leading success factor for businesses today is to be a lean enterprise, quickly adapting to changing market opportunities and efficiently responding to customer needs. Fast-spreading Internet connectivity, the rise of call centers, and global competition have fueled this move to an integrated, volatile, worldwide twenty-four-hour economy. To achieve and sustain an adequate level of flexibility to cope with Internet-driven business demands and growing competitive market pressures, organizations are focusing resources on their core competencies and, as a result, outsourcing nonvital business activities, such as selected aspects of information technology (IT).

A number of elements contributed to the solid growth in IT outsourcing in the late 1990s: year 2000 preparations, e-business opportunities via the Internet, the IT worker shortage, and the rapid pace of technology change. As enterprise software is an increasingly sophisticated, multilayered assembly of interconnected applications, managing and developing these critical elements has become the primary focus of many corporate IT departments.

Business success in today's information-intensive marketplace depends on a company's ability to acquire and fully utilize the latest advances in business-critical applications. The ability to provide the workforce with access to data whenever and wherever they are needed is indispensable for positively impacting a company's profitability, by driving revenue-enhancing opportunities and creating and sustaining a competitive advantage over competitors. Unfortunately, deploying these computer-based information applications often means initiating a stream of increasing costs and complexity when done with internal staff. This approach often leaves little time, money, or resources to focus on core strategic initiatives. Using an alternative approach, by having these applications delivered as services over the Internet or other dedicated line systems, can mean lessened demands on company IT staff and increase the ability to get complex software into use immediately, with the potential for easy upgrades and modifications, continuing its strategic value over the long run.

Within this context, a new outsourcing business model called ASP, or application service provider, has emerged that is transforming how businesses access and leverage software applications.

Acknowledgments

Research and writing demand countless lonely hours, yet the outcome depends upon the involvement of others.

I first want to thank my husband and best friend, Claudio Maccelli. I am ever so grateful for his unwavering love and support throughout this process and for ultimately making this book possible.

Special thanks go to Dr. Robert J. Mockler. He was always available to me, always treated me as a scholar in my own right during the first developmental stages of the book, and constructively critiqued my ideas, without imposing his own. Definitely, he is the best writing partner I could ever dream of, and I look forward to another opportunity for developing ideas into a common frame.

Special thanks also go to Marc Gartenfeld for actively contributing in this transatlantic book project with his critical insights, his brilliant ideas, and his enthusiastic participation in endless conversations about the most challenging elements of the book's architecture.

Thank you to Max Tomassini of St. John's University, Rome campus, for connecting me with Dr. Mockler and for contributing to initiating the collaboration that has also developed into this book project.

Thanks to my mother and my father and to the friends who were there for me during the difficult research and creativity moments, and helped me find the strength to go on in the research and writing.

To Claudio, Valerio, and Tiziano with endless love.

ABOUT THE AUTHORS

Luisa Focacci, MBA, is the Administration and Business Resources Manager for a Fortune 500 global company, which she began working at in 1994 as Office Manager. She was previously employed by an English school in Rome and was designated the Head of Students' Administrative Office in 1992. She has co-authored three publications about application service providers. She earned her BA in cultural anthropology in 1998 and went on to complete her Master of Business Administration in 2001.

Robert J. Mockler, PhD, is the Joseph F. Adams Professor of Management at St. John's University's Graduate Business Program, Tobin College of Business. He is the Director of the Strategic Management Research Group and its Centers of Case Study Development and of Knowledge-Based Systems for Business. He has authored/co-authored over 60 books/monographs, over 230 case studies, and over 320 articles, book chapters, and presentations. He has lectured, consulted, and taught MBA courses worldwide, has received national awards for innovative teaching, and is a Fulbright Scholar.

Marc E. Gartenfeld is an Adjunct Instructor in the Marketing Department of St. John's University's Tobin College of Business. He is Associate Director of the Strategic Management Research Group and the Center for Case Development and Use. He has co-authored and edited over 70 books, monographs, textbook instructor's guides, book chapters, journal articles, conference presentations, and case studies. He is the recipient of the 2001 Teaching Excellence Award and Professor of the Year Award, both from the Tobin College of Business.

Chapter 1

Application Service Providers: An Overview

INTRODUCTION

This chapter provides a general introduction to application service providers (ASPs) and the business context in which they operate. It gives various definitions of ASPs, describes the diverse functions individual ASPs perform, and provides a focus on a commonly accepted general definition. It also describes the main features of the ASP business model and its benefits to end users and the rising market need for ASPs globally, through a discussion of the multiple dynamic drivers underlying ASPs' formation and development. The chapter then examines the broad variety of ASP offerings. A brief literature review of this dynamic phenomenon is also included, followed by an overview of its anticipated substantial opportunities and potential market growth, looking beyond the severe industry shakeout and consolidation in 2001. Then the multinational nature of the ASP industry is discussed. This perspective reflects the inherently global nature of the ASP industry and the multinational orientation of its major successful players.

Research indicates potentially many opportunities for application service to survive and prosper in the current and future business environment. These opportunities have also generated intense debate among analysts and information technology (IT) industry leaders. Problems noted in this debate especially include lack of homogeneity in functions and services provided, which have led to this book's multidimensional analysis of the ASP model.

ASP DEFINED

This section examines various kinds of ASPs and provides a commonly accepted definition of application service providers. The ASP

Industry Consortium, a global advocacy group that was formed in May 1999 to promote the industry, defines ASPs as companies that host, deliver, and manage computer software applications and services from remote data centers to multiple users across a wide area network (WAN) via the Internet or other private dedicated networks. An ASP provides computer applications and the infrastructure (physical infrastructure: IT plus delivery and communication networks; human infrastructure: skilled and well-trained workforce) and support services necessary to deliver them to customers on a subscription basis (ASP Industry Consortium, 2001a). There are, however, other definitions of ASP. International Data Corporation (IDC), for example, defines an application service provider as a company that gives a contractual service offering to deploy, host, manage, and provide access to computer software applications from a facility other than the customer's site.

Another useful definition is offered by Gartner Group's Dataquest, which defines an ASP as the provision (and servicing) of business process-enabling applications delivered over a network via a subscription-based outsourcing contract. Not included in this category is the providing of pure infrastructure—the physical systems and networks necessary to deliver the application from the ASP to end users. The infrastructure provider does not become an ASP "until there is some application functionality" being delivered (Haskins, 2000). In essence, what characterizes the ASP is the provision and management of business software applications on behalf of the end user, a somewhat incomplete definition given the study of actual ASPs in this book. In light of the later discussion of actual ASP developments, which also involves some important ASP Industry Consortium initiatives, the ASP Industry Consortium's description of ASP characteristics is used as a formal definition in this book.

ASP MODELS' MAIN FEATURES

The basic value function of ASPs is that they rent out technology rather than sell it, get revenues from the sale, and deliver it online, either over the Internet or via other private or dedicated networks. ASPs are a way for customer companies to outsource some or sometimes almost all aspects of their IT-related needs. The main difference between an ASP and a traditional outsourcer, which underlies its power, is that ASPs manage commercially available application servers in a centrally controlled and remotely managed location rather than on a customer's site. The defining characteristics of an ASP are as follows (Mizoras, 2001; Stanco, 2000; Gillan et al., 1999):

- *Application centric:* ASPs provide access to, and management of, an application that is commercially available or especially developed for the ASP.
- *Renting application access:* ASP services offer customers access to a new application environment without making investments in licenses, servers, people, and other resources. The ASP either owns the software or has a contractual agreement with the software vendor to license access to the software.
- *Centrally managed:* ASP services are managed from a central location rather than at each customer's site. Customers access applications remotely, such as over the Internet or via leased lines.
- *One-to-many offerings:* The ASP often partners with other vendors to package standardized offerings that many companies will subscribe to over a specific contract period.
- *Delivering on the contract:* The ASP is responsible, in the customer's eyes, for delivering on the customer contract, ensuring that the service is provided as promised.

Common features in formal ASP services are, therefore,

- owning and operating software applications;
- owning, operating, and maintaining the servers that run the applications;
- employing the workforce needed to maintain the applications;
- making applications available to customers everywhere via the Web (Internet) or other dedicated networks; and
- billing the service on a per-user basis.

ASPs give customers an alternative to procuring and implementing complex information and enterprise management systems in-house, which can be very costly and time-consuming. These costs include up-front capital expenses, implementation tasks, and a constant need for maintenance, upgrades, and customization. With data processing performed off-site by a third party, organizations have time and resources to adequately and efficiently focus on their core business without diverting their attention to support activities. In some cases, ASPs even provide customers with a comprehensive, fully customized solution, which gives customers the ability to control more precisely the cost of technology use and ownership through scheduled payment programs. Generally the ASP owns the software license and gives the end user access to the application, so costs associated with application ownership are spread over the lifetime of the contract, thus lowering the up-front entry costs. Recently, licenses have also been sold separately to give end users a more secure relationship with software developers.

ASPs supply not only hardware- and software-related services but also human assets and expertise that may be unavailable or prohibitively expensive for companies to acquire individually. This is especially true for small and medium-sized firms or high-growth companies of all sizes, where large investments are required—but where resources are restricted—for IT. The ASP model simplifies life for companies that would rather not, or are unable to, purchase the software applications, buy the computer, storage, and networking systems, or hire experts to install and maintain their own entire system.

ASPs evolved from a concept that was in fashion approximately thirty years ago—the computer bureaus that emerged in the 1970s, when the high cost of computing made companies rush to rent computer-processing time from external suppliers. The (re)birth of the ASP model was, in part, due to Traver Gruen-Kennedy, who founded the ASP Industry Consortium in 1999. He devised the concept in 1997 while working as a consultant and took it to Citrix Systems. He spent most of 1998 talking to companies that would provide the essential components of an ASP: telecommunication companies to provide the links between the applications and the clients; hardware providers and data centers to host the applications; and software companies that would have to customize their software to run in an ASP environment (Howarth, 1999).

The following timeline shows the evolution from hosting to ASP (Marks, 2001):

> 1969: The U.S. Department of Defense commissions ARPA-NET, the first variant of the Internet, developed by the Advanced Research Project Agency (ARPA).

1979: ARPA establishes the Internet Configuration Control Board, a further significant step toward the Internet.

1982: The TCP/IP (Transmission Control Protocol/Internet Protocol) model for connectivity in telecommunications networks, developed by the U.S. Department of Defense in 1972, is established as the protocol suite for ARPANET, leading to one of the first definitions of "Internet."

1984: DNS (Domain Name System, a hierarchical system of servers maintaining databases enabling the conversion of domain names [the unique name of a node on the Internet] to their IP addresses) is introduced. By the end of the year, there are over 1,000 hosts.

1986: The Internet Engineering Task Force and the Internet Research Task Force are established.

1987: By the end of the year, there are over 10,000 Internet hosts.

1989: With seventeen countries online in the National Science Foundation Network (NSFNET), the number of Internet hosts breaks 100,000.

1991: The World Wide Web (WWW) is released, and the National Science Foundation (NSF) lifts restrictions on commercial access to the Internet.

1995: Mobile code, such as Java (a programming language developed by Sun Microsystems, designed to run on any computer or computing device regardless of the specific microprocessor or operating system it uses) is developed, adding online interactivity to e-commerce.

2000: ASP technology comes of age. Microsoft unveils its .Net Strategy (a new way to deliver applications), expected to turn many of its applications into ASP services by utilizing XML (eXtensible Markup Language) protocol-based Web communication code, which makes information in documents usable in computer programs.

The discussion so far has highlighted the basic ASP delivery model's features and some of the benefits to end users. The following section describes various interconnected factors that contributed to the origin and expansion of the ASP phenomenon.

ASP DRIVERS

This section presents the major drivers underlying the formation and development of the ASP business model. These factors are not exclusive to the ASP environment, as they are encountered in most developing IT-related industries.

ASPs and the robust physical infrastructure necessary to support them are being driven by the desire to meet the specific needs of businesses that do not have the time, money, or resources to purchase, deploy, and manage software applications on their own. These businesses need software to help run their companies more efficiently, improve customer service, and gain competitive advantage. Application hosting and remote management as performed by ASPs are the solution for many businesses, especially small and medium-sized ones.

Fundamentally, ASPs have become possible because of advances in technology, notably the Internet. Basically, it takes only an Internet connection and a Web browser for the end user to be able to utilize ASP-managed applications. The end user is freed from the need to build or control all the infrastructure elements required by a traditional IT-related system. ASP growth, then, is being driven by several converging dynamic forces, including financial, technical, and market dynamics (Gartner Group, 2001a; Sound Consulting, 2000; CIO.com, 2000):

Financial Dynamics

- Desire for predictable cost streams at business level
- Increased computing complexity
- Escalating IT infrastructure and application costs; rapidly evolving business environments; rapidly changing technology
- Ability to reach new customers with minimal cost through the Internet

Technical Dynamics

- Increased reliability and security of the Internet (on which software, IT services, and telecommunications industries have converged)

- Pervasive, high-speed access from virtually every computer anywhere in the world, which allows users to link into a massive network, backed up by growing standards
- A user interface—the Web browser—widely embraced by end users everywhere thanks to new, higher-level functionality/performance
- Server-based computing advancements

Market Dynamics

- Demand for simplicity and business focus driven by the e-business transformation
- Desire to access greater application capabilities and value-added services around the application
- Difficulty in hiring IT staffs
- Competitive differentiation drives
- Recognition of value-added services tied to outsourced software applications

Figure 1.1 summarizes and dynamically captures these multiple dynamics.

In particular, the broad acceptance of server-based technologies has been instrumental in the development of the ASP market. Server-based computing enables existing applications to be deployed, managed, and supported 100 percent from an off-site server. Server-based computing incorporates a multiuser operating system that allows multiple, concurrent users to log on and run standard applications simultaneously in separate sessions—each session being insulated, to prevent accidental or malicious third-party intrusion—on a single server. Server-based computing has successfully overcome many of the bandwidth and management limitations that have historically caused high expense and fast obsolescence associated with providing extensive connectivity over wide area networks (Sound Consulting, 2000).

The ASP market was also made possible because cost-effective delivery methods became available to interconnect ASPs with enterprises. In the early 1990s, when dedicated connections and high-speed Internet access were affordable only for the largest enterprises, the ASP market was nonexistent. Large enterprises had IT staff to

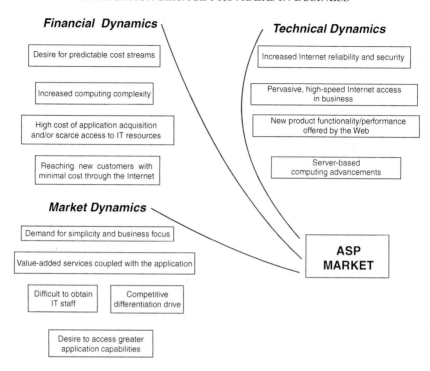

FIGURE 1.1. The birth of the ASP market. *Source:* Adapted from Sound Consulting (2000). "Understanding the ASP Market," Software Information Industry Association, June. <www.siaa.net/software/pubs/GASP-00.pdf>. Accessed September 29, 2004.

write or customize software to meet internal needs and ample cash processes to pay for expensive private or frame relay networks. Smaller enterprises could not afford the expense of complex enterprise management application systems, such as enterprise resource planning (ERP) or customer relationship management (CRM). With the emergence and wide availability of affordable bandwidth to corporations of all sizes, ASPs are now able to offer valuable applications and related services that are also financially appealing.

Beyond specific technological advances, what has played an important role in the growth of ASPs is the push to tailor technology to individual business needs. Of all the resources available to a business, computer-based applications for the management of business functions and resources are among the most critical. These applications enable organizations to generate more revenue in that they maximize the company's internal efficiency and strengthen ties with customers, and thus boost new and repeated sales by offering new and better services, increasing levels of user knowledge, and enhancing overall productivity. However, many internal and external barriers prevent organizations from fully exploiting mission-critical applications, which make the ASP business model a necessity and a cost-effective solution, since many kinds of ASPs not only can provide a more efficient employment of software applications that reduces costs and increases productivity, but also can adapt them to specific individual company needs. Outsourcing to ASPs the delivery and management of applications enables business entities to specialize and grow faster.

When studied by experts from another perspective, top drivers of ASP application outsourcing include the following end user demand factors (ASP Industry Consortium, 2001b; Sound Consulting, 2000; Corbett, 2000):

- *Focus:* Executives know that anything that distracts the company from its core expertise should ideally be moved outside the organization. Such operational freedom is probably the most fundamental justification underlying the adoption of the ASP model in any industry or company. ASP contracts put the responsibility for the application in the hands of the ASP.
- *Speed:* Organizations are finding they simply cannot by themselves upgrade infrastructures or adopt technology fast enough to keep pace with the changing technology mix. Such upgrading projects consume already limited IT resources that could be used to pursue more strategic business goals.
- *Reach:* Organizations compete in more countries than ever before, serving an extended workforce that often requires round-the-clock access to the same applications available at headquarters. To conduct business faster, more conveniently, and more cost effectively, organizations find they must provide their employees, customers, partners, and vendors with reliable, secure, high-performance, and timely access to business-critical applications that ASPs can provide.
- *Connectivity:* E-sourcing turns supply chains into fully integrated trading networks.

- *Flexibility:* Businesses, particularly small and medium-sized ones, are looking for flexibility with respect to software licensing and billing options in order to more accurately reflect their specific needs and use of technology services and applications. Subscription and usage-based licensing, as well as consolidated billing options, offer compelling alternatives to building and maintaining in-house systems. The ASP model creates a true plug-and-play approach to acquiring advanced business capabilities, reduces fixed costs, and lowers overall expenses (by 30 to 60 percent) for hardware, applications, and their management.
- *Scalability:* The right solution can be put in place first and then easily grown and adapted, as the customer's needs change. Scalability is also applied to the fee structure used by most ASPs since it is based on the number of users per month.
- *Reduced risk:* With no capital expenses for software, hardware, and IT personnel, organizations can implement new technology with minimal impact on their existing environment and profitability. Companies using ASPs enjoy much higher levels of technology upgrading without continual investment in new technology. Trial and adoption are simplified.
- *Predictability:* Operations, particularly business-critical ones, must perform reliably and to the required service level on a continuing basis. ASPs apply their vast experience to implement best IT practices for higher levels of availability, security, backup, disaster recovery, and support services.
- *Cost-effectiveness:* Lower total cost of ownership and shorter time-to-benefit are important to business success at all levels.

It is not by accident that ASPs have emerged during a period of key technological and cultural changes. According to Chris Phoenix, vice president and general manager of Citrix iBusiness, ASPs enable enterprises to implement global e-commerce and other strategies, allowing their employees the freedom to work anywhere and anytime on any device, regardless of connection or network. This kind of flexibility is crucial to the success of companies in the digital global age (CIO.com, 2000).

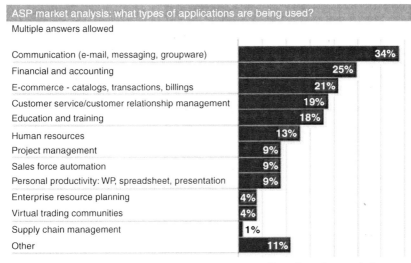

ASP market analysis: what types of applications are being used?

Multiple answers allowed

Communication (e-mail, messaging, groupware)	34%
Financial and accounting	25%
E-commerce - catalogs, transactions, billings	21%
Customer service/customer relationship management	19%
Education and training	18%
Human resources	13%
Project management	9%
Sales force automation	9%
Personal productivity: WP, spreadsheet, presentation	9%
Enterprise resource planning	4%
Virtual trading communities	4%
Supply chain management	1%
Other	11%

Percentage of respondents

FIGURE 1.2. Specific functional applications in use by customers. *Source:* Adapted from ASP Industry Consortium/2001). "ASP Industry Consortium Releases Fourth Quarterly Tracking Studies." ASPstreet, February 1. <www. aspstreet.com/pr/a.taf/idpr,16891>. Accessed September 23, 2004.

A VARIETY OF OFFERINGS

Virtually any type of application can be accessed through an ASP. Figure 1.2 shows which types of specific software applications customers were most commonly using through the ASP delivery model at the end of 2000. The percentages indicate that the most frequently outsourced applications were those enabling communications, those enabling the streamlining of financial and accounting functions, those enabling e-commerce and customer service/customer relationship management, and those associated with education and training functions.

Depending on business functional requirements, ASPs may provide relatively basic kinds of applications, such as e-mail for personal or collaborative communication as well as complex applications such as ERP, CRM, and human resource management (HRM) systems (ASP Industry Consortium, 2001a). The following is another useful way to group ASP applications, ranging from simple to complex ones (Gillan et al., 1999):

- *Personal applications:* include Office suites such as Microsoft Office and consumer applications (e.g., games, home productivity)
- *Collaborative applications:* Groupware, e-mail, and conferencing applications
- *CRM applications:* Segments such as sales force automation (SFA), customer service, and marketing applications
- *ERM applications:* Accounting, materials management, and facilities management
- *Vertical applications:* Any industry-specific applications, such as management resource planning (MRP) in the manufacturing industry, patient billing in the health care industry, and claims processing in the insurance industry
- *Analytic applications:* Any applications built to analyze a business problem (e.g., financial analysis, Web site analysis, and risk analysis)

Viewed from another perspective, although the ASP market is still developing very quickly, most ASP service offerings at this time fall into one of the following categories (Gillan et al., 1999):

- *Core services:* These include the basic services an ASP must provide to manage the application environment and provide a base level of customer satisfaction. These services include application updates and upgrades, $24 \times 7 \times 365$ monitoring of the application, network, and servers on which the applications run, and basic customer support.
- *Managed services:* These services include all of the core services plus additional services and guarantees involving support, security, application performance, and data redundancy. They include service-level agreements (SLAs) about uptime (guaranteed application performance) and data security, dedicated technical support staff, and daily backup of an application and its data.
- *Extended services:* These services include all the managed services plus additional professional services such as application configuration and extension, strategy and planning, and training

and educational support. Although the extended services approach a custom-delivery model, they are still delivered in the context of the ASP one-to-many model.

Since customers' needs are highly diversified, depending on product life cycle, internal and external requirements, market type, and competition in the market, there may be virtually as many customer requirements for ASPs as there are customer types. These customer types include

- individuals who want personal, collaborative, or wireless applications;
- small to midsized companies that want minimally customized applications;
- large organizations in need of complex niche applications that they cannot afford, in terms of money or time, to develop themselves; and
- vertical industries that need B2B (business-to-business) e-commerce services or industry-specific software functionality or performance.

ASPs' actual and potential business customers include the whole range of business-to-business and business-to-consumer enterprises. Companies in every industry, ranging from start-ups to Fortune 500 global corporations (Rutherford, 2000), have been using ASPs. The two extremes of business customers are large corporate clients who need complex application management (CRM, ERP, and accounting software) on one end and smaller companies and individual consumers of Web applications such as free e-mail on the other end.

On the one hand, large enterprises (more than 500 employees) can also benefit from the third-party ASP model to manage the complex systems and software required to support a large firm, which are difficult to build and sustain internally. Corporations that do not formally partner with ASPs are already using a sort of internal ASP, some even using bill-back systems for each of the various departments or subsidiaries. These enterprises are increasingly open to using ASPs, since large firms have recently become strong proponents of IT. On the other hand, the ASP market can also effectively meet the demand created by the smaller "application gap" customer (Sound Consulting, 2000) in need of outsourcing—organizations with fewer than 500 employees, whose IT-driven overhead costs on software acquisition and maintenance can well exceed their profits. These customer companies could greatly benefit from the competitive advantage offered by software efficiencies, and the cost predictability offered by the ASP model is an optimal solution for them. The degree to which current ASPs have been able to satisfy this market need is a discussion topic in Chapter 2.

In the ASP model, according to the defining characteristics presented earlier in this chapter, a key success factor is the relationship with the individual customer, who relies on an ASP as a true business partner to run its data as a trusted third party and sees the ASP as its single contact for the overall delivery mechanism. As such, client businesses expect the ASP to have an intimate knowledge of their business needs and the markets they serve (Torode, 2000b). They must know what is expected of each other in detail. As Craig Pennington, director of PSINet, noted, "Basic questions such as who, what, why, when and how" need to be answered "to ensure the customer gets the service expected" (Nicolle, 2000). Chapter 2 examines the necessary relationships that underline the how, who, what, why and when factors within the complex ASP model and also examine the extent to which these partnership relationships are fulfilled by existing ASPs.

REVIEW OF ASP INFORMATION SERVICES

Since the industry is relatively young, academic studies of the subject are minimal. The most important sources for information are leading market research firms, industry research companies, and specialized IT Web sites. This section discusses significant ASP information and perspectives found in these sources.

In 1997, IDC noticed growing buyer interest in the new application delivery model, whereby clients would rent access to the most popular enterprise software applications. Its early research confirmed interest in the ASP concept, not just in small to midsize enterprises (SMEs) but in large companies. Early on, IDC recognized in the ASP model a "disruptive innovation" threatening to intrude on and displace existing ways of doing business for all sorts of IT vendors (Gillan et al., 1999). Clayton Christensen had already spoken of disruptive innovations and the positive consequences they generate for customers, in that they generally package and deliver existing technologies/solutions in a unique way that proves to be simpler for end users than prior approaches. According to Christensen (1997), history shows that disruptive innovations have introduced changes that eventually have "toppled the industry's leaders" (p. 15). The fact that IDC had rated ASP as a disruptive innovation showed its belief in the model's ability to change the course of IT and the way end users might employ technology in the future. Whether this is true is one primary focus in this book, where possible future scenarios are explored in the final two chapters.

ASPs represent a small proportion of the outsourcing business in general and of the IT services market in particular, as their revenues account for a tiny percentage of the $150 billion market for computer software goods and services (Rudy and Corridore, 2001). Yet their emergence is considered more revolutionary than the PC was in the 1980s. In a report titled "Packaged Software Rental: The Net's Killer App," analyst Phil Wainewright (2000b) asserts that the packaging of application services for delivery through online rental computing "marks a new shift in the evolution of information technology, more significant than the advent of the personal computer." In this perspective, the ASP business model is expected to radically change the status quo and become "the engine of a new, networked economy" (The Euronet, 2000).

For the Yankee Group, ASPs represent a new delivery, implementation, and pricing model for the distribution of critical business applications. ASPs are defined, and in some successful cases fully act (as Chapter 3 shows) as the "general contractors" that bring together, and are directly responsible for, a number of different software-related services (Yankee Group, 2000). In 1999, Ben Pring, senior ASP analyst at Gartner Group's Dataquest, noted that the ASP model had already emerged as one of the foremost global trends driving phenomenal growth in the application outsourcing market. This new model incorporated "infrastructure, implementation, and management services into one bundled, monthly price point" (Gartner Group, 1999). Gartner Group studies support the view that over time this model has the potential to become a significant catalyst of growth in broader strategic solutions, such as customer relationship management, supply-chain management, and e-commerce.

Dave Boulanger of AMR Research, Inc., recognized in 2000 a maturation process for the ASP market, which he expected to continue and evolve over time. He also noticed that many new applications are now being offered only on a hosted basis, thus acknowledging that end users and suppliers are endorsing the viability of the ASP business model. Combined with the increase in value-added services and application suites targeted to specific sectors, Boulanger is convinced that "hosted models present a viable alternative for mainstream companies to embrace leading technologies" (AMR Research Inc., 2000).

In a 2001 report, *Standard and Poor's* illustrates the ASP sector's unique areas of expertise, and notes that while the ASP core business may seem similar to the other IT services, there are indeed fundamental differences (Rudy and Corridore, 2001). The report highlights the fact that ASPs take responsibility for all the investments related to a particular application, whether they involve licenses, personnel, or technology. The study also emphasizes the positive level of standardization in methodologies and processes the ASP delivery model can offer to customers. In addition, Katie Ring, author of "Application Service Providers: Opportunities and Risks," published by European market researcher Ovum, notes that one of the crucial advantages of ASPs is a center of excellence in managing computer systems, which leaves ASPs' customers free to concentrate on pursuing their strategic business objectives (Ovum, 2000).

Not only are ASPs reportedly filling gaps in market demand they are also being perceived as the generators of a new way of thinking about business. They are rated as having the know-how to best enable business processes and, in an increasing number of cases, to connect these processes across a company and among all its mission-critical partners. Chris Phoenix, Citrix iBusiness' vice president, believes the ASP model's goal is to enable more effective and efficient business process management and to aggregate best practices across companies and industries. He claimed ASPs will change the in-house IT landscape "from a break-and-fix mode" to a more strategic IT entity—"from a constant upgrade cycle to a strategic relationship management function" (CIO.com, 2000). Traver Gruen-Kennedy, ASP Industry Consortium's founder, echoes this view, in his conviction that ASP outsourcing is "substantially different to the way that most companies are computing today" (Newing, 2001a).

Gartner Group's research director, Bruce McCabe, noted the ASP model is essentially an extension of the trend toward IT outsourcing, as companies continue to extract themselves from noncore activities. McCabe is among the analysts who liken the way ASPs provide software to the way utilities supply power and water, and the underlying opportunities in the similarity of demand in the two sectors. As he observed, "there are a lot of businesses out there that wish they didn't have IT, and if you give them an opportunity to get that application delivered in the power-and-lights scenario, then a lot will take the philosophy" (Howarth, 1999). The ability to deliver applications the same way a utility company delivers power and light to consumers is rated by some analysts as the best way to achieve market share. Whether and which ASPs have been able to perform as effectively as a utility firm is the focus of the following two chapters.

Another vote of confidence in ASP as a better way of delivering computer applications came early in ASP development from Scott McNealy, Sun Microsystems chief executive officer. In 1999, he predicted that by 2004, "if you're a Chief Information Officer with a head for business, you won't be buying computers anymore. You won't buy software either. You'll rent all your resources from a service provider" (The Euronet, 2000).

The following are some industry insiders' views about the ASP model (PC Dealer, 2001). According to Maria Cappella, vice president of product management at XO Communications, lots of companies are trying to understand what it means to be an ASP. This observation accurately reflects a current ASP marketplace characteristic—absence of uniform functions and services provided by individual ASPs. This is a critical issue and its most striking components and consequences are noted in Chapter 2. Looking forward, Cappella foresees a scenario where "loads of new ASP start-ups end up merging into the traditional companies they set out to replace. ASPs are able to spin on a penny, while traditional companies have stability. A merger is good for both." Such possible future scenarios are developed in Chapter 5.

Margaret Hopkins, principal analyst at telecommunication consultant Analysys, is convinced that SMEs are the big challenge for ASPs, their main raison d'être. In her view, however, it is also essential to work hard and have great economies of scale in order to make headway in the highly demanding larger corporate sector, especially because many SMEs have no comprehension of the ASP model. These difficulties in penetrating the SME market—the lack of customer awareness of the model and the need for ASPs to find ways to improve—are developed in later chapters. They are part of the analysis, in Chapter 2, of the challenges ASPs face, and are also discussed in Chapter 4, which provides some insight into current ASP efforts to educate customers to the benefits of ASP-delivered services.

This literature review indicates potentially major opportunities for application service providing in the current and future business environment, as well as potential negative factors that may impact ASP market growth.

TRENDS AND ESTIMATED WORLDWIDE MARKET GROWTH

To help the reader better understand the huge potential in the ASP sector, this section discusses significant trends and ASP market growth forecasts. Chapter 5 extends this discussion by looking into the predicted future of various ASP models.

To gain an appreciation of trends in this industry, it is useful to first refer to the pressures that emerging and rapidly growing markets generally face in their high-velocity environments. The major challenges are (Thompson and Strickland, 1999) as follows:

- uncertainty about how the market will function, how fast it will grow, and how big it will get;
- conflicting judgments about which of the several competing services will gain the most customer attention (wide differences in product quality and performance exist in the market);
- low to moderate entry barriers;
- strong experience curves that produce significant cost reductions as business volume grows;
- customer resistance and concerns about performance, features, and conflicting claims of rival firms; and
- a wait-and-see approach by customers. First-time users often prefer to be followers rather than early adopters.

Over the 1996-2000 period, the U.S. economy grew at an exceptional rate. According to CE Unterberg's ASP research team analyst Bill Dering, outsourcing and technology—ASP specialties—were major factors in that exceptional growth. The Internet, for example, has created a publicly accessible infrastructure that connects users to off-site applications worldwide and provides an environment where information can be exchanged cheaply and seamlessly. Analysts at Gartner Group confirm this trend. In an August 2000 report on the worldwide ASP marketplace, Dataquest forecast explosive growth for this industry, both in the United States and worldwide (Flanagan, 2000b). In addition, Dale Jorgenson, an economics professor at Harvard University, has predicted that outsourcing IT could increase the efficiency of technology investment by 20 percent (Burrows, 2000).

Costs can exert substantial pressures in a softening economy, yet some market experts regard a slowing economy as a potential benefit to ASP growth, a way to maximize available resources. In addition, for entities challenged with developing a new business or business focus in a tight market, time-to-benefit can be a compelling driver favoring the ASP approach (Gilmore, 2001a; Torode and Hagendorf, 2000).

A number of trends favorable to ASP growth were noted in 2000, such as (AMR Research Inc., 2000)

- an established growing ASP adoption curve, including dot-com startups, high-tech manufacturers, and small to midsize companies;
- ASP providers beginning to segment based on target company size and requirements;
- business models being developed to focus on maximum value components for specific customer companies;
- the establishment of general go-to-market strategies focused on specific industries;
- increasing focus on individual company business development, and growing recognition of the role of IT as a business development factor; and
- smaller ASP players beginning to consolidate as partnership benefits are recognized.

The strategic importance of some of these trends as the moderating factors that can make or break an ASP emerges from discussion in the following two chapters. In particular, Chapter 2 examines the present structure and dynamics of the ASP market and discusses the business models that have contributed to the shaping of the aforementioned trends so far.

According to surveys conducted in 2000 (ASP Industry Consortium, 2001b; Gilmore, 2000c; CIO.com, 2000; ITAA, 2000), growing interest in ASP services is being manifested by small and medium-sized companies looking to outsource noncore functions, in order to stay focused and enhance their opportunities for growth. They are realizing that ASPs have the potential to enable internal IT specialists to take care of tactical and strategic business issues and, through this function, to give businesses a better chance of balancing competing forces (Nicolle, 2000). According to these studies, potential and actual customers are gradually noting the value of ASP-based application outsourcing to provide their business with more flexibility and more available resources, so they can better respond to competing pressures. The validity of results from these surveys is not in doubt; however, the discussion in Chapter 2 provides a broader perspective about this complex environment.

The ASP market generated $986 million in revenue in 2000. Overall growth has been and remains strong, with revenues increasing at an annual rate of 89 percent (Moran, 2001). By 2005 the ASP market is expected to have grown exponentially. Growth depends on several factors, among which are wider availability of broadband communication (technology driver) and marketplace education (sociocultural driver, tied to the acceptance of the delivery model and its wide adoption), whose impact on the ASP market is analyzed in Chapters 4 and 5. IDC forecasts that by 2005, worldwide spending for ASP will reach $24 billion annually. The Gartner Group estimate of growth calls for $22.7 billion in expenditures for ASP solutions in 2005 (Moran, 2001; CIO.com, 2000; Gartner Group, 1999; Haskins, 2000), close to the Forrester Research forecast of more than $23 billion for the same period (Foremski, 2000).

The Phillips Group estimates that services to large companies will grow to 58 percent of the total ASP market by 2005. Giant IT companies have demonstrated interest in the ASP model, which reveals the potential inherent in this new software application provisioning mechanism. Among them, Microsoft and IBM have welcomed and supported the ASP business model.

In July 2000, for example, Microsoft announced a $10 million investment in the sector, and chief executive officer Ballmer introduced the ASP Service Delivery Initiative, designed to facilitate partnerships between hosting service providers, Microsoft resellers, and ASPs (Gilmore, 2000c). According to some analysts, Microsoft's .NET strategy shows a commitment to the ASP model that will drive demand for ASP services worldwide (Gilmore, 2000b). Also, during this period IBM launched the ASP Prime program designed to transform software developers into ASPs. Jan Jackman, who is in charge of ASP Prime, recognized the importance of ASP as a way to foster and develop a promising new industry: "The focus is helping to legitimize [ASP] by providing the infrastructure necessary to ensure its credibility" (Gilmore, 2001b). This in turn is expected to give IBM other revenue channels and substantial return on its early ASP-related efforts.

Along with huge predicted growth, the Gartner Group warned in 2000 that there would be a very high failure rate among ASPs in 2001. Sixty percent of ASPs were expected to be acquired or go out of business within a year or two because of poorly developed business models and inadequate partnership strategies, and because of the inability to execute marketing strategies, market consolidation, and changing market requirements (Gartner Group, 2001a; Stobie, 2000). Signs of severe burnout and consolidation appeared in 2001, with many companies either changing their names, as they were acquired/merged, or actually getting out of business. The press and specialized ASP portals reported on the industry shakeout frequently (Flanagan, 2001; "Gathering Steam," 2001; Mears, 2001c; Cirillo, 2001). Despite the problems, Gartner believes the ASP model will in some form continue and grow with the increased use of outsourcing by IT users (Moran, 2001; Stobie, 2000).

A MULTINATIONAL PERSPECTIVE

As the evolution from hosting to ASP shows, ASPs emerged from advanced Internet and e-commerce applications and technologies. Although the Internet began within the United States in 1969, the Internet of today, which provides the platform from which ASPs are run, cannot be considered a domestic marketplace technology. The global nature of the Internet and e-commerce, therefore, makes the ASP industry inherently multinational in scope. That does not mean that there are no U.S.-based ASPs that serve only domestic partners (e.g., smaller ASPs, such as Employease.com, which serve SMEs operating only in the United States). The large majority of the 1,600 U.S. ASPs at the end of 2001 served domestic as well as international partners. Examples include Interliant, Corio, Outtask, Portera, and Jamcracker. In addition, many U.S. and non-U.S. firms are served by overseas ASPs. For example, TeleComputing, Europe's largest business ASP, serves, among others, the U.S. consulting firm Global Knowledge Consultants, and U.K.-based iFuel provides its applications and services to many firms across Europe.

This book focuses mainly on those larger ASPs that serve the multinational marketplace, reflecting the inherently multinational nature of the ASP industry. As we will show, the leading ASPs in the industry are used to define and discuss the five business models presented in Chapter 2 independent of their country of origin. Also, one of the market requirements is global-scale expertise. This continuing trend of general globalization as a whole and the common drive toward unified cross-cultural technology applications and implementations in the area of IT in particular build the basis for ASPs to be multinational in orientation, if they want to be major successful players in the industry.

Therefore, a multinational perspective underlies the discussions in all chapters. Within this multinational perspective, an international ASP can be defined as "an ASP that serves partners both within and without its own domestic marketplace," which includes almost all of the ASP examples discussed in this book.

CONCLUSION

Research has revealed that at the moment there is no single comprehensive ASP model beyond some key common features discussed in this chapter. This is true because ASPs serve business needs, which vary considerably from company to company and industry to industry. A comprehensive model covering the multitude of ASPs worldwide at the end of 2005 is not only impossible to develop but also unrealistic given the rapid changes in the industry. In addition, new ASP business sectors emerge continuously, driven by the industry's high growth potential and by competition. Research results especially point to a lack of homogeneity in functions and services provided by individual ASPs.

ASP has become one of the most debated technologies of the twenty-first century. Major questions are: Which specific ASP business models are workable? In what forms will ASPs remain with us? The future of the ASP business concept appears very promising, as its general business model provides a degree of flexibility that software vendors alone cannot supply. "Plug in, switch on, and pay only for what you use" is a viable marketing formula. This is the seductive offering of ASPs, which promise to take the pain out of implementing software applications (Moran, 2000). But what does the reality of current ASP businesses look like? The worldwide ASP market is going through what ASP Industry Consortium chair Paula Hunter calls a "trough of disillusionment" (Moran, 2001), meaning that customers are uncertain and not wholeheartedly adopting ASP, after its initial enthusiastic welcome—better defined as "hype"—by the press and industry analysts.

This book aims to substantiate the broad consensus that the survival of the ASP industry is not in doubt, moderated by the fact that a one-dimensional analysis does not fully explain the phenomenon in both its current nature and expected future form. Our overall goal is to reaffirm the viability of the core ASP delivery concept and to identify successful and unsuccessful contingent ASP business models as implemented by individual players, and then to explore future scenarios for current ASP business models.

Contingency factors, such as satisfying differing customer needs, have led to this book's multidimensional analysis of the ASP model, which has two main objectives. The first is to provide a structure for understanding the present ASP business environment, which is developed by identifying the multiple relationships among the diverse market participants, discussed in Chapter 2. The second is to point ahead, by looking into what, who, why, when, where, and how the ASP marketplace will develop, which is pursued in Chapters 2 through 5.

Chapter 2

The ASP Marketplace: Structure and Overall Dynamics

INTRODUCTION

The objective in this chapter is to identify the multiple dynamic forces at work in the current global ASP marketplace to provide some structure for the wide range of different ASP business models. First we identify and discuss three important analytical areas of interest in the current ASP environment. One concerns "ASP-enabling" relationships—that is, the roles and contributions of diverse market participants to the complex ASP business model. The second focus is describing general ASP business model characteristics and identifying the main categories of ASP models in the marketplace. The third focus involves the analysis of different specific ASP business models within the present environment. Several business-critical dimensions are identified and a general analytical framework is developed for the discussion of the contingent specific ASP business models that have been implemented to date. This structure is based on an analysis of both private and public existing ASPs.

The analysis then moves to the challenges faced by existing ASP models. The discussion highlights the areas where most models have been inadequate or inappropriate relative to customer requirements. Research results indicate many ASPs have not lived up to the high expectations of the new application delivery model early in the ASP life cycle. It is also argued that the failures have been responsible for a backlash toward the ASP model as a whole and account for much of today's uncertainty surrounding the ASP concept. Finally, the chapter presents an overview of the state of market acceptance and adoption of application services.

THE CURRENT ASP MARKET ENVIRONMENT

The perspective of this section is that the ASP business model should not be looked at in isolation from its actual business context. Our aim is to present a more realistic view of the model in relation to its environment than can be developed by studying its general characteristics and user benefits only. This view is necessary to pursue a multidimensional analysis of the ASP business model and the industry at present. The analysis also involves looking at its possible future developments (see Chapter 5). To gain a broader, systematic perspective, the section analyzes and structures the current global ASP marketplace by discussing and clarifying the individual roles and contributions of various market participants that together form the general ASP delivery model.

The basic description of the ASP delivery model's features given in Chapter 1, although following the official ASP Industry Consortium's definition and guidelines, does not fully capture the complexities found in today's marketplace. Research results indicate the current ASP environment is made up of almost as many specific models as there are combinations of applications, service offerings, and underlying business-enabling relationships. To start making sense of the models' variety, this section discusses several underlying functions and relationships that enable application service providers to perform and deliver services.

ASP-Enabling Relationships

This section discusses the complex relationships that enable the ASP model to function and deliver value to end users in the present environment. To understand the market, this section examines the ASP value chain and clarifies its diverse components. By discussing mission-critical relationships, the various roles that together compose the ASP delivery model can be identified and help explain why and how it has been implemented by individual ASPs in different forms.

Today's ASP marketplace consists of many different types of providers working together to create contingent models, which provide different solutions of varying scope. Broadly speaking, an ASP is a service provider that deploys, hosts, manages, and rents access to one or more software applications through the Internet or other private lines/networks directly to an end user. To execute these functions, application service provisioning requires a broad range of competencies, including skills and expertise from the services, networking, and application fields. With a multibillion-dollar market on the horizon, many IT vendors in these areas have developed ASP market-entry strategies. The result is that the current marketplace is very fragmented. This fragmentation arises partly from the model's inherent complexity, which this analysis describes. It is also a result of the diverse provider and customer companies participating and competing in the ASP arena.

Due to the strong real or perceived opportunities in the ASP market, many providers with diverse backgrounds have been driven to enter this new IT niche. This has led to confusion about which enterprises truly are ASPs and which are just partners with ASPs. Confusion has resulted in a common mistake, as indicated by the research— the inclusion of ASP suppliers and partners in a single category labeled "ASP"—which is partially justified by the fact that the line between the various categories is often blurred.

ASP models are rooted in functional core competencies in such areas as application infrastructure, storage services, network services, telecommunications, hosting services, systems integration, capacity services, hardware, software, and Internet services (Gillan et al., 1999). Box 2.1 describes these providers, or ASP value chain participants, based on the core function they perform.

Based on the synergy of some of these core functions, the first wave of ASP models (each one including two of the previously discussed core function providers) emerged as follows:

- Data center providers (application infrastructure providers; storage service providers)
- Network providers (network service providers; telecommunication companies)
- Hosting providers (hosting service providers; systems integrators)
- Infrastructure providers (capacity service providers; hardware vendors)
- Software providers (independent software vendors; value added resellers)
- Internet protocol/virtual private network providers (Internet service providers; network service providers).

BOX 2.1. ASP Value Chain Participants by Core Function

Application Infrastructure Providers (AIPs)

Offer Internet-based infrastructure and applications services and in some cases complete portfolios of services, including hosting and e-commerce applications.

Network Service Providers (NSPs)

Provide part of the infrastructure (bandwidth) and manage wide area network links necessary to deliver applications to customers.

Hosting Service Providers (HSPs)

Provide all services and infrastructure necessary for the development of a Web site or Web presence and for the management of data center facilities, and also host applications for ASPs.

Capacity Service Providers (CSPs)

Own and operate the data center infrastructure that ASPs need to function, such as the hosting of powerful servers.

Independent Software Vendors (ISVs)

Develop and market software applications, including those specifically designed for ASPs.

Internet Service Providers (ISPs)

Provide companies and individual users with an account and a phone number to dial in and gain access to the Internet.

Storage Service Providers (SSPs)

Offer hosting and access to storage devices and technology. They bundle services, software, and the storage devices formerly sold directly or through other vendors' channels.

Telecommunication Companies

Provide the "last mile" physical links between the applications and end users.

Systems Integrators (SIs)

Offer applications implementation, maintenance, and outsourcing business.

Hardware Providers

Supply the computing and networking hardware that resides in the data center. They also provide consulting and support services associated with the hardware system framework.

Value-Added Resellers (VARs)

Solutions-oriented vendors providing integrated hardware and software systems, often including consulting, design, and implementation services.

These models can be defined as the legitimate ASP business model "enablers." At a simple level, the various ASP business model enablers that interface with an individual ASP act as illustrated in Figure 2.1. The following is a brief discussion of their primary characteristics and roles in the ASP model and their mutual relationships within the

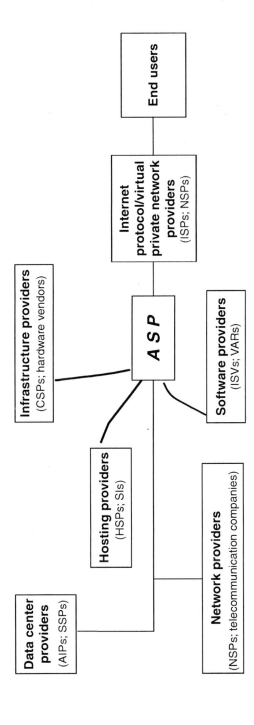

FIGURE 2.1. ASP core business-enabling relationships. *Source:* Adapted from Yankee Group (2000). "Executive Summary of Application Service Providers: Evaluating Strategies for Success." <www.yankeegroup.com>. Accessed May 31, 2001.

ASP environment. The analysis also highlights the fact that these business-enabling relationships have created, or may create, direct and indirect competition within the young and transitioning ASP marketplace. This may shape new business models and their characteristics in the future.

1. *Application infrastructure providers (AIPs)* are companies with expertise in managing large data centers. They operate hosting centers that are specially equipped for application hosting. AIPs provide Internet-based infrastructure and applications services, and in some cases a portfolio of services, including hosting and world-class e-commerce applications, delivered through the ASP model. Digex, Qwest Communications, and Intel Online Services have moved to the AIP model (Wainewright, 2001b; Sovie and Hanson, 2000; ASPstreet, 2001).

2. *Storage service providers (SSPs)* offer hosting and access to storage devices and storage area network technology. SSPs bundle services, software, and the storage devices formerly sold directly or through other vendors' channels. For instance, JAWS is a data center and storage provider for businesses and for ASPs, which employs the ASP model to provide secure data storage management to diverse customers in the IT industry (Greenemeier and Maselli, 2001; Lepeak, 2001).

3. *Network service providers (NSPs)* are companies that manage network resources. Traditional NSPs are phone companies, although Internet service providers (ISPs, number 11) such as AT&T are service providers that also provide network connections. In the simplest versions of the ASP model, delivery of services occurs through the Internet. Although this makes services very easy to access, the performance of those services is subject to the performance of the Internet links between the ASP and the customer and so is not totally predictable. For companies seeking a secure connection to their ASP, NSPs can provide dedicated links between the data center and the customer site through virtual private networks (VPNs). An example of an NSP is AT&T Global Network Services, which provides managed network services, advanced Internet Protocol-based solutions, and custom network outsourcing services (ASP Industry Consortium, 2001b; "Technique: ASP Infrastructure," 2000).

4. *Telecommunication companies* provide the "last mile" physical links that allow connection between applications and clients. Examples of such providers are AT&T, Bell Atlantic, and BT Ignite. Because of the increasing network complexity resulting from remote application hosting and management, they are vulnerable to being relegated to a decentralized role in IT-based industries. Therefore they are qualified to target, and compete within, the ASP market (Wainewright, 2001b; Sovie and Hanson, 2000).

5. *Hosting service providers (HSPs)* traditionally have provided all the services and infrastructure necessary for the deployment of a Web site or Web presence and for management of data center facilities. More recently, some HSPs have tailored hosting services to fit the ASP-based application delivery model and to meet the hosting services' expected performance along the ASP value chain. This has required complete reengineering of their approach to fit the hosting services model, as well as much internal work to add value to services and ultimately retain ASPs as a growing customer group. Examples are Exodus and Verio (Wainewright, 2001b).

6. *Systems integrators (SIs)* carry out technical integration work necessary to ensure that new software solutions integrate seamlessly with a customer's legacy—that is, old or existing—information systems. They supply applications implementation, maintenance, and outsourcing business. In addition to working with ASP customers, SIs also play a role in integrating the business solutions of participants in the ASP value chain. Given their critical application integration and management skills, they see the ASP market as a natural extension of their core expertise. SIs can be powerful gatekeepers in the customer selection of applications, solutions, and infrastructure. EBtech is an example of an SI that also offers Web-based application solutions through the ASP model (Wainewright, 2001d; Sovie and Hanson, 2000).

7. *Capacity service providers (CSPs)* own and operate the data center infrastructures that ASPs need to survive, such as the powerful servers that host valuable customer information. Companies in this sector range from super giants, such as Exodus, IBM, and Qwest, to smaller players, such as TeraBeam

Networks. The larger firms play a major role as facilitators in a company's transition to the ASP model, as does IBM with its ASP Prime Program. CSP services include, but are not limited to, leasing the use of their infrastructures to an ASP (Torode, 2000a; Gilmore, 2001b).

8. *Hardware vendors* are infrastructure providers that supply the computing and networking hardware that resides in the data center. They often also provide consulting and support services associated with the hardware system framework. Hardware vendors have the potential to enter the ASP marketplace directly. As an example, Fujitsu Siemens (2001) supplies hardware equipment and has also created its own ASP division. Other hardware and networking technology providers, such as Sun Microsystems have targeted the ASP market as a revenue channel, and have been partners in providing ASPs the necessary hardware since the early stages of the ASP industry (Sun Microsystems, 2001a; Compaq, 2001).

9. *Independent software vendors (ISVs)* are owners, providers, publishers, or rights holders of the software or content that an ASP customer/end user wishes to access and use. Typically, ISVs have written software applications that can be either purchased through retailers and value-added resellers (discussed next) or accessed through ASPs and other solution providers such as SIs. To be available to a business user, the ISV's software/application must be hosted at a data center and delivered to the end user via a public or private network using the IP standard (ASP Industry Consortium, 2001b). One ISV that has successfully set up and maintained an ASP division is Oracle. Other ventures have not experienced the same success. J.D. Edwards opened and shut its ASP business in less than one year (ASPstreet, 2001; Luening, 2001).

10. *Value-added resellers (VARs)* are resellers of software that also provide software training and integration services. They are solutions-oriented vendors providing integrated hardware and software systems, often including consulting, design, and implementation services. For a complex business application such as enterprise resource planning, a VAR's role is essential in bringing a practical understanding of the application and blending that knowledge with the details of the customer's business

processes and needs. In areas where the ASP model is young, such as Europe, VARs are often the only channel between ASPs and end users. An example of a VAR is Unisys Services (ASP Industry Consortium, 2001b; Total Telecom, 2001).

11. *Internet service providers (ISPs)* supply ASPs with connections to the Internet or to the dedicated private networks created by NSPs. Companies such as AT&T Worldnet supply business and consumer clients with an account and a phone number to dial into and gain access to the Internet. Many ISPs bundle access along with a basic suite of hosted applications. PSINet is among the ISPs that are expanding their activities with an ASP-like model of renting services to differentiate and gain new market share (Stanco, 2000).

In essence, to effectively support customers, ASPs must handle delivery, integration, maintenance, and support for software that works in the customers' unique business environment. To do this, they work with and through many partner relationships. For example, according to hardware and networking services giant Cisco, ASPs spend 40 to 60 percent of their cash flow on partnerships with NSPs such as Exodus and with telecommunication companies such as AT&T (Maselli, 2000b). Most, if not all, ASP operations depend on the strength of partner networks that are built to support underlying specific ASP models. To ensure delivery of the services promised, ASPs need partners that have high technical skills, developed through serving customers in the past (Gillan et al., 1999). Underlying the ASPs' new delivery mechanism is thus a complex stream of business models made of numerous vendors, partnerships, and alliances necessary to put all the pieces together and match end user requirements.

General ASP Business Model Characteristics

As discussed in Chapter 1, the advent of ASPs and the infrastructure to support them was driven by the desire to meet the needs of businesses that do not have the time, money, or resources to purchase, deploy, and manage needed applications. These businesses need software to help run their companies more efficiently, improve customer service, and create competitive advantages.

The ASP business models implemented to date have several common characteristics. They make software applications hosted in a data center available over the Internet or other private networks to multiple users both from within company facilities and/or from anywhere via mobile phones and laptops. They are an optimal solution for small to medium-sized enterprises because they free companies from the burden and complexity of acquiring and managing IT staff and computer systems. ASPs also save capital by allowing these organizations to pay for the use of applications through a monthly rental scheme on a "per user, per seat" basis. They also give these businesses access to software that they could not normally justify due to their high costs, and spare companies the need to subsequently upgrade systems as they grow. ASPs generally purchase and manage software licenses from software vendors, and hardware from hardware vendors. A few ASPs have developed their own software to provide the degree of customization and integration that organizations are increasingly demanding. Many of these benefits are also important to larger companies.

Initial ASP offerings may consist of applications that would previously have been purchased directly by a business customer and installed and managed on a server at the business's premises. Other early services included the outsourcing of specific applications that manage a function within the organization, such as online travel services and the outsourcing of HRM. Beyond these general characteristics, however, are multiple combinations of expertise and business goals that respond to diverse business requirements, resulting in a multitude of ASP models with different specific features. A few primary models are identified as significant to understanding the present ASP marketplace and providing a foundation for developing a larger basic perspective. These models result from research and analysis of the existing marketplace by many experts (PR Newswire, 2001; Wainewright, 2001d; ASPstreet, 2001; ASPnews, 2001b; "Reshaping IT," 2001). These models can be grouped into four primary categories, which encompass all but a few of the ASPs presently in operation:

1. *Business ASPs:* These typically supply low-end, generic standard software applications for general administration activities to support business processes and/or collaborative applications (which enable simultaneous access to, and sharing of, informa-

tion, data, and projects by multiple parties, such as a firm and its suppliers or partners) to customers in any industries. Because of this, most have a horizontal customer focus.

2. *Enterprise ASPs:* These typically provide high-end software applications, such as ERP and CRM, developed by established software vendors and e-commerce applications, and supply extended application management-related services. They are both horizontal (expertise in functional applications) and vertical (expertise in specific industry applications and solutions) in terms of customer target as their primary focus is the management of enterprise-level applications.

3. *Specialist or function-focused ASPs:* These specialize in one or a few business functions and provide the software application, management, and related support and services required to completely manage the business functional areas they choose to serve. They tend to have a horizontal customer approach, as their primary focus is function-driven application management in a wide range of industries.

4. *Vertical-market ASPs:* These focus on applications that can thoroughly address the requirements of the industry or industries they choose to serve. They implement software applications and manage related solutions and services that are targeted for specific industries. The applications they manage are designed to address a wide range of industry-driven challenges.

An emerging category of ASP models that is also discussed here, because of its interesting implications for both the current and future direction and forms of the ASP business model, is:

5. *ASP aggregators or AASPs:* These bring together or aggregate numerous underlying ASPs and are designed to provide customers with a wider range of software applications and related services than a single ASP can provide. An AASP is in essence an ASP with a wide strategic and operational scope.

These five models are significant for this analysis as they represent existing, contingent forms of the general ASP delivery model that have been tested and implemented to date. They have characteristics in common with the general model yet show unique dimensions, which together illustrate the multifaceted reality of the present ASP environment. The following section first presents the analytical framework used to approach these ASP models' characteristics and then describes the specific contingent models.

SPECIFIC CONTINGENT ASP BUSINESS MODELS

Overview and Analytical Framework

Although most ASPs currently in operation do not have the internal resources to provide all the layers of services necessary to deliver applications to end users, a few ASP companies are able to provide complete, end-to-end solutions. Discussion of contingent ASP business models thus must necessarily include analysis of the degree of value chain integration that specific ASP models pursue—the extent to which individual ASPs can handle all the application-related delivery tasks, either internally or through effective partnerships. This is a critical business dimension and an important differentiating factor in the ASP market, as explained further in Chapter 3. It also has long-term implications, which are explored in Chapter 5.

Owning a data center involves a substantial up-front capital investment. ASPs that do not own choose to be flexible and, as the market and technology progress, avoid being locked into supporting their acquisitions and investments and so are better able to adjust to customers' rapidly changing requirements. A growing number of ASP firms are developing a service offering encompassing tighter control over infrastructure elements, as well as additional services such as IT consulting, systems development and integration, and hosted services, either through direct acquisitions and mergers or through partners. ASPs that had been exclusively concentrating on applications have added these skills, in some instances by acquiring small, specialized IT service providers, in particular those with expertise in implementing ERP, e-commerce applications, and e-business development competencies (Total Telecom, 2001; Gilmore, 2000d). The range of tasks and services an ASP can provide, alone or through partners, is significant for the long-term viability of the ASP models discussed here, and is discussed further in Chapter 5.

Because of the variety in ASP contingent specific business models, and to reflect the unique combination of ASP internal competencies, objectives, and customer requirements, the analytical framework includes a discussion of the following mission-critical dimensions:

1. *Application offerings:* This is the primary business dimension that defines an ASP model. The extent to which ASPs delimit the types of applications they offer, deliver, and manage on behalf of customers determines the model and the strategic focus. A broad variety of application offerings, designed to serve diverse end user requirements across industries, is referred to as a horizontal ASP focus. A more narrowly specified application offering for one or a few selected markets is referred to as a vertical market-focused ASP. Examples of these ASP types are given later.

2. *Customer selection:* This is a second business dimension that determines and differentiates one ASP model from the others. The breadth and depth of an ASP's customer and industry targets also determines a specific business model and the degree of strategic focus. ASP business models that only target some industries or some segments of an industry adopt a focused market strategy, while those serving customers of any size, in any market have a broadly focused (or not focused at all) market strategy.

3. *Operations:* The operational scope is another critical strategic dimension, which is tied to the ASP's core competency focus and strategic intent. The decision ASPs make to build and manage internally all the components involved in serving their customers—such as application development, physical network infrastructure, and data center and servers—versus partnering for these components with a third-party channel also helps define the specific ASP model's scope. Operational focus ranges from limited service (ASPs whose core activity is the implementation of computer application-based solutions that are remotely managed, as defined in Chapter 1) to full service (ASPs that either own or tightly oversee all the underlying components of their business model to provide extended services, as defined in Chapter 1). Within these two extremes are many intermediate combinations. The operational focus also addresses the geographic scope, domestic versus international, that the ASP model covers.

4. *Strategic fit:* This dimension, which determines the specific ASP models discussed in this chapter, arises from the contingent way in which ASPs match internal goals and core competencies—the choice of applications, the target customers, and the operational scope—with diverse individual market and customer requirements. Strategic fit, or match, involves focusing on customer, quality, cost, performance, and competition, and individual ASP models have shown varying unique strategic fits. At this stage, the analysis of this dimension is information oriented and does not explore the degree of success in the match, which is the focus of Chapter 3.

A further dimension is provided in a summary at the end of each discussion of the five selected ASP models, where significant elements of the four business dimensions are highlighted. The comments serve as a basis for the long-term considerations studied in Chapter 5. The following sections discuss in detail the five ASP business models through analyzing existing representative ASP companies.

Business ASPs

Business ASPs typically supply low-end, generic standard software applications, generally acquired from established software vendors, that support general business administration processes or online collaborative business applications (such as e-mail and conferencing applications). Business ASPs also provide brand name prepackaged application services to the general business market, and some have also developed or acquired core application-related skills to integrate with optional third-party services. Most business ASPs provide core services, which are the basic services needed to manage the application environment and ensure a base level of customer satisfaction. Only a few large business ASPs offer a portfolio of applications and related services to match a variety of business requirements, and provide managed services (all of the core services plus additional services and guarantees involving support, security, application performance, and data redundancy) to extended services (all the managed services plus additional professional services such as application configuration and extension, strategy and planning, and training and educational support), as defined in Chapter 1.

Although most business ASP models have been horizontal, working across many industries with a preference for small to medium-sized clients and limited services, recent evolutions, both new start-ups and incumbents that have modified their existing models, show some degree of defined vertical market focus or full-service operational scope.

Interliant

Interliant is a business ASP and part of NaviSite, offering a broad range of outsourced business applications including Exchange/Outlook and Domino/Lotus Notes, complemented by comprehensive Web hosting solutions, to support virtually every Web-driven requirement. Its customers of all sizes worldwide are in various industries, such as food manufacturer Eagle Family Foods Inc., online encyclopedia World Book Online, Financial Services advisor Beacon, and entertainment giant Rank Group—a horizontal perspective. Its operational scope is global, with headquarters in the United States and activities in the United Kingdom and France, and it is full-service oriented. Its in-house talent pool is combined with the expertise from acquired companies and strategic partners for applications. It has the necessary infrastructure, such as Microsoft Windows NT, Unix operating systems, and Sun Microsystems' Solaris, to ensure a complete or full service to customers. Its strategic fit comes from providing the design, implementation, deployment, and management of cost-effective, fully integrated Web-based solutions, which deliver uninterrupted access to applications, total reliability, flexibility, and speed (Interliant, 2001b).

FutureLink (Part of Charon Systems)

FutureLink offers a variety of business application offerings and solutions, including Microsoft Office for back-office administration and Outlook for e-mail. It also manages any existing applications that are Microsoft Terminal Server or Citrix Metaframe compliant, and provides integration services. Its clients in various industries and sizes include manufacturers KIK Corporation and Enerline Restorations, and service organizations such as the National Multiple Sclerosis Society, Goodwill Industries, and Watsonville High School. Its operational focus is international, with activities in the United States, Canada, and Europe. It manages a core or limited-service operation, relying on partnerships with industry leaders such as Compaq, Citrix, Microsoft, and Sitara Networks to provide efficiency, cost-effectiveness, simplicity, speed, and top-level service. Its strategic fit arises from offering a wide range of applications and services to a diversified customer base, including large companies that are in a strategic position to match and use the wealth of FutureLink's solutions, and from providing immediate implementation, continuously optimized performance, and regular updates, supported by expert personnel (FutureLink, 2001).

Mi8

Mi8 offers business administration and collaborative applications, including Microsoft Exchange/Outlook and Office along with enhancements such as wireless access, e-mail-to-fax, and an Office 2000 Virtual Desktop, enabling users to require only a Web address to access their personal computing environment from anywhere. Its customers, small and midsized organizations in different industries, include venture capitalist ARCH Venture Partners, law firm McConnell and Associates, entertainment business Metropolitan Entertainment Group, and Cornell University's Johnson Graduate School of Management. Its operational focus is international, with offices in New York and London. Mi8 has an internal limited-service focus and relies on partners such as Microsoft and ThinAirApps for application solutions and Compaq, Cisco, Digex, AT&T, and Citrix to have a powerful infrastructure. Its strategic fit arises from a fast and flexible problem resolution process, aimed at guaranteeing easy access, free and unlimited support to customers, full system functionality, and constantly improved performance (Mi8, 2001).

TeleComputing

A leading business ASP in Europe, TeleComputing, offers over 200 business and customer-specific applications, including Microsoft Exchange and Office 2000—one of the largest portfolios in the ASP industry. Customers are end-user business clients: over 400 midsized companies in various industries such as manufacturers Bergen Tanker Brothers and West Fish Norwegian Salmon, business services firm Confex, and U.S. consulting firm Global Knowledge Consultants. It serves NSPs, telecommunication companies, and other service providers through a private label designed to address multiple needs. This ASP, which has operations in Norway, Sweden, and the United States, has a full-service approach, built on strategic alliances with Microsoft, Citrix Systems, Exodus, and Compaq. Its strategic fit derives from providing a complete end-to-end application services delivery package—including a technology system framework, consulting, design, development, and managed services—usually deployed in only four weeks, a time frame that generates immediate benefits to customers and their end users (TeleComputing, 2001b).

Summary

These business ASPs show unique features that differentiate each from the others within the same model category. However, they have some common characteristics that help define the business ASP model. Business ASPs are defined by service choice and management of business applications, and most show no preference for a particular industry in choosing to offer and deliver business-driven applications to satisfy a wide range of business requirements. Most are limited-service oriented and need to partner for the missing components of the ASP value chain they do not develop internally. Although the discussed ASPs generally possess the characteristics of business ASP models, and are fairly successful in strategically matching their goals and internal capabilities with customer needs, many are deficient in some key business characteristics.

Research results based on studies of a wide range of business ASPs indicate that most business ASPs do not adequately focus on the development of customization (modification of applications to individual customers' needs) and integration capabilities (enabling customers' old systems to integrate with new, upgraded, Web-based systems). Only the most established business ASPs, including the ones discussed in this section, do approach and resolve the integration and customization requirements of their customers, mainly by capitalizing on partners' capabilities and expertise. Furthermore, only a few seem to be able to offer a range of services to complement the remote management of the applications offered. The implications of these characteristics are evaluated further later in this chapter and in Chapter 5.

Enterprise ASPs

The broadest and most familiar form of ASP (Wainewright, 2001d) in 2001 was the enterprise ASP. Market researcher IDC defines enterprise ASPs as those that provide managed or extended services supporting such business processes or functions as ERP, ERM, CRM, and e-commerce business applications (Newcomb, 2001b). Unlike business ASPs, enterprise ASPs choose to run and manage these more complex applications. Their focus is to meet the individual requirements of larger clients and/or the challenges of more complex business environments. In addition, enterprise ASPs differ from business ASPs in that enterprise ASPs provide high-end software applications and extended application management-related services, such as additional configuration and customization as well as consulting services. Many to date have offered a portfolio of complementary suites and applications. Most enterprise ASPs are horizontal in targeting either midsized or large customers in all industry segments.

Some serve just one customer size, such as growing medium-sized customers, in more selected industries. Recent enterprise ASP evolutions have shown a more narrowly defined vertical market focus by concentrating on customers in specific industries or industry segments. In terms of operational scope, they can be both limited-service and full-service.

Agilera

Agilera, part of BlueStar Solutions, Inc., offers a broad range of top-tier integrated applications, including e-commerce from Ariba, BroadVision, Oracle, CRM from PeopleSoft, ERP from Lawson, and Supply Chain Management from J. D. Edwards. Its target customers are selected emerging and midmarket companies in specific industries (retail, manufacturing, distribution, financial services), such as manufacturers Flash Electronics, LumiLeds Lighting, and MD Helicopters, and human resources (HR) provider SCI Companies. Its operations are limited to the United States, with offices in several states. It has a full-service operational focus, achieved through tightly controlled partnerships that bring Agilera experience and expertise in implementation and integration (CIBER) and in Internet hosting infrastructure (Verio). Its strategic fit arises from a highly customer-centric focus and a quality- and scalability-driven approach, which provide integrated applications environments, best-of-breed solutions, a single point of contact, a powerful and protected network, comprehensive service-level agreements, and scalability. In early 2001, Agilera acquired Applicast to offer a new range of application products, such as Siebel CRM and Agile (collaborative manufacturing) tools and business support, and to continue offering expertise in key business areas (Agilera, 2001).

Corio

Corio implements, integrates, and manages a suite of enterprise software applications from leading vendors such as Ariba, People-Soft, Oracle, Microsoft, and SAP for ERP, Siebel Systems for CRM/marketing, and Commerce One and BroadVision for e-commerce. It calls this suite an Intelligent Enterprise. Among its target customers are midsized companies, such as Internet portal Excite@Home and consultant Peppers and Rogers Group, and also large companies, such as utility consortium Enporion, which actually constituted the majority of its customers at the end of 2000. Corio operates internationally and was working to become a global company in 2001. Its application-driven, core service model hinges on a strong partnership strategy, having shifted infrastructure management, rated a non–core competency, outside. Its strategic fit involves constantly focusing on the application management process, promoting integration, and building economies of scale into the process, which produce rapid delivery, affordable solutions, and extensive expertise to support clients' growth and their ongoing challenges (Corio, 2001a).

Interpath

Interpath focuses on world-class enterprise application management and remote managed services, including SAP-based ERP solutions, CRM application services, e-commerce solutions, and e-business development services and support. Customers are companies of all sizes (some with worldwide operations) in every industry, such as pharmaceutical manufacturer Bayer, service provider Greenville

Utilities, employment service Manpower, express courier UPS, and media firm MJI Broadcasting. Its main operations are in the United States, with offices in the Pacific Rim. It began a global expansion with the August 2000 acquisition of a leading Australian ASP. It has a full-service operational focus, with its own proprietary data and network center. Interpath partners with companies that are leaders in their market, have proven methodologies, and share its commitment to excellence in customer service, infrastructure (Cisco Systems, IBM, Nortel Networks, Sun Microsystems), and applications (Microsoft, Pivotal, and Vignette).

Interpath's strategic fit involves providing secure data environments, flawless application service management, staff experience, a single trusted source, and an increasing portfolio of applications and services. For example, it acquired Interliant's ERP hosting and related services in July 2001, which meant the addition of a team expertise and ERP business offering that Interpath rated a must to address its customers' requirements (Interpath, 2001; Newcomb, 2001c).

Summary

Although these ASPs undoubtedly show unique characteristics stemming from individual core competencies and organizational goals, they also possess common elements that together form the main body of the enterprise ASP model. Enterprise ASPs are defined by the choice, implementation, and management of powerful, complex applications and their support-related services designed to handle IT systems and business functions within medium to large customer organizations that may have critical connections of their own with nationwide, international, and even worldwide business partners and customers. They show a much stronger focus than business ASPs on customization, integration, and supplementary value-added services, either developed internally or added through acquisition strategies that provide quick access to highly demanded solutions. The best enterprise ASPs of 2000, including those discussed, operated full-service models by tightly partnering for the components of the ASP value chain they had not developed in-house and maintaining full control over them.

Although the ASPs discussed here seem to have successful business models, others not included are deficient in some important characteristics. Research results indicate many enterprise ASPs targeting customers have application offerings that are too broad, which results in a lack of adequate internally developed core competencies, which in turn results in lack of focus. Such ASPs fail to thoroughly understand their customers' present and future business needs, and they have difficulty in improving their customer service to strategically fit their customers' objectives. Only the most established enterprise ASPs, including the discussed ones, seem to be broad enough to build a winning strategic fit yet agile and focused enough to be flexible and adequately responsive to rapidly changing market requirements. The implications of these characteristics are evaluated further in this chapter, and in Chapter 5.

Specialist or Function-Focused ASPs

Specialist or function-focused ASPs provide applications that serve a specific professional or business activity, such as customer relationship management, human resources, financials, sales force automation, messaging, and Web site–related services. They differ from business and enterprise ASPs, as specialist ASPs focus on selected areas of expertise, in which they become full experts in understanding, developing, streamlining, and managing, thus delivering a complete, end-to-end solution that reengineers the business process and solves function-driven challenges. Specialist ASPs offer their customers one or a few applications that require special expertise to manage and operate, such as intensive data analysis or high-volume document management. They employ in-house experts who recognize and thoroughly understand the requirements of their specialist user base. Because their main focus is particular areas of expertise, their target customer group is usually horizontal, and they serve customers in any industry segment and of varying size who need to outsource these particular functions. Some, however, are vertical and combine specialist applications with a narrower customer target, one to five industries.

Employease.com

Employease.com provides HRM software applications that it develops and markets itself, as well as a suite of related services, for managing HR departments in companies with up to 3,000 employees. It sensed an opportunity to offer an alternative to expensive and complex HR applications to small and medium-sized companies. Among its customers are Amerisure Insurance, Inc., Works.com, PSS/World Medical, Inc., and Cabrini College. It operates across the United States, and its full-service approach focuses on keeping costs down to maintain affordability to its target clients. Behind this is a robust network that warehouses all employee and benefits information in one central, shared database, protected with fully encrypted sessions. Its strategic fit arises from being a service, not a software company, which intimately knows its market segment. To ensure satisfaction, it wraps implementation, professional services, training, and ongoing support around its network to make applications easy to implement, learn, and use (Employease.com, 2001).

NetLedger

NetLedger specializes in finance (accounting) functions. The target customers are individuals with small home offices and small, growing businesses, such as Alan George and Associates, Milo Inc., and Open Door Technology. The company has offices in the United States and Canada. Operations rely heavily upon an integrated partnership with Oracle. As of June 2001, NetLedger and Oracle were jointly offering an integrated business management service under the new brand Oracle Small Business. NetLedger also used selected business partners to reach a variety of vertical markets, such as Stamps.com, 3rdSector.Net, and ADP Payroll Services. It formed partnerships with several companies such as OfficeMax, ADP, and Yahoo! to distribute and market NetLedger's suite of applications. Its strategic fit derives from the use of a completely integrated Web-based service that saves customers' time and money and enables clients to run their company more efficiently. NetLedger is committed to providing real-time, anytime, anywhere affordable access to Fortune 500 equivalent business-enabling power (NetLedger, 2001).

Outtask

Outtask is a multispecialist ASP that offers a portfolio of functional applications either as single-point solutions or powerfully integrated portfolios, from financials to SFA, from HRM to travel and payroll management. Customers are companies of all types, any size: bricks and mortar, consumer-based, new economy, manufacturing, and professional services, across the United States, such as Chicago Board of Trade, Electrolux, Ericsson, Polaroid, Perceptual Robotics, and McKinley Marketing Partners. Operations support delivery of a total solution that is configured toward flexibility to meet customers' unique business needs. Partners are selected from among industry leaders in technology, business applications, and office services, such as CyberCFO, Grant Thornton, Exodus, and Primus, to ensure Outtask delivers a broad portfolio of solutions that meet any need, along with dedicated support and training (Outtask, 2001).

Its strategic fit arises from eliminating IT barriers, which provides operational simplicity, as well as from providing top-level cost-effective performance delivered with knowledgeable people and secure and reliable systems. In July 2001, Outtask announced the acquisition of Aspen Technology's ASP division to strengthen its specialist base and add Aspen's complete Siebel CRM application suite to its multispecialist offering menu (Mark, 2001).

United Messaging

United Messaging is 100 percent focused on Web-delivered messaging functions, based on Microsoft Exchange and Lotus Domino. It concentrates on the broad needs of the business enterprise. Among its customers, of any size in any industry, are Thomas Jefferson University, biopharmaceutical manufacturer Centocor, worldwide real estate firm Grubb and Ellis, and insurance firm Trustmark. United Messaging has international operations, with headquarters and several offices in the United States and activities in London. Its full-service scope revolves around the power of strong relationships, which it has built with leaders in the IT industry, such as Sun Microsystems, to ensure that every solution is built from best-of-breed products and technologies and to guarantee an end-to-end service. Its strategic fit derives from providing a mix of world-class people, processes, and technologies that rapidly deliver the business-critical messaging applications and services businesses most need. Its distinctiveness is in the delivery process, which United Messaging seems committed to constantly mastering and improving (United Messaging, 2001c).

Summary

The ASPs described in this section have concentrated individual efforts on diverse areas of expertise. At the same time, they share common elements that characterize the specialist ASP model in general. Specialist ASPs are defined by the choice, implementation, and management of software applications, in many cases designed and developed internally, which are required to manage specific business departments and functional areas of expertise. Because they specialize in one or a few business functions, they are horizontal in terms of the customers they typically serve, choosing to focus on the function more than on any specific industries. Therefore, they tend to have a broad, diverse customer base, which may have widely different business requirements. The high learning curves of specialist ASPs involving one or a few processes enable them to charge affordable monthly user fees and at the same time allow the best ones, including the discussed specialist ASPs, to address and accommodate specific customer objectives.

Specialist ASPs implement a broad-focus differentiation strategy and manifest a commitment to ultimate customer satisfaction. They develop processes, technologies, and people that are needed to manage specific areas of expertise, and repeat processes over a large user base, thus becoming more and more specialized experts and potentially very competitive. To ensure the optimal performance of applications, processes, and technologies, they adopt a full-service approach, achieved through strong partnerships. The commitment to have the best people and processes, in order to attract well-informed clients, seems to imply a good business approach in the ASP marketplace.

Although the discussed specialist ASPs seem to have a successful business model, others not included in the analysis have not. Research results indicate most specialist ASPs are young enterprises that have not reached profitability yet. Also, those that develop their own software, which they also manage as an ASP, might be at risk of losing focus by investing time and energy in traditionally separate fields, software sale and software rental. The implications of these characteristics are also evaluated further in this chapter and in Chapter 5.

Vertical-Market ASPs

Vertical-market ASPs are different from the previous models in that the vertical market ASP's primary business dimension is the choice of applications that aim to fulfill the complete requirements of one or a few selected industries or industry segments. These ASPs tailor solutions to the needs of one or a few specific industries, such as banking, health care, education, engineering, financial services, and professional services. With management typically drawn from the industry they serve, vertical-market ASPs aim to be a one-stop source of applications and online services designed to complement, streamline, or reengineer their customers' existing business activities. However, what differentiates vertical-market ASPs from the other models is their objective of addressing specific challenges in specific industry sectors for which they have become highly sought-after, effective problem-solving experts. They evaluate customers and build application solutions to support the customer's industry-specific business objectives.

Their application offerings range from single software application-based solutions, used to manage one function in one industry segment for a limited-service vertical-market ASP, to a variety of applications, either acquired from software vendors or developed internally, for full-service vertical-market ASPs, whose goal is broad to full coverage of the selected industries.

Portera

Portera provides integrated combinations of Web-hosted professional services automation (PSA) applications and services for the professional services industry. Its over 250 customers around the world, such as AvantGo, CrossWorlds Software, and McLaren Consulting, are professional service organizations serving industries such as public relations, advertising, and taxation as well as professional services departments in large, multinational enterprises. It has an international market presence—twenty-two offices in twelve countries. Portera relies heavily on partners such as Oracle (primary business partner for applications), Microsoft Great Plains, Avasta, Cisco Systems, and Storage Networks to provide its PSA solutions. Its strategic fit is enabled by an in-depth knowledge of the target customer and its market, whose requirements are fulfilled through totally Web-based, industry-tailored, integrated solutions, delivered as a unified process, which increase the productivity of dispersed teams, as well as by acting as a single point of support when applications are running (Portera, 2001).

TriZetto Group

TriZetto Group is a fast-growing health care technology company, whose vertical-market ASP division provides services to all the businesses and end users within the health care market segment. Among its over 150 customers, serving approximately 70 million patients, are Talbert Medical Group, Eye Clinic of Wisconsin, and Kelson Pediatric Partners. It has operations across the United States, with regional offices in several states. Its full-service approach is built on tightly controlled partnerships to provide complete solutions to its selected vertical market. TriZetto relies on over seventy-five application and technology partners to deliver a combination of the best capabilities of traditional, industry-established applications with the foremost e-business technology and processes. Its strategic fit arises from TriZetto's three business units working in concert to provide seamless communication and complete tailored solutions, through bundling of infrastructure, primary software applications, and information access and reporting. The company delivers value via a combination of market-specific expertise, infrastructure, technology, and world-class customer service (TriZetto Group, 2001a).

LearningStation.com

A vertical-market ASP that delivers educational content through personalized Web-based desktops to the education market, LearningStation.com serves 144 schools with a total of 23,000 students, such as Cotswold Elementary School and Lowcountry Day School. It also offers on-site training, online assessment, and professional development tools, and provides students and teachers access to instructional applications and professional development programs through any Web-enabled device. It has activities in the United States and Canada and affiliations in Australia, with a full-service approach reflecting its aim to provide the most cost-effective technology solutions for academic achievement. To this end, it maintains close partnerships with Microsoft, Inspiration, and Tom Snyder for applications, and Time Warner, Qwest, and EarthLink for technology. Its strategic fit involves delivering a highly comprehensive suite of education-oriented content to enable its customers to meet industry requirements. By operating some of the most popular software applications to meet a variety of instructional and management goals for schools, it has customized its tools with the resources users need, delivering them where and when they are needed (LearningStation.com, 2001a).

Fullscope

Fullscope provides collaborative design support solutions, complemented by Internet-based and networked IT technologies and business services, to the manufacturing and engineering service industries. Its service delivery architecture integrates diverse online services (document management, collaborative CAD visualization, project management, SFA) into a single interface. Among its customers are market leaders and innovators such as Komatsu America. Fullscope operates throughout the United States and has adopted a full-service approach by partnering with providers that have effective business models, market viability, and high-quality features and functions. Among these are UpShot Inc. for sales force automation and Sunset Direct for technology. Its strategic fit is enabled by its management expertise in targeted industries, which offers a common look and feel across application solutions, and by consolidating and simplifying access to the offered solutions, which reduces product development time and related costs, lowers investment risk, and offers a one-stop service for billing and all service/support needs (Fullscope, 2001; PR Newswire, 2001).

Summary

Vertical-market ASPs differ from previously discussed models in that vertical-market ASPs' primary business is customers in one or few selected industries or industry segments. The primary characteristic of the previous models is the choice of applications that fill varied business needs; in particular, the specialist ASPs provide applications that solve specific function-driven challenges. For vertical-market ASPs, the choice of selected customers, which have industry-specific business challenges, determines the design and development (or purchase if they do not do this in-house) as well as the implementation and management of business software applications that are selected to serve the customers' specific requirements. In choosing to focus on the customer first, the structure of their models is the reverse of that of the specialist ASPs. They choose to thoroughly know their customer's industry and fully address its market-dictated requirements, which they become experts in.

Deep knowledge of and experience in the customer's industry is often either acquired through staff previously operating in the same industry or developed by operating in the same sector, where the ASP developed its own applications to solve industry-specific needs (Maselli, 2000a). Research results indicate that vertical-market ASP models, which appear to be successful, represent the strongest ASP model, given their primary focus on selected markets and high degree of focus. The implications of these characteristics are also evaluated further in this chapter and in Chapter 5.

ASP Aggregators or AASPs

ASP aggregators (AASPs) are, as the name suggests, an aggregation of numerous ASPs, which may have diverse underlying models themselves. They are designed to integrate software offerings from multiple ASPs and provide a single sign-on access, as well as unified billing and administration tools. By bringing diverse ASPs under one umbrella, AASPs are meant to provide clients with a wider range of software applications and thus fill voids in the ASP value chain as a single ASP cannot. They also enable small, limited-service ASPs to compete effectively. Unlike all previously discussed models, ASP aggregators represent the interests of disparate ASPs and multiple service providers and act as the single point of contact for their customers. These customers may shift from one ASP to another within the AASP as their business and market requirements change, without the need to break or modify existing contracts or initiate new relationships with their ASP vendor. AASPs enable clients to choose among a larger number of providers and options.

Jamcracker

Jamcracker provides businesses of any size and type with multiple IT and ASP services through a single source. It supports multiple application and service vendors in each service category, including market leader ASPs and software/technology vendors. This gives Jamcracker's customers the ability to switch to any vendor as the need for specific solutions arises. Among its more than 100 customers in several industries are online marketing service B2Bworks, Inc., designer and manufacturer Vitria, and IT service provider Digital Island. Jamcracker's operations, which are international, are based on multiple-level partnerships (business and technology consulting partners, such as Accenture, application partners, such as Oracle, and service partners such as Appshop and UpShot). The underlying architecture is designed to add or to replace multiple, dispersed service providers. The result is access to a leading Internet-based architecture that would cost millions to build internally. Jamcracker is a business, enterprise, specialist, and vertical-market ASP and also an infrastructure service provider. Its strategic fit derives from providing customers with access to a breadth of service and application offerings with the flexibility to move to different vendors, as customers are not locked to fixed-term contracts with the individual vendors (Jamcracker, 2001a).

eZigma

eZigma's AASP program provides comprehensive and flexible solutions for growing businesses of any size, such as Newhomesmedia. It has made deals with several ASPs to offer applications in HR, accounting and finance, business management services, sales and marketing, international trade, invoicing, fulfillment, and inventory from a single source. It provides a wealth of underlying expertise, software, and services that are readily available through the Web, thus sparing clients the considerable time, money, and inconsistent quality associated with custom-built solutions. Its main operations are in the United States (California, Texas, and Nevada) and in the United Kingdom. Not only does eZigma partner with multiple ASPs for the delivery of solutions, it also partners with IT service providers for the necessary supporting technology. Its strategic fit derives from providing the breadth of Internet resources and tools collected through diverse providers, and instant access to its Web-based applications, all of which is achieved through superior, twenty-four-hour customer support, which allows clients to be efficient in using all the information, tools, and software they access (eZigma, 2001).

iFuel (Part of iRevolution)

iFuel is a fast-growing AASP, launched in November 2000, which enables ISVs to deliver their applications, whatever their design or build, through iFuel's direct or indirect channels, in an ASP style, on a pan-European scale. Beyond this main customer target, iFuel also delivers ASP services to business customers, such as the entertainment company Really Useful Group. It has over 11,000 contracted users, which access more than thirty fully hosted applications from leading ISVs, such as Onyx Software. iFuel's model is not exclusively focused on business customers and end users but is also designed to add value to the ISV segment and its channels, allowing ISVs to provide software as a service and to supplement their revenues with an ASP offering. iFuel enables end users to access up to fifty leading applications across various industries through a network of iFuel partners, such as Citrix and RSA Security. Its strategic fit is enabled through providing secure access to a broad variety of applications from anywhere in the world, complete support, and a single source of responsibility for the entire back-end infrastructure (iFuel, 2001).

Summary

Although the discussed AASPs exhibit many special individual characteristics in terms of customer target and scale of operations, the analysis of these AASPs shows some common elements. ASP aggregators are defined by the aggregation of numerous ASP providers and other service providers that complement the ASP value chain under one company name. The AASP model is dedicated to offering an ASP outsourcing solution for access, management, integration, and support for Web-enabled applications from any source. This solution is designed to be less expensive, more flexible, and much more powerful, in terms of guaranteed performance, security, and reliability, than any single ASP. AASPs so far have been implemented thanks to a large network of partnerships and are characterized by a number of disparate business entities, each with diverse portfolios of offerings that together form the largest ASP companies.

By joining an AASP, small and start-up ASPs and ASP value chain enablers can provide their specialized, core-competency contribution and enable customers to switch to any AASP partner whenever business and market requirements dictate a change. The benefit for the customer lies in the ability to use as many ASP vendors as needed at zero switching costs.

The most established AASP, Jamcracker, utilizes best-of-breed partners in all areas, such as industry leaders Siemens for on-site support and McAfee for antivirus and security tools. It also partners with established ASPs, such as vertically oriented enterprise ASP Surebridge for its PeopleSoft HRM and Siebel CRM solutions, with vertical-market ASP Portera for its PSA solutions, and with specialist ASP Employease for its HRM and benefits administration suite. This type of partnership approach indicates that many established ASPs need the AASP model to give their own customers more choice, flexibility, and higher guaranteed performance than they can provide alone. This fact also shows how the AASP model can be viewed as another revenue channel for individual ASPs, a sort of association that produces a win-win situation, through facilitating the meeting of ASP suppliers and clients.

Although the discussed ASP aggregators seem to have adequately successful business models, research into other AASPs shows other interesting aspects of the model. On one hand, AASP signal a strong market demand for providers that can offer a one-stop solution and a single point of contact. The existence of AASP indicates a perceived lack of flexibility in the contractual terms individual ASPs have offered their customers. Such contracts bear high switching costs and may be among the major reasons for the limited adoption of ASPs so far, as briefly discussed in Chapter 1. On the other hand, as the ASP market matures and the strongest ASP models survive, the marketplace may no longer have a need for AASPs. As ASPs strengthen their business processes, increase their market share, and gain customer confidence, individual ASPs may no longer need to join an aggregator.

Furthermore, some AASPs have experienced mixed results. Agiliti, once considered an aggregator, discarded that model in 2001 to focus on infrastructure and e-commerce services. According to Agiliti's chief financial officer, Mark Payne, "the model was ahead of its time" (Mears, 2001a).

The various ASP models and their business partners and enablers can now be better appreciated as significant elements of a multifaceted ASP environment. The next task is to identify the contingent ASP business models' problems to provide additional understanding of the ASP market.

ASP MODELS' CHALLENGES

This section discusses significant problems many ASP models have experienced throughout the short history of formal application service provision. This discussion provides further insight into the marketplace's structure and dynamics.

Overview

Although ASPs are prospering, they have not achieved the spectacular growth predicted by analysts. A few highly publicized ASPs such as Pandesic, Red Gorilla, and HotOffice, which had attracted much media and industry attention, have even failed, leaving their customers in trouble.

The premise, and high-profile promise, was that ASPs would relieve companies of the burden of maintaining internal client-server networks and application integration. By outsourcing all the hosting and application-related services, ASPs would let enterprises access the same tools on the Internet through a VPN. ASPs would scale up to provide the same benefits to many clients. In reality, ASPs had a hard time proving they could effectively and efficiently deliver cutting-edge applications over the Internet. Although part of the problem lies in the general downturn that hit global IT sectors in 2001 as a result of the dot-com companies' collapse, most of the fall was due to the following specific shortcomings in technology, marketing, and management (Lipschultz, 2001):

- The Internet has not performed with the robustness and security of private internal corporate networks.
- Small and medium-sized companies have not been receptive enough to ASPs' offerings.
- Software was not effectively Web-enabled for distribution over the Internet.

- Most ASPs have failed to understand their customers' specific needs.
- The high costs of building ASP infrastructure have been underestimated.
- The difficulty of factoring in all ASP-related costs has produced pricing schemes that proved far from clear to customers and far from being comprehensive enough for ASPs to make money.
- ASPs have failed because, as a result of all these factors, they could not get and retain sufficient numbers of customers.

These limitations underscore a gap between the ASP business model and the state of the market (Moran, 2001).

Many potential customers are uncertain about ASP issues such as pricing, security, performance, and service levels (Lepeak, 2001; Flanagan, 2001). The ambiguity in what ASPs are and do has led to further confusion and uncertainty. It is, then, not by accident that more and more new or merged companies entering the market have carefully avoided dubbing themselves ASPs (Pring, 2000), in an effort to create distance from pioneering, and in most cases challenged, ASPs. However, beyond general issues facing the industry, it is necessary to examine the real challenges that specific models have been dealing with.

Problem Issues

This section discusses the following significant problems in the implementation of ASP business models, as identified from research on existing ASPs:

- An undefined market and customer focus, which resulted in early ASP models offering to remotely host and manage any applications, for any size business, without diversifying application offerings and/or trying to understand the specific needs of selected customer groups in order to reach out to customers most in need of their solutions.
- Tied to an undefined business focus, the too-broad approach of some specialist players that developed their own software and then marketed it through the ASP model, failing to establish and maintain a clear, narrowly defined market strategy.

- Ineffective communication about the ASP model and its delivery mechanism, which resulted in limited understanding, or misunderstanding, by customers of the advantage of outsourcing software applications and related services to an ASP.
- Market resistance to relinquishing control over internally managed mission-critical data and systems, which resulted in failure to proactively deal with customers' internal IT staff concerns about the perceived ASP threat—a failure to manage the "people barrier."
- A lack of effective transfer of knowledge to clients' employees by many ASPs, particularly enterprise ASPs that dealt with complex applications, which resulted in lack of participation by customers' staff and in their inability to truly benefit from the ASP solution. A particularly challenging area involves inadequate training of customers' staff.
- Tied to insufficient familiarity with the ASP concept and to the fear of relinquishing control over proprietary mission-critical data, the failure by many ASPs to attract a sufficient number of customers to become profitable soon enough to enable expanding, differentiating, and gaining competitive advantages. Without enough customers on which solutions can be tested and verified, ASPs were not able to demonstrate their capabilities, create a reference base, and match fast-changing market requirements.
- Stemming from failure to adequately lay out business goals and implement them in a way consistent with the ASP strategy, and tied to the already noted inadequate communication about what the ASP is all about, the inability by many ASPs to attract their true "sweet spot"—firms with up to 250 employees.
- The inadequate level, or total absence, of customization, integration, and other services by early ASP models, particularly business and enterprise ASPs, which resulted in failure to match existing market requirements and in dissatisfied customers.
- A multilevel failure to understand the ASP delivery mechanism, its performance, and its complexity, which often resulted in underestimating the value-chain enablers' role, in poor execution of the basic ASP delivery model, and in failure to meet customer requirements. Among the most common noted problems are

—inadequate or ineffective partnerships that made many ASPs fail in terms of application delivery, because individual ASPs did not have access to, or badly utilized, the necessary technology and application system framework to provide a robust service overall;

—the high costs of network access for many start-up ASPs, which resulted in failure to build an adequate technology base to support growing market/end user requirements;

—multiple infrastructure and performance issues, which have made many ASPs fail to deliver the promised service and resulted in major disruptions of customers' business activities;

—poorly defined SLAs default on the SLA terms because of ineffective partnerships or infrastructure and performance issues;

—lack of a single point of contact, a person or team within the ASP organization that the customer can rely upon anytime and is fully accountable in case of problems;

—insufficient attention to ASP mission-critical security planning and management;

—failure to deliver the promised (but unrealistic in the early stages of the ASP life cycle) significant cost savings, which resulted in extreme dissatisfaction and general negative backlash against the ASP model overall; and

—the issue of ASP durability, which has created concerns among ASP value-chain enablers and vendors, who are often reluctant to partner with ASPs for fear they will get out of the market soon.

Some problems that involve long-term considerations are also part of the discussion in Chapter 5.

Many pioneer business and enterprise ASPs have not communicated to customers, clearly enough, what their application offerings are. There is not a broad understanding of what is meant by an application. In addition, customer targets and offerings have not always been spelled out clearly. The major problem with the first wave of ASPs was that they would host everything for any customer, in a desperate pursuit of business, claims Linda Rose, founder of vertical-market ASP RoseASP (McCausland, 2001). This observation points to the lack of a defined business plan in the early stages of the industry and the need for a clearer market focus to succeed and develop, which vertical-market ASPs seem to have adopted as a strategic foundation for their model, as noted in the previous section.

A related issue concerns specialist ASPs that have developed their own applications, as some appear to have mixed two traditionally separate fields, software development and software utilization and management, although the mix enabled them to offer additional customization, integration, and deep functional expertise in their application solutions. The problem for many specialist ASPs developing and offering their own software is the risk of losing business focus. For example, enterprise ASP Surebridge's chairman Khurana believes this problem is so great as to represent a real threat for them, even foreseeing a point "where you [the specialist ASP] have to decide if you're going to be good at developing code or delivering a service" (Torode, 2001). Some specialist ASPs also appear to be in a weak position to compete with established software brands, which also indicates a lack of clear market focus. As Meta Group analyst Dean Davidson noted, it is very hard for ASPs to gain a foothold in the market that is not already filled by a well-known vendor. As he emphasizes, most companies are still making buying decisions "based on brand name and looking for a hosting provider second" (Torode, 2001), which does not help start-up specialist ASPs.

Tied to the lack of focus on application offerings and too broad customer targets is limited end user understanding of what the ASP does in the first place. The marketing tools were utilized badly or not at all in the early stages of the ASP phenomenon, with the result that few IT managers at corporate levels are sure how this business model is supposed to work. For instance, an ASP Industry Consortium survey published in late 2000 showed that ignorance of the model itself was one of the top five reasons for foregoing the use of ASPs (ASP Industry Consortium, 2000).

End users also may resist relinquishing control over business-critical applications. Although no significant statistical evidence is available to corroborate this, many customers have indicated that when the electronic connection is interrupted, for example, there is little possibility for ASPs to regain control over the data. For instance, Ben Reytblat, president of Web host Quadrix Solutions Inc., is vehement about how painful a poor ASP experience can be in this area: "I advise against ASPs for any application you can't live without for a

few hours" (Hall, 2000). Another warning comes from Indian Motor-
cycle, which has avoided using them so far. "I want to be in control of
the applications that are affecting the company, and ASPs don't totally promise that yet," says F. Wagenseller, company's chief information officer (Lipschultz, 2001). This degree of customer suspicion
is also tied to the use of new technologies—common to new, fast-
growth industries. As Julia Legge, marketing director of Emerald
Lizard, observes, "people do not want to be the first to try" (Allen,
2001b).

An important implication of this discussion is the failure by many
ASPs to proactively deal with network managers' doubts and questions about the perceived threats of ASPs to their job security
(Newswire, 2001). IT staffers are voicing these concerns. For example, Mike Lucas of Compuware notes, "Network managers who fear
outsourcing themselves out of a job are one of the factors that are
holding back the ASP delivery model." John Tonnison, a consulting
partner at ASPassist, a professional services firm that helps end users
understand the ASP market, agrees. In his view, the main issue is that
"the IT department could see the ASP as a threat." Tonnison cites IT
resistance as one of the top ASP problems. To him, IT managers need
to understand that the ASP would supplement their department, not
supplant it (Newswire, 2001; Mears, 2001d).

A major issue for ASPs is what can be defined as a people barrier.
From a long-term perspective, it is essential to find ways to educate
existing and potential customers about the value of application service provision. Given its importance, and because of recent educational efforts —identified as a critical element for the growth of the
global ASP market—Chapter 4 develops this topic.

Another challenge particularly concerns enterprise ASPs, which
typically deal with more complex applications than business ASPs.
They often have not provided for an effective transfer of knowledge
to the customer's internal staff, including IT employees and technology users, before any project begins and during implementation. According to Gartner Group's Richard Hunter, "The mechanics and
strategy of knowledge transfer on enterprise resource planning implementations are fairly complex. Knowledge transfer takes time to
document what's being done, and it takes time to train one's own people to use the documentation" (Ruber, 2000). The amount of training
provided to customers varies among ASPs, yet what most have of-

fered to date is quite limited. ASPs have typically included the cost of limited training as part of the implementation fees; additional training costs more. For example, consultant firm Engage.com's Colin Britton observes, "Many people treat training as a one off hit, and until you experience the application for a period of time, you won't know exactly what you need out of the training. You are still going to require additional training, and you're going to have to pay for that" (Maselli, 2000c). Therefore, many ASPs have not anticipated either such a customer approach to training or the actual need for training to enable staff to access complex applications. Many ASPs have failed to make their applications understandable, usable, and accessible by end users.

Another complex issue is that many ASPs have failed to attract enough customers to enable their own growth (Kerstetter, 2001). For example, outsourcing firm ITNet, which moved into the ASP market offering SAP-based ERP software in 2000, only announced its second customer over a year after signing the first one (Moran, 2001). In addition, when ASPs manage to attract customers, they often fail to deliver the goods. For instance, Ben Young, owner of Web design firm Big Blue Hat, thought he had found a great deal when he signed with Red Gorilla to keep track of his billable hours for clients. The service was cheap. But just as he was about to bill a client for a labor-intensive project, Red Gorilla abruptly shut down because it had run out of money. "I guess you get what you pay for," Young reckons (Kerstetter, 2001).

Being a cheap application provider is not always a sustainable strategic move for an ASP, and to many observers it signals lack of market focus. Research indicates that the best ASP models have instead crafted and implemented a clear market (applications, customers, and partners) strategy.

Another weakness stems from failure to lay out business goals and implement them consistently with the ASP strategy, the strategic and operational fit. Many ASPs have missed their best customer size— firms with up to 250 employees—as their preferred target has been businesses with over 250 employees. The problem is that the latter generally have an IT manager. In this respect, Katie Ring, author of the report "Application Service Providers: Opportunities and Risk," notes that it is "almost a sociological fact" that IT managers often focus on "building an empire" in the company they work for, and one of their enemies is outsourcing (Newing, 2001b). In contrast, smaller companies most often do not have an IT manager, and their overburdened staff would be more likely to gladly offload some functions to ASPs. Clearly, many ASPs have not carefully selected their target market and thus have missed a strategic opportunity. A few have done so, and have achieved significant results, as shown in Chapter 3.

Some ASPs have been criticized for their "one-size-fits-all" or generic solution approach, and for delivering "plain vanilla" prepackaged solutions with no customization (Newing, 2001a). Many limited-service business ASPs have not developed customization and integration capabilities internally, as their core business is to manage applications on behalf of end users. This lack of customization, coupled with lack of communication about each other's expectations, can lead to a negative experience. For instance, Thomas Morrison, Internet information server manager at data specialist ATL, recalls,

> In a previous job, [we] outsourced our technical support to a third party. It became clear that a terrible mistake had been made. We brought it back in-house immediately. I wonder if ASPs have the expertise and understanding of the business needs of individual companies. That kind of experience is gained over many years. (Newswire, 2001)

Concentrating on the customer's view is a primary key to ASP success. The ASPs that are able to match their customers' needs and business challenges have been the most successful in the global market, as Chapter 3 illustrates.

The lack of application customization is also evident in enterprise ASPs that target medium-sized customers. A frequently noted issue is the mismatch between their ability to offer ready-made complex and expensive applications in a matter of weeks and growing customer requirements for greater customization and postimplementation support, which cannot be delivered within such short time frames. According to Mitch Kristofferson, Corio's vice president of marketing, "It's not that out-of-the-box isn't valuable to those customers. But to get an organization of that magnitude to change its legacy processes [quickly] is not practical. They have to scale to make that investment" (Fonseca and Jones, 2001). Enterprise ASPs have so far specialized in fast implementation of complex solutions, and many have not adequately accounted for extensive customization required by large customers and/or medium-sized customers with complex business challenges. Market requirements seem to dictate the need to focus on this capability to achieve a winning strategic fit, or a match of an ASP's internal goals and skills with customer requirements.

Also, poor execution is another major problem stemming from the number of subparts in the ASP delivery model that must be managed and integrated, which has led to the inability to keep up with customer expectations (Flanagan, 2000b) and may pave the way to failure. To AASP Center 7's CEO K. Phillips, "the model has proven more complex than originally believed, and many companies did not build this complexity into their business plans" (Flanagan, 2001). Many ASPs have underestimated their task. The fact that an AASP claimed a shortcoming exists in other models is not surprising. AASPs were developed to fill in gaps in existing ASP models. This seems to indicate that some models may not be fit to survive over the long run. Roger Barkerville of Citrix, a leading supplier of application server software and services, also witnessed as an ASP partner the fact that many ASPs have misunderstood or underestimated the complexity of the model and its challenges, observing that "a lot of people jumped in," yet they "didn't have enough IT experience" (Moran, 2001).

The ASP failure rate also depends on the decision to outsource noncritical layers of the delivery model, per se a strategically sound move. The result of outsourcing to the wrong partners or providers can be a disastrous execution. For example, the apparel retailer OshKosh B'Gosh Inc.'s online store appeared open to customers—they could place orders, but the orders went nowhere. The communication link between the customer and the ASP, Pandesic, managing its Web site had been lost. The problem was worsened by the number of parties unrelated to the outsourcing agreement and by the ineffective, uncontrollable, network of partners Pandesic had established. OshKosh struggled for several days to reestablish contact with its Web server, which was managed by Digex, Pandesic's hosting service provider partner. Digex in turn had to rely upon another party, OshKosh's telecommunications carrier, to finally reestablish communications (Anthes, 2000), thus making a relatively simple connection problem a lengthy one to resolve, which resulted in substantial damage to OshKosh.

Another problem is the high cost of network access to very small organizations, coupled with the restricted internal resources of small, limited-service ASPs that prevent many from being able to build and sustain substantial technological investments in-house in order to adequately perform their service throughout the value chain. For instance, David Angwin of European ASP Vistorm cites the "considerable" resources needed to be up and running, and stresses the importance of adopting and operating structures that resemble those of telecommunication companies, which have "the deep pockets" to build a strong model (Newing, 2001b). The implications of alliances between ASPs and telecommunication companies for the growth of ASPs, and competition from telecommunication companies, are explored in Chapter 5. Among the ASPs studied, those with a too-broad customer focus—that is, no clear market focus—and a variety of business and enterprise application solutions to satisfy diverse customer requirements were found unable to sustain at the same time the necessary costs of network access, and were likely to be among the failing ASPs over the short term.

Financial stability and profitability to create the necessary technology architecture is therefore a major issue ASPs have to address to win larger market shares (Bradbury, 2001). As discussions in Chapters 3 and 5 indicate, ASP size—a result of having enough revenue to grow their technology base—is a differentiator in today's environment, and a key factor for survival and future growth. Most ASPs have yet to prove that they can actually make money. Even specialist ASPs, which have a clearer, leaner operational strategy than horizontally focused business and enterprise ASPs, are having profitability problems.

A number of important issues concern infrastructure. Many ASPs have failed because of poor strategic partnerships in the area of infrastructure or because of the exorbitant costs (for people and equipment) connected to maintaining a high-level infrastructure (Flanagan, 2000b). Market participants agree with such analysts' views. For example, Bill Joss of AASP 7 Global notes that at the moment there are infrastructure and server issues in almost every ASP deal. "The ASP model has created a false expectation in the customer's mind that you can pick a nice application, wing it down the wire and expect it to run properly." With his twenty years of experience in outsourcing, Joss sees this proposition as inaccurate, as in his mind the ASPs that take this route shift the task of solving infrastructure issues to the client (Harrington, 2001). This observation signals the likelihood that single ASP models might be weaker than AASP models, as the latter can provide a stronger infrastructure tied to their larger networks of partners. Whether this is true in the long term is a topic of Chapter 5.

Another major challenge involves guaranteed performance or uptime. The issue has implications for ASPs with limited scope and inadequate supporting partnerships, such as small business and enterprise ASPs, which cannot control their performance on the Internet. According to Steve Sopko of Agreement Design, a company that negotiates SLAs between users and vendors, the 99.999 percent application uptime guarantee that many ASPs offer is virtually impossible to deliver. Market insiders confirm this. For instance, George Khater, hosting provider Navisite's director of strategic projects, claims that more than 30 percent of application failures are due to unreliable performance, because "many ASPs are promising better performance than the application itself can give" (Maselli, 2000c).

The absence of objective performance metrics is a related challenge. An ASP can claim the ability to provide 99.999 percent performance, but how can one measure it, and what does it include? In a Forrester Research survey of fifty "Global 2500" companies, 43 percent of respondents complained about a lack of objective data for measuring application and systems performance, which forces them to make investment decisions based on soft information ("Reshaping IT," 2001).

Even large enterprise ASPs may face performance issues because they lack some internally managed services. For instance, Corio, an enterprise ASP, cannot offer local presence and support in many regions such as Asia, nor can it offer multilanguage capabilities. In spite of the fact that Corio was ranked sixth among the top ten ASPs of 2000 (Whalen et al., 2001), its enterprise ASP model is not inherently immune to challenges. Enterprise ASPs have a broad array of applications, yet they cannot supply the broadest application-related service packages to customers these days. Such a comprehensive model may not be sustainable for a single ASP. This has implications for the future of some enterprise ASP models, which are discussed in Chapter 5.

Also, in the area of performance, one of the greatest challenges facing both application providers and their customers is establishing clear SLAs that protect the integrity of the application and the various players along the ASP value chain. The results of an April 2001 forum organized by IDC confirm this is a serious problem. "Defining a meaningful and balanced SLA" was the fourth greatest reported challenge in the ASP buying process for early adopters who participated in the forum (ITAA, 2001a). Many potential customers are concerned about letting a third party run their business and their clients' data because of unclear service levels (Haskins, 2000).

A useful example of the ambiguity in SLA management is offered by Elite.com, which rents business applications for time and expense tracking and billing services over the Web. It offers a 99.5 percent uptime guarantee, ensuring "commercially acceptable performance" of its application. But what does "commercially acceptable" mean? President Mark Goldin says, "If it's so slow you can't perform any normal business process, we will grant the company service credits." But according to its SLA, Elite.com will provide credits only if the service is shut down completely because of a failure in its software, servers, or network connections. In addition, the SLA does not cover the network provider's last-mile connections to the end user's site (Maselli, 2000c).

Tied to unsatisfactory performance, particularly for the business and enterprise ASPs that do not exhibit a clear, narrowly defined market strategy and have not developed strong partnerships to become full-service oriented, is the lack of a single point of contact, that the customer can rely upon anytime and is fully accountable in case of problems. The importance of such a role has been ignored or neglected by many ASPs with a generic delivery model and an unsystematic operational strategy. A director of management information systems at Hoyts Cinema Corporation has observed that the ASP's role is not just hosting an application in a data center, "because anyone can do that." Instead, the key to an ASP's customer service and strategic fit is to take "responsibility from the application level down to the last mile" (Torode, 2000b). The problem, as Art Williams, analyst at Giga Information Group, correctly observed, is that many ASPs "have been long on technical depth and short on business sense." He contends the market is full of technology experts who know what they are doing, but in the end "customers should really be able to rely on a user advocate" (Anthes, 2000).

One difficulty certainly lies in getting business, IT, and legal managers to view the relationship with an ASP from a unified perspective.

However, what is still missing in many processes, particularly for limited-service business and enterprise ASPs, is a single person or a team within the ASP whose task is to keep the customer happy. Chapter 3 shows that most of the successful ASPs studied have adopted and fully implemented a strategy using a single point of contact. Chapter 4 provides additional rationale for such a strategy.

Security concerns are the major issue that ASPs have yet to resolve. Based on an early 2001 survey conducted by Zona Research on behalf of the ASP Industry Consortium, security remains the top concern for existing and future ASP customers. These fears are not without foundation. The survey results indicate that only 36 percent of its members provide user-based access control and authentication, and only 22 percent support and provide intrusion detection ("ASP Industry Consortium," 2001; "Survey," 2001; Gilmore, 2000g). Some ASPs use shared servers. The implications are easy to see. For instance, ChannelWave's Ron Schmelzer notes that a list of customers or salaries could be dumped into a database containing the same information from fifty competitors renting the same program (Hall, 2000). Also, John Safa, chief technical officer at security vendor BitArts, emphasizes that until security thinking evolves, users have good reasons to be concerned over external hacking threats, as most security today "takes a reactive rather than proactive approach" (Allen, 2001b).

Security is also the biggest issue for European ASP users. Only 25 percent of current ASPs have the majority of European customers connected through VPNs, whose security and reliability is higher than Web connections. In Europe, this is a major challenge and serious inhibitor to the mass adoption of ASP, given the perceived high risks of Internet connection coupled with a lack of robust legislation regulating the Internet (Total Telecom, 2001).

The hosting of data at an outside facility is recognized as a risk by almost two-thirds of respondents to the November 2000 Software Information Industry Association survey ("ASP Gaining Awareness," 2000). This is related to the fact that most ASPs have not had adequate resources and business focus needed to control security components in-house. ASPs that do not adequately account for security because it is not their core competency—this is true for all ASPs based on existing models—or because of scarce resources risk going out of business, unless they effectively partner for these key components.

The link between security focus and long-term viability of existing ASP models is examined in Chapter 5.

Another challenging issue faced by ASPs involves the promise, at the early stages of development, of significant cost savings. Paola Bassanese of European market researcher Ovum, for instance, blames the industry for making unrealistic promises: "Those marketing the ASP model have foolishly opted to promote it as a way to reduce costs" (Allen, 2001b), yet renting services was seldom less expensive than buying them outright. This view is widespread. The results of a Lucent Technologies–commissioned survey of current and potential ASP users indicates 40 percent reported "cost unpredictability," along with the already discussed difficulty of defining and negotiating clear service levels as the leading factors preventing repeated use of ASP (Arlen, 2000). An interesting story in this regard involves U.S. apparel manufacturer Norm Thompson. Vice president of IT systems Matthew Abraham investigated both Corio and USi service options and decided not to go for an ASP, because he would actually spend 20 percent more per year with an ASP than if he handled everything himself, providing he could bear the investment cost (Kerstetter, 2001).

A case in point that summarizes and highlights some of the main challenges a less-than-robust ASP will almost certainly face concerns Pandesic, a business and enterprise ASP established in 1997 by two of the three largest, richest technology companies, SAP and Intel. Pandesic did not establish a defined customer focus and eventually attracted the customers it needed least: small, unproven dot-com start-ups with no revenues and little to lose. In addition, it chose not to bill its customers for "traditional" consulting services, but instead charged 2 percent on its customers' margins. Pandesic tried to bury those costs in a flat monthly fee, which ultimately hindered the revenue stream needed to sustain its business. This ASP closed its doors in early 2001, primarily because it could not foresee "timely profitability" due to "slower than anticipated market acceptance of business-to-consumer electronic commerce solutions" (Kerstetter, 2001; Bradbury, 2001; Flanagan, 2000b). The second reason behind its failure was that although the company had probably the most complete ASP package available on the market, it still could not address all customer requirements (Koch, 2000).

The lessons from Pandesic's failure are useful. Many of the first-generation ASPs, particularly business and enterprise ASPs, have realized that operating a widely horizontal ASP may not bring long-term success, and they understand the need to urgently rethink their scope. Business ASP Interliant, for example, announced in early 2001 the layoff of 14 percent of its workforce in an effort to narrow its scope. Its executives said it would offer services only where they see the greatest demand. Also, as a result of lower than expected earnings, FutureLink announced the decision to step away from its ASP business and focus on professional services (Interliant, 2001b; Future-Link, 2001). Also, enterprise ASP Corio was trying to understand in 2001 how out-of-the-box software can be more focused and addressed to specific industries' business requirements, in an effort to narrow its application offerings, to diversify, and to remain competitive (ASPstreet, 2001). Horizontal ASP models were thus evidently taking steps toward increased focus and clearer scope.

Finally, another key issue is the perceived durability of ASPs, which is negatively impacting ASPs' relationships with their value chain suppliers and enablers. "Every day you read a report that says 60 percent of ASPs won't be here soon," says Adam Juechter, vice president of sales and channel management at ASP Mi8. In his view, ASP value chain partners are rightly tempted to think twice before establishing relationship with an ASP, reasoning, "I don't want to hitch my wagon to someone [an ASP] who won't be there in six months" (Flanagan, 2000a). ASPs must significantly strengthen their ties with partners to remain in the market over the long run. Chapter 5 explores such related scenarios.

The discussion of a variety of end users' actual or perceived problems connected to the ASP application delivery method is a major step in defining the state of the industry. Recognition of these challenges also highlight the strategic areas in the ASP delivery model that specific models must fulfill to succeed. Some have, and their winning approaches are discussed in Chapter 3.

ACCEPTANCE AND ADOPTION OF ASP SERVICES

This section presents the state of market recognition and acceptance of ASP services, which is a high general familiarity with the business model and its benefits among IT decision makers, counterbalanced by limited detailed knowledge, resulting in low acceptance and adoption rates. This analysis focuses on the U.S. and European markets because more extensive data is available for these areas than for the Asian, Australian, and Latin American markets (where the ASP phenomenon is quickly catching up).

The literature contains multiple reasons for the still low acceptance and even lack of awareness of the ASP business model. The global ASP market is now reconciled to lower growth than expected in 1999-2000. Despite over 100 ASP success stories, documented by a major ASP Industry Consortium study conducted in 2000, the industry is still dealing with a slower than expected adoption rate. A study developed by U.K.-based PMP Research, with information gathered from 868 organizations equally distributed among EU countries and fifty ASPs across Europe, contains interesting facts. Awareness of ASP services in Europe ranges from 40 percent (in France) to over 80 percent in Scandinavia and the United Kingdom, with Germany and Italy in a 60 percent range. In the United States, organizational awareness and likelihood of using ASP services as of August 2000 ranged from 50 percent for small businesses to about 65 percent for medium enterprises and approximately 75 percent for large businesses (Total Telecom, 2001; Gilmore, 2000b).

Regarding adoption rates, a distinct difference can be noted between the two regions, due to the different stages in the life cycle of ASPs in Europe and in the United States, as well as region-specific factors. The ASP Industry Consortium's second tracking report, released in early 2001, found that two-thirds of U.S. firms, already familiar with ASP and interested in the outsourcing concept, were actually using ASPs (ASPscope, 2001b). The European ASP market was at a lower development stage, with approximately 150 ASPs operating, as opposed to approximately 1,500 in the United States, and usage ranging from nonexistent to low depending on the specific country. However, almost nine out of ten European firms were considering using an ASP in the future. This was actually a better result than in the United States (Total Telecom, 2001; Gilmore, 2000b). A significant point is that most European organizations that have an interest in ASP services are taking a cautious approach. Slow adoption reflects the specificity of the EU whose countries still have to reconcile their legislative and cultural diversity, and an EU data protection law dating back to 1995 that is hindering ASP development in Europe (ASPscope, 2001a; Gold, 2001).

A wider picture of the current awareness and adoption rates emerged from the initial results of a global ASP tracking survey. Unlike the previous tracking study, which focused attention on respondents already interested in the ASP concept, this further study is wider and less biased. The most significant preliminary findings are as follows (Newcomb, 2001a):

- Almost 70 percent of respondents are aware of the ASP delivery model, and almost 25 percent of businesses are already outsourcing applications in some form.
- Although only 8 percent of respondents are currently purchasing or renting applications from an ASP, close to one-fourth express a likelihood of doing so in the near future.
- No marked differentiation exists between regions globally with regard to awareness and willingness to utilize the ASP model. There appears to be consistency in awareness and willingness among both business types and business size.
- The primary reasons indicated for not using an ASP are "the wish to keep IT in-house," "no business case," and "not yet considered."

In summary, awareness of ASPs is rather high and widespread in the United States and Europe. There is a wider gap in the adoption rate, which mostly depends on the differences in the life cycle stage of application service provision in the United States relative to Europe.

CONCLUSION

This analysis indicates that many ASPs have failed to match diverse and unique customer requirements with their own strategic internal goals—what has been called the strategic fit. Major issues are the failure to properly plan, organize, implement, and monitor an appropriate contingent business strategy—one that makes sense for the specific situation at hand. This in turn results in backlash against the ASP delivery model as a whole. Challenges such as system security and integrity for remotely stored data will likely continue to represent a major obstacle to broad acceptance of the ASP model over the intermediate to long term (Gerwig, 2001; Borck, 2000; The Euronet, 2000). Chapter 5 examines further the implications of the anticipated challenges for the five described ASP business models. Over the short term, ASPs require clients and business partners to take a leap of faith on a relatively unproven model. To succeed over the long run, ASPs must convince end users and partners not only that individual ASPs can execute their task, but also of the validity of the ASP concept itself.

Although diverse models exist to satisfy customers' desire to focus on their core business and to outsource everything else, it is necessary to truly provide the services that enterprises are seeking. This is why the underlying relationships that form the complex ASP business model were covered in this analysis. Most ASPs must learn to tightly partner, integrate applications, and ultimately provide end users with a single-source perspective into whatever application or information they need. Customer satisfaction arises only from meeting the expectations of the customer and its end users (Mears, 2001d). In most cases, the ASP industry is not there yet. However, research results indicate that a few ASPs have managed successful and fulfilling business relationships with customers. To this end, Chapter 3 discusses optimal ASP performance, as well as the different models that have met customer and market requirements, essentially a contingency-based perspective.

Chapter 3

ASP Performance Experiences:
A Contingency Approach

INTRODUCTION

The objective of this chapter is to examine successful ASP performance in the current global market environment. Using a contingency approach, different models and strategies are identified that have been implemented to develop and manage successful ASPs servicing specific groups of customers. The chapter first discusses the contingency-based approach to success at a general level, by presenting both the demand side, diverse customer requirements in a variety of situations that ASPs are asked to fulfill, and the supply side, different ASP models developed to meet varying customer and market needs. The analysis then moves to a more specific company level to explore, through stories of existing ASPs, how different ASP models have actually performed successfully in contingent situations, in order to highlight the unique ways they have created value for customers.

Research substantiates the conclusion that the ASP business model can deliver value as long as individual ASPs pursue the model and approach appropriate for the specific situation. The discussion shows the top performers are, not coincidentally, those ASPs that have developed their business models in ways that fully address diverse specific business requirements. Overall research results provide evidence of the fundamental value of situation-based guidelines for ASP success and show that most often the underlying approaches of various models, rather than a single model, are conducive to successful performance. The conclusion is that survival of the ASP industry is not in doubt, but is dependent on the ability of individual ASPs to strategically meet specifically identified market requirements, the strategic fit. Success is also contingent on the specific combinations of outstanding implementation of business-critical fundamentals, which some ASPs have put to work, the operational fit.

THE RIGHT SOLUTION
FOR THE SPECIFIC SITUATION

The objective in this section is to explore the direct relationship between success in the current environment and different ASP models' ability to meet diverse market and customer requirements with solutions that are appropriate for the specific situation. In other words, the goal is to discuss how success in the ASP environment to date generally has been contingent on how business-critical dimensions have been effectively blended together in specific models, both the strategic and operational fit. Specific substantiating evidence is presented in the second section. To assist in the process of understanding how both demand and supply are driving a multifaceted ASP marketplace toward a broad variety of offerings and solutions, this section presents the demand side—diverse customer requirements that need to be fulfilled in today's ASP market. Later sections discuss the developing and managing of successful ASPs—the supply side.

Current and Anticipated Major Customer
and Market Requirements

The following is a partial list of the major existing and anticipated ASP market and customer requirements, which was developed from the literature and field research.

1. *Broad range of applications/application portfolios:* Many organizations do not want to deal with multiple vendors. A growing number of both SMEs and large corporate clients are looking for a single-source provider that offers a broad range of applications to meet diverse needs at varying times. Dev Ittycheria, vice president and general manager at enterprise ASP Breakaway Solutions, emphasized the fact that customers are "looking for people who can offer the widest breadth of solutions" (Clancy, 2000) that meet their specific individual business requirements.

2. *Full range of services:* Customers physically moving their mission-critical data outside their organizations require a service provider for a range of functions and tasks, from handling mundane, overlooked back-office functions to overseeing entire processes. Requirements go beyond reliability, security, and problem solving. Customers often need a broader expertise in integration and management, as well as adequate customer support.

3. *Customization:* Information systems can be built using software from ISVs, either purchased directly or leased via the ASP model, that include a set of prewritten, precoded application software programs. Customers at times require applications and services to be adapted to their specific business requirements. Application customization capabilities allow ASPs to modify software applications to meet an organization's unique requirements without destroying the integrity of the underlying software (Laudon and Laudon, 2001). Customization is a value-adding service that customers are increasingly looking for in their ASP relationships, since most information systems require some degree of customization to adapt to current business processes.

4. *Total responsibility:* Many customers may have little or no internal IT systems management in place, or outdated systems. They may require a sophisticated, comprehensive solution and have no desire to handle related problems internally. They can require an integrated operating system or technology platform to control scattered resources and multiple communication channels. They want to outsource complex systems to get IT to help, not hinder, their opportunities in the marketplace.

5. *Strong ASP-customer alliance partnerships:* Companies looking for ASP solutions are very often looking to effectively partner for selected aspects of IT via the ASP model. ASPs must operate closely controlled value chain partnerships themselves in order to provide a full menu of top-class products and services to their customers and in order for customers to view their ASP as a true partner. As Zona Research vice president G. Blatnik noted, "If there's a silver bullet for ASPs, it's an element of the service. The system must be bulletproof" (CIO.com, 2001), indicating that in order for the ASP to be-

come a true partner for its customers, it must ensure it can provide the same strong system a customer would like to have in-house.

6. *Experienced ASP management team:* Customers often require an ASP to be a reliable process contributor for the management of mission-critical data, in order to avoid concerns on performance, security of data, and problem solution at the customers' end. Many customers rate their relationship with an ASP as a value-adding relationship, not just a customer-vendor association (Mizoras, 2001). The ASP must show a willingness to work with customers and the ability to execute expertly. Effective sharing and transfer of knowledge is an associated requirement that only an expert team can provide to the customer.

7. *Single point of contact:* Since ASPs need access to a substantial range of technical expertise, from data centers and applications to agile infrastructure and a comprehensive breadth of skills coordinated from a number of strategic partners, customers need to be confident that the "best in class" package they are hiring will work for them. This can be done in a coordinated way through having one ASP person or team as the customer's point of contact.

8. *Access to a powerful solution at a variable cost:* Customers turn to outsourcing as a more cost-effective alternative to building applications internally, for example, to avoid locking themselves into IT investments that may restrict their investment in other ventures and to find experts who could run internal IT functions at lower cost. This is true both for SMEs that have limited funds for IT development and also for large organizations that increasingly outsource noncore competencies to avoid IT implementation, upgrading, and maintenance concerns.

9. *Global-scale expertise:* Many companies of all sizes and scope—from those in high-growth, high-velocity markets such as online portals to large, established brick-and-mortar enterprises expanding into e-commerce—are exposed to the global environment-driven challenges in the business marketplace. As they expand into foreign markets by widening their online accessibility and direct investments or strategic alli-

ances, they increasingly require an ASP with global-scale expertise.

10. *Ability to grow with business growth, or scalability:* Customers need reliable information system performance to meet current requirements, as well as additional capabilities as their business grows, coupled with the ability to manage incremental variable costs matched with incremental benefits. Flexibility is an essential requirement to remain competitive, and customers look for ASPs that understand present and future needs and demonstrate the ability to solve related current and future complexities.

11. *Speed in implementation:* Customers may have time-to-market constraints, and the implementation of early mover strategies to positively affect the introduction of their product or service with their own clients is vital to them. They need fast implementation of IT-based and Web-based solutions that support their rapid growth and mission-critical objectives.

12. *Deep industry knowledge and experience:* Customers may require solutions for industry-specific business challenges in such areas as project management, financial services management, health care-related process management, and the like. A growing number of ASPs are finding an essential requirement for success is deep knowledge of a client's specific industry-driven objectives and related business challenges. The savvy ASPs are working to develop and increase their expertise in vertical markets (Maselli, 2000b).

13. *Deep functional (process) knowledge and experience:* In-depth expertise in one or a few particular processes underlying application hosting and management is a critical business requirement for some companies, especially if the function is mission critical and takes up a considerable amount of the internal IT staff's time. Efficiencies result from learning and implementing on a wide basis applications that are meant for specific functions.

All ASPs cannot be all things to all customers. Demand for application service provision can be quite broad and is fueled by a variety of customer needs and market requirements. For companies that wish to outsource applications and the activities to support them, finding the appropriate ASP for the specific requirement at hand is a critical business dimension. As the following section shows, a few ASP business models that have been implemented to date provide the optimal match for the described requirements. They have developed the skills necessary to meet the above-mentioned market and customer-dictated requirements.

Different ASP Models to Meet Diverse Customer Requirements

The following are the ASP models, discussed in detail in Chapter 2, that have been identified as effective:

1. Business ASPs
2. Enterprise ASPs
3. Specialist or function-focused ASPs
4. Vertical-market ASPs
5. ASP aggregators or AASPs

Research indicates that these five models have thus far met or exceeded customer expectations, in situations where they hold tight control of all the elements of the new application service delivery model in unique, specific, and ultimately effective ways designed to meet the current market outlook and related specific customer requirements.

Market research also indicates that success has come where individual ASP firms have adopted and adapted one of these models to more fully meet customer requirements. Success has thus been contingent on providing customer value. Ultimately, this first depends on an effective and efficient strategic fit between the implemented model and customer expectations—one that has worked. Customer value also depends on the ability to execute systematically and repeatedly all the components of the ASP delivery model, the operational fit. The following section discusses each of the five models and shows in practice how they differ in meeting customer requirements in significant analytical areas. The analysis is based on existing successful ASPs and the ways specific customers and their requirements were thoroughly addressed.

CONTINGENCY-BASED PERFORMANCE IN ACTION: HOW DIFFERENT ASP MODELS HAVE FULFILLED DIVERSE CUSTOMER EXPECTATIONS

This section, as well as the discussion of problems and failures in Chapter 2, develops a contingency basis for the best-practices discussions in Chapter 4.

Strategic Analysis Overview: Strategic and Operational Fit

To systematically analyze the ASP market, the following discussion is organized by model type. In general, once ASP management determines the market type it wants to work within and their target customer group, it has to develop plans that enable adapting what and how they deliver within their model framework to specific customer requirements.

Because success is situation-based, it is not possible to provide a priori a generalized overall, comprehensive analysis that explains the strategic match for every ASP being examined. As the stories illustrate, each successful performance is contingent on the situations faced, and is the result of a unique, effective strategic and operational fit, which stems from having the right solution, approach, and implementation for the specific situation facing the customer. The value-creating strategic and operational match results from specific focus by the ASP on business-critical capabilities needed to meet customer requirements:

- *The ability to provide a broad range of applications or application portfolios,* involving quality-oriented application depth and breadth focus, which enables the ASP to provide the needed applications without diffusing internal resources on too many applications or application types that do not solve real business needs.
- *The ability to provide a full range of services,* involving a defined ASP core competency focus, one that establishes what is to be developed in-house and what is to be acquired via value chain partnerships, which enables the ASP to effectively meet

the real customer and market requirements, such as extensive customer support, at any given point in time.

- *The ability to provide application customization,* involving an optimal balance between significant customization and internal business objectives (a one-to-many model reflecting application process standardization), which enables the ASP to efficiently and effectively adapt applications and services to its customers' specific business requirements without disrupting its internal resources.

- *The ability to provide total responsibility,* arising from an integrated operating system or technology platform supported by robust infrastructure elements and from a high level of customer responsiveness, which enables the ASP to deliver the required range of services and customer support around remotely managed applications.

- *The ASP's ability to form and maintain strong customer alliance partnerships for selected aspects of IT with their customers,* involving an ASP having a full-service approach and a bulletproof application delivery and management process, arising from the ASP either managing its data center and mission-critical infrastructure directly or operating closely controlled value chain partnerships, which enables the ASP to become a trusted partner to its customers, one that provides the same strong application performance and system reliability its customers would like to have and control in-house.

- *The ability to provide an experienced ASP management team,* involving deep ASP value chain expertise, developed internally or acquired via partners, which enables the ASP to deliver the needed applications and services within secure data environments and per the agreed SLAs and also to provide the required postimplementation support, such as training.

- *The ability to provide a single point of contact within the ASP,* arising from the ASP's full-service approach and involving a customer-centric approach to the client's business and its needs, which enables the ASP to provide its customers an accountable support interface.

- *The ability to deliver access to a powerful solution at a variable cost,* involving the availability of IT experts within the ASP who have deep knowledge of the required applications and a strong application configuration methodology, which enables the ASP to manage its customers' internal IT functions at less cost and in shorter time than customers' internal IT staff could.

- *The ability to provide global-scale expertise,* involving effectively controlled networks of value chain partnerships established by the ASP, which enables the ASP to manage complex software-based applications that solve multiple, geographically dispersed, often unrelated business-driven needs.
- *The ability to provide an application that can grow with the customer's business,* involving ASP expertise in the complex technology and hosting capabilities needed to provide the optimal level of performance required by the specific business situation at hand.
- *The ability to provide speed in implementation,* involving ASP focus on mission-critical integration and customization skills, developed over a sufficiently large number of implementations, which enables the ASP to gain significant learning curves and efficiencies to lower implementation time and related costs.
- *The ability to provide deep industry knowledge and experience,* involving a clearly defined vertical-market focus and core competency, combined with in-depth understanding of customers' industry-specific challenges.
- *The ability to provide deep functional (process) knowledge and experience,* involving in-depth expertise in processes underlying application hosting and management, developed over numerous implementations that strengthen the specialization approach.

Successful ASPs have developed most if not all of these skills and have built them into their application delivery model. The following sections discuss these matches in practice. Equally important is reference to how these ASPs managed to overcome problems they encountered.

Business ASPs

Business ASPs typically supply low-end, generic standard software applications for general business administration activities that support business processes and/or online collaborative solutions.

TeleComputing

This is the largest business ASP in Europe. It offers over 200 business and customer-specific applications, including Microsoft Exchange and Office 2000. A more detailed profile of this ASP is given in Chapter 2 (TeleComputing, 2001b).

In 1997, Norwegian Confex ASA was a leading independent company that arranged conferences, courses, and exhibitions for executive management in the public sector, with aggressive expansion plans at the international level. Fast growth meant Confex needed a substantial upgrade to their internal network. Lack of the upgrade threatened to put a stop to the company's growth plans unless it was done quickly. Confex was tied down to the infrastructure and maintenance of its IT network, and sought an ASP-based solution that would give the company a broad range of applications, a full range of services, and guarantee speed in implementation and scalability, supported by the ASP's total responsibility. TeleComputing had the right solution for Confex. This ASP offered a complete application services delivery package, including consulting, design, development, and managed services, necessary to overcome Confex's system upgrade problems. Its quality-oriented application depth and breadth focus and its integrated ASP operating system or technology platform supported by robust infrastructure elements managed through its infrastructure and application partners enabled it to rapidly implement a scalable ASP solution (TeleComputing, 2001b).

TeleComputing gave Confex remote access to Microsoft Office, Outlook, Internet Explorer, Project and Caesar Business Systems, guaranteed Confex users 99.7 percent uptime, and was able to deliver a turnkey solution, which was deployed in a few weeks and generated immediate benefits to the customer, thanks to its defined ASP core competency focus and a strong application configuration methodology. Confex was looking for a solution like this. TeleComputing was quick to implement the service, thanks to its focus on mission-critical integration and customization skills, which lowered its implementation time and related costs. "We were up and running within two months," an extremely satisfied Nicolaysen says (Citrix, 2001a, p. 189). Confex's applications could now be accessed remotely from anywhere in the world, and the Norwegian enterprise could now concentrate on its core business. Confex raised user productivity through increased performance and more effective network management as managed by TeleComputing, and whenever there was a problem, Confex could call TeleComputing's desk and get it resolved, often in a matter of minutes (Citrix, 2001b).

The working strategic and operational fit between TeleComputing and its client appears to be effective. This is because TeleComputing's full-service business model had the robustness necessary to guarantee the substantial technology upgrade that Confex needed quickly.

FutureLink

This is a business ASP offering a variety of business application solutions, including Microsoft Office and Outlook. It also hosts any applications that are compatible with its technology platform. A profile of this ASP is given in Chapter 2 (FutureLink, 2001).

In 1998, Enerline Restorations Inc. was Canada's leader in pipeline liner systems for corrosion and production tubing liner systems for progressive cavity and rod pumping, injection, and disposal well applications, aimed at oil and gas producers. As a fast-track company, it was facing a serious time-to-market challenge due to lack of a centralized information infrastructure that could be easily accessed by all employees. It found itself with only one computer shared among thirty staff members. To sustain top-line growth, Enerline considered making the required significant capital investment—which proved cost prohibitive, due to the company's early stage of growth. It started looking for access to a powerful solution at a variable cost, a broad range of applications, and speed in implementation, among its critical strategic requirements. FutureLink had the optimal solution to overcome Enerline's problem (FutureLink, 2001; Laudon and Laudon, 2001).

FutureLink was open to hosting any software application if its experts were given four weeks to successfully test the new software in Enerline's environment, given its strong application configuration methodology allowing customization at the user's end, which made its applications compatible with any technology platform or operating system. The ASP gave Enerline access to a wide range of applications, from Microsoft tools to a sophisticated PriceWaterhouse-Cooper accounting system. It also gave its client a full range of services, such as Internet access, consulting, maintenance, and system backup activities and full-service twenty-four-hour support, reflecting its defined core competency focus. Enerline was up and running on FutureLink services within thirty days, thus meeting its requirement for speed in implementation. FutureLink's solution provided fast access to current production schedules and inventory levels, and production decisions were now made more quickly and easily based on timely and accurate information (FutureLink, 2001).

Enerline gained higher productivity and significant organizational improvements, such as being able to generate internal financial statements by using exported data from the existing accounting system in a matter of hours instead of weeks, resulting from FutureLink's focus on mission-critical integration and customization skills (FutureLink, 2001). Enerline's requirement for access to a powerful solution on a variable cost schedule was met by FutureLink, which reduced its customer's overall fixed cash outflow. Chief financial officer Ron Hozjan defined the positive experience as follows: "Thanks to FutureLink, we have quickly evolved from a one-computer shop to fast-paced customer oriented business" (FutureLink, 2001).

FutureLink was also the right solution for KIK Corporation, North America's second largest bleach manufacturer in the late 1990s. Rapidly growing KIK's business challenge was to standardize the IT and application systems used by its various manufacturing plants. A major problem was the fact that each plant had its own applications and procedures for handling accounting and financial issues. KIK therefore needed unified, centralized business applications and a dependable WAN solution to support its high growth. Its requirements included a broad application portfolio and a full range of services to support a desired comprehensive system in order to meet its own large customers' (such as Wal-Mart) needs, speed in implementation to support its rapid growth, and an experienced management team with documented ASP expertise in the required areas to support all its key objectives. FutureLink set up and implemented a Citrix-based centralized system at KIK's site, fully integrated with existing systems. All KIK locations were set up to access the company's unified data and applications (FutureLink, 2001).

All data previously maintained at individual plants was now securely stored and managed by FutureLink's Toronto office. The centralized solution gave KIK's 200 end users fast and easy access to the full suite of their hosted business and desktop applications. This was possible because of FutureLink's quality-oriented application depth and breadth focus, focus on mission-critical integration and customization capabilities that enabled fast implementation, and a core competency focus in the business application sector (FutureLink, 2001).

The solution overcame KIK's existing poor IT system performance tied to disparate processes in each manufacturing plant and created a unified, centralized, accessible process. Other main benefits were knowledge sharing with and transfer to KIK employees, and the synergies resulting from FutureLink's deep ASP value chain expertise, enabling FutureLink to achieve management team collaboration with KIK. "The people at FutureLink worked with us and shared their knowledge with us openly. They were patient, professional and saw us through every step of the project," acknowledged Sam Porcasi, KIK's IT manager. As a result of the new computing system, KIK managed to save $200,000 on the cost of computer hardware, and estimated IT support staff savings in the range of $100,000 annually. As Porcasi recognized, "a decentralized solution would have meant technical staff to handle nine separate upgrades in nine different cities." In addition, "by the time we would have been done, we would have had to start all over again because the next version would be out" (FutureLink, 2001).

This is an example of a winning strategic and operational fit between a business ASP and its client's internal and market requirements, which arose from a broad application portfolio, a full range of services, the necessary integration skills to ensure fast implementation, and an experienced management team.

Interliant

This is a business ASP with a broad range of comprehensive outsourced business applications, including Exchange/Outlook and Domino/Lotus Notes. A more detailed profile is given in Chapter 2 (Interliant, 2001b).

In 1999, Eagle Family Foods Inc. was a manufacturer and distributor of high-profile, national food brands that had been pursuing an aggressive growth strategy, often through acquisitions. Its human resources department faced serious operational challenges resulting from fast growth and acquisition-based strategies, which had put together disparate cultures and systems. The greatest challenge, and a major problem to overcome, was effectively tracking and managing employee benefits across the organization. Eagle was looking for access to a powerful solution at a variable cost, and an application package that would grow with expected internal growth, providing a minimal investment for the present. Interliant had the solution that satisfied Eagle's quest for value maximization and scalability, and also satisfied its critical requirement for a strong ASP-customer alliance partnership, because it had the full-service approach and the same bulletproof application delivery and management process Eagle desired to have internally (Interliant, 2001b).

The strong partner relationship with Interliant allowed Eagle to access the vast capabilities of the adopted PeopleSoft HRM solution, including a comprehensive set of standard reports that spared Eagle's users the need for customized reporting, a main solution to Eagle's problems, possible because of Interliant's operating closely controlled value chain partnerships that enabled it to be Eagle's only partner for IT. As Eagle's HR vice president Jim Byrne noted, by using Interliant's solution and support, Eagle quickly gained confidence in using the system and was up to speed "in no time." This was possible partially because of Interliant's robust infrastructure elements, which made its integrated ASP operating system fully available to its client. The immediate result was improved business agility and accuracy in tracking employee benefits. A main capability at Interliant's end was also a deep value chain expertise that fulfilled Eagle's experienced ASP management team requirement and freed Eagle's internal staff from the burden of IT maintenance (Interliant, 2001b).

Byrne rated Interliant as "the organization best equipped to meet each of our selection criteria," and the ASP partner that has "delivered consistently per promises." The desired scalability also translated into access to a powerful solution at a variable cost that proved more cost effective than if Eagle had developed the same core competencies in-house (Interliant, 2001b), thus exceeding Eagle's initial requirements.

Mi8

Mi8 offers business administration and collaborative applications, including Microsoft Exchange/Outlook and Office and enhancements such as wireless access and e-mail-to-fax. A more detailed profile of this ASP is given in Chapter 2 (Mi8, 2001).

In 2000, CPA2Biz was a start-up Internet-based service provider for certified professional accountants (CPAs). As a new business, CPA2Biz needed to grow quickly, to reach out to the U.S.-based association of CPAs with 450,000 members, and to support its plans for acquisitions to have an office presence in every state. It needed a solution that would guarantee speed in implementation to quickly resolve the frequent outages and painful interruptions resulting from an in-house deployment of Microsoft Exchange for e-mail communications, which created major workflow challenges for its 150 scattered employees. It was also looking for a system that would grow along with its planned fast growth. Yet CPA2Biz did not want to focus resources on building an internal communications infrastructure, and was looking for an ASP with a strong experienced management team to assist its staff and a full range of services to manage all of its present and future needs and guide CPA2Biz through the implementation process and beyond. Mi8 had the optimal solution for all these needs and worked to implement a Microsoft Exchange application (Mi8, 2001) that successfully integrated with CPA2Biz's systems.

Mi8 deployed and implemented a robust, scalable, and secure application package in one week with minimal expenditure of time and resources for CPA2Biz, therefore meeting a major requirement— access to a powerful solution at a variable cost. This was possible thanks to Mi8's expertise in the complex technology and hosting capabilities and its optimal level of performance. CPA2Biz was able to secure and maintain an ongoing active connection with Mi8's data centers, and easy access with no interruptions and a continuous workflow across the organization. In addition, Mi8 eliminated the lost productivity and frustration connected to the previous failures, improving CPA2Biz's system performance from less than 90 percent to over 99 percent. It followed CPA2Biz's staff throughout the implementation process thanks to its strong application configuration methodology, designed to guarantee consistently high performance and a fast problem resolution process (Mi8, 2001).

Along with these benefits, Mi8 provided a full range of services: twenty-four-hour customer support through a help desk, secure access to the Internet, and wireless access for many CPA2Biz's remote employees as an enhancement to their Exchange server-based connection. These services enabled CPA2Biz's processes to increase productivity and provide an even communication workflow among employees and its online-based customers (Mi8, 2001). The details of this ASP solution summarize the working match between customer requirements and Mi8's capabilities to satisfy them, resolving an urgent nationwide expansion need that, unless achieved, would have undermined CPA2Biz's growth plans, and stemming from Mi8's defined core competency.

Enterprise ASPs

Enterprise ASPs provide managed or extended services supporting ERP, ERM, CRM, and e-commerce applications. Enterprise ASPs run and manage more complex applications.

Corio

Corio implements, integrates, and manages a suite, named Intelligent Enterprise, of enterprise software applications acquired from leading vendors, including CRM and e-commerce. A profile of this ASP is given in Chapter 2 (Corio, 2001a).

In late 1999, Excite@Home was an online portal—providing an initial point of entry to the Web along with specialized content and other services—which had experienced dramatic growth in just a few months since inception. At the same time, the online media industry had gone through swings and Excite needed to be flexible and responsive to changes. It lacked the expertise and resources required to run the desired complex PeopleSoft application suite in-house. It looked for an ASP with a broad application portfolio and experienced management team, which would guarantee significant customization to adapt the complex software application to its fast-growth, Internet-driven business. Excite did not want to undergo the capital expense of an in-house application deployment and desired access to a powerful solution at a variable cost, and also needed speed in implementation (Mizoras, 2001). Corio's solution matched Excite's requirements.

Corio dramatically accelerated Excite's time to market by implementing the application service in less than seven weeks and provided access to scarce and costly IT personnel at a variable cost. This was possible because of Corio's strong application configuration methodology. Based on results and due to the growth experienced,

Excite even expanded the relationship with Corio to include additional users and applications. Hank Mahler, Excite's director of business systems, rated Corio as "ahead of the game" in supporting customers. Corio helped Excite establish clear-cut procedures for users, make changes to the system, and ensure security (Mizoras, 2001).

Corio also had the appropriate model and the right solution for Enporion, a consortium of seventeen large energy companies that joined together in August 2000 to provide a global online business-to-business marketplace for the procurement of direct and indirect goods and services for the electricity and gas industries. Given that it was a new separate entity formed by several companies, the challenge was to develop an integrated IT infrastructure. Major requirements were fast implementation and the experienced management team to host and manage a complex application, its supporting technology, and its seamless integration across the online marketplace, essential to guarantee a secure environment to be accessed by a large number of users. Enporion selected a comprehensive enterprise resource planning application from SAP, and chose Corio from among six other ASPs on the basis of Corio's documented expertise with complex software, such as SAP, arising from its focus on mission-critical integration and customization skills, which gave it a proven track record of delivering applications and services within secure data environments, and also in-depth functional expertise in understanding the specific process underlying e-procurement, needed to support the new business-to-business e-marketplace Enporion required (Corio, 2001a).

It took Corio only ten weeks to implement the required solution, which provided integration features and the secure environment needed for widespread user access. This was possible because Corio was successful in applying its strong application configuration methodology to a completely new environment, such as a business-to-business marketplace platform. Scott Dawson, director of exchange strategy at Enporion, acknowledged the positive results: "We asked them [Corio] to do a lot in a short time frame. We set a date and figured we could push, and we weren't convinced ourselves if they could do it because it was so aggressive" (Swoyer and Maselli, 2000). Yet Corio overcame the challenges related to building an entirely new technology platform to support its integrated application suite, and Enporion's positive experience was even strengthened by the realization that Corio could support the online e-marketplace scalability requirements. A second version of Corio's implemented solution, as well as its focus on hosting scalable applications, assured Enporion that the solution would accommodate the marketplace's growth along with Enporion's development (Mizoras, 2001; Willan, 2001; Swoyer and Maselli, 2000).

The strategic and operational fit between Corio's approach and its customers' market and business challenges worked well because Corio's model was robust enough to guarantee the expected results associated with diverse business requirements.

USinternetworking (USi)

USi is a full-service-oriented enterprise ASP that offers a vast array of enterprise applications, from ERP to e-commerce, selected from among leading vendors. It targets midsized businesses worldwide. Its operations reflect a full-service approach and a global scale. USi owns and tightly controls the entire necessary physical and human infrastructure to provide an integrated, end-to-end solution. USi maintains global-scale data centers in North America, Europe, and Asia and has built effective value chain partnerships with market leaders, both for applications, such as software vendors Ariba, PeopleSoft, Siebel, and Oracle, and for technology, such as Sun Microsystems, in order to offer a top-level service. USi takes complete responsibility for the full cycle of the application solution, backed up by a written customer satisfaction guarantee, and assigns its customers a dedicated client assistance team, a single point of contact that understands and quickly meets their individual requirements. It offers and delivers the highest service-level guarantees in the industry, 99.9 percent for its entire service, and has a proven record of delivering to that level (USi, 2001). It ranked first in the top ten ASPs in 2000 with estimated $100 million revenue, in the list published by IDC (Whalen et al., 2001; Rosenthal, 2001).

A new customer in 1999 was the American Cancer Society (ACS), the U.S. nationwide community-based health organization dedicated to eliminating cancer. ACS wanted a single point of contact and total responsibility guaranteed by a strong SLA. ACS's top priority was customer satisfaction, and its focus on a robust SLA reflected this business imperative. Its major problem was to find an ASP with the same customer-centric and full-service approach, capabilities USi had. ACS's chief information officer Patterson worked with USi to make certain the agreement included the high level of service ACS wanted to fully address its cancer patients', volunteers', and donors' expectations (USi, 2001).

The result was a clearly defined total responsibility backed up by a comprehensive SLA in which USi was tightly focused on ACS's business goals, and which fully satisfied ACS and overcame its initial concerns. This was possible because USi had an integrated ASP operating system or technology platform, supported by robust infrastructure elements, for the most part owned by USi. USi's deep value chain expertise enabled it to deliver applications and services per the SLA, having clearly defined the business service it was offering to ACS and what exactly it was going to be responsible for (Shand, 2001; USi, 2001).

In contrast, for John Vogus, chief executive officer of AllBooks-4Less.com, getting an SLA did not matter when the company chose USi. AllBooks4Less was a leading online bookseller, with revenues exceeding $15 million in 2000. What drew Vogus to purchase a Microsoft-powered suite of applications to be managed by USi was the level of trust USi gave Vogus, arising from USi managing its data center and mission-critical infrastructure. Also, what Vogus was looking for was the ability to truly engage in a strong ASP-customer alliance partnership, as this requirement was more important to him than the percentage of guaranteed performance or the amount of credit AllBooks4Less would get if something went wrong. AllBooks-4Less.com's major challenge and problem was finding a trusted partner to take care of its mission-critical data. Turning to USi proved to be a good choice for his company objectives (USi, 2001).

Vogus and his employees were able to stop worrying about the system's management complexity, thanks to USi's proprietary data centers, networks, and priority communication, which reflected USi's full-service approach, mission-critical capability, and bulletproof application delivery and management process. The requirement of a full range of services, of which a critical one for the online bookseller was customization, to increase its chances of maximum utilization of the outsourced Microsoft suite, was met by USi, and also resulted in total responsibility at the ASP's end, thus exceeding Vogus's expectations and overcoming all his company's present and anticipated concerns.

USi proved to have the ability to deliver the required range of services and customer support around the remotely managed applications. Finally, it provided a dedicated team acting as a single point of contact for AllBooks4Less (USi, 2001). The two customers' experiences are examples of the successful operational match USi was able to achieve with two very different customers, a clear example of the contingent approach most often needed for ASP success.

Qwest Cyber.Solutions (QCS)

QCS, which is profiled in this section, offers a variety of enterprise application solutions from leading vendors (Ariba, Captura, Oracle, PeopleSoft, SAP, Siebel, and others) and extended services for ERP, CRM, sales automation, and business-to-business e-commerce, targeted to medium-sized and large companies in any industry worldwide. These customers have included JDS Uniphase, Redback Networks, and Expanets. Its main operations are in the United States, with global extensions through value chain partners. A joint venture between technology/infrastructure provider Qwest Communications International and consulting giant KPMG, QCS's ASP model is predicated on a tight, strong partnership with its parent companies. QCS leverages Qwest's state-of-the-art Internet protocol broadband network and data centers, while KPMG provides access to consulting and software integration expertise. QCS is also an authorized reseller of Oracle software, which reflects QCS's commitment to a quality-driven service experience overall (Qwest Cyber.Solutions, 2001b).

In 2000, Rochester Institute of Technology (RIT) was a strong career-oriented university, ranked by *U.S. News and World Report* as one of the leading universities in the United States in terms of academic reputation, which wanted to focus internal IT resources on its academic mission rather than on the management of its administrative functions. RIT needed a full ERP implementation to reengineer its twenty-five-year-old homegrown system combined with a new Oracle suite of applications that had been incorporated to comply with year 2000 deadlines. It also needed a tailored application suite, which would include significant customization to enable its staff to fully manage RIT's financial operations, including those aimed to serve students better. RIT's challenge arose from its inability to attract and retain the IT staff resources to support the complex technology needed to provide education services. It was looking for a broad range of applications and a full range of services to support its entire administrative function built on the complex-to-manage Oracle suite. It was also seeking a strong experienced ASP management team to operate a smooth transition to the new system overall with no business disruption (Paul, 2001a).

QCS had the necessary knowledge of Oracle and other enterprise applications and quality-oriented depth and breadth focus, as well as the expertise to provide an experienced management team that efficiently supported the integration and customization features needed to make the Oracle suite a comprehensive, yet usable, application. In spite of the technical difficulties of migrating the application suite from a 10.7 version to an 11i version, and the incremental costs associated with the huge resources required, the process was highly successful, with no business interruption during the transition. Thus, RIT's problems and concerns were overcome by QCS's bulletproof application delivery and management process. RIT quickly realized the big advantage of a strong ASP-customer alliance partnership with QCS. The staffing challenge, for instance, was overcome. "QCS has a level of expertise to be able to solve problems immediately," said Jim Fisher, RIT's vice president of finance and administration (Paul, 2001a).

QCS also met the critical requirement for a single point of contact for RIT's staff. "If they can't solve [problems], they are the ones dealing with Oracle for the fixes. That has been a tremendous advantage for us," Fisher added. Ultimately, QCS's team provided RIT "the peace of mind" needed to "efficiently and effectively maintain the strong reputation of the University as an innovative institution dedicated to excellence" (Qwest Cyber.Solutions, 2001b; Forbes.com, 2001). This experience illustrates how QCS's model successfully matched RIT's quality-driven educational goals.

Oracle

Oracle is a software vendor, which has developed and deployed 100 percent Internet-enabled enterprise ASP solutions with its Oracle Business Online ASP business. Oracle Business Online offers application solutions and services for any size business, from small offices to large businesses with multinational operations. Its operations reflect a global scale and a full-service model. Through its value chain partnership with specialist ASP NetLedger, Oracle Business Online provides functional ASP services (financials) to small-business customers in any industry. Through its exclusive partnership with Sun Microsystems, it has built the top-end technology platform necessary to support complete business client solutions. As a full-service-oriented ASP, Oracle Business Online not only provides Oracle applications but also offers solutions to the entire range of customer business requirements: application development and decision support tools, and integration and management services such as customization, to give customers a one-stop solution. By managing its data center facilities directly, it provides the levels of responsiveness, availability, and security to support any-size customer requirements (Oracle, 2001; Sun Microsystems, 2001b).

A new Oracle Business Online customer in 1999 was Cigna International, a $2 billion subsidiary of Cigna Corp., a provider of health care, insurance, and financial services on a worldwide scale. With a goal of getting a complex ERP system up and running in twelve months, a major challenge given traditional implementation times for this software type, Cigna considered an ASP to carry out the total solution, and had clearly in mind what the ASP should provide. "We're a tough client," stressed Nick Amen, senior VP of Cigna International operations and technology, which required total responsibility (Oracle, 2001). Cigna evaluated at least six leading ASPs, and Oracle Business Online was selected because of its effectively controlled networks of value chain partnerships, which enabled it to provide multiple support centers around the globe. Speed in implementation, coupled with global-scale expertise and the ability to support multiple languages, handle Cigna billing in multiple currencies, and host applications in twenty-six countries with 150 worldwide users on a twenty-four-hour basis, were the mix of applications and services Oracle Business Online offered (Oracle, 2001).

Oracle Business Online succeeded in delivering in a short time frame a complex system that fully met Cigna's objectives thanks to the considerable customization features it included, which were essential given Cigna's high expectations (Oracle, 2001). The result for Cigna was rapid access to robust, reliable online services with global-scale availability, which solved its time-to-market considerations and its requirement for a solution that would grow with the company (Oracle, 2001; Maselli, 2000b). These were the elements that provided the winning operational fit between Cigna and Oracle Business Online's model.

BlueStar Solutions

Formerly eOnline, BlueStar Solutions provides management and technology services for enterprise applications, with a particular focus on SAP enterprise solutions. It supports 20,000 users in over twenty countries. Its customers, such as Electroglas (services provider for semiconductor process manufacturers), chemical company Astaris, and e-businesses eBay and ZoneTrader.com, range from emerging e-businesses to Fortune 100 companies with multinational/ global operations. BlueStar has established value chain partnerships with leading technology providers, such as Compaq and Cisco. These key relationships enable BlueStar Solutions to provide customized solutions for various vertical markets, and reflect its decision not to develop customization skills in-house. Global operational scope is reflected in BlueStar's ASP model, which aims to provide speed in implementation, coupled with high-level technology and innovative methodology, and customer responsiveness, key elements appropriate for the needs of large and fast-track companies. BlueStar positioned itself among the ten best ASPs of 2000 (BlueStar Solutions, 2001; Whalen et al., 2001; Mears, 2001c).

In 1999, Autodesk was a software design company with a clear focus on the future. It was aggressively expanding into the Internet and e-commerce marketplace. Its internal SAP-based environment installed in 1994, initially as a number of separate highly customized modules, had expanded into a complex system, a major problem for its management, which needed immediate action. It became apparent that Autodesk would benefit from combining the individualized modules into a unified environment. Autodesk sought an ASP with the experienced management team to host and manage their complex SAP R/3 application and the required supporting full range of services, of which optimizing the SAP customization features was critical, and also needed an ASP that would guarantee speed in implementation. Another need was access to a powerful solution at a variable cost, as significant customization features in the original SAP environment had resulted in high maintenance and operation costs. Since BlueStar specialized in hosting SAP, it had the deep ASP value chain expertise, the defined core competency focus, and the robust infrastructure elements to "effectively optimize our SAP environment," as chief information officer Joe Cardenas recognized (BlueStar Solutions, 2001).

BlueStar Solutions provided a customized solution, rapidly delivered and quickly accessible by end users, without disrupting its internal cost structure, thanks to a high level of customer responsiveness, which proved critical in supporting Autodesk's staff to manage the extended SAP functionality as part of Autodesk's total responsibility requirement, and thanks to a bulletproof application delivery and management process. Autodesk was impressed by BlueStar Solutions' outstanding infrastructure, but its experienced ASP management team proved to be the single most important factor. Autodesk quickly benefited from the direct and indirect effects of the required strong ASP-customer alliance partnership, which allowed it to "confidently turn over all aspects of our SAP environment to the BlueStar Solutions team," as Autodesk's James Dunn, director of global infrastructure, acknowledged (BlueStar Solutions, 2001). One major advantage was instantaneous access to SAP software releases, impossible before. BlueStar Solutions dramatically reduced Autodesk's costs, improved the complex application's performance through optimizing its customization features, and proved to be "the turn-key solution we were looking for," according to Dunn (BlueStar Solutions, 2001).

A winning fit or operational match between this ASP and its client's complex business needs tied to speed and variable cost considerations was achieved also because, in addition to providing all the necessary supporting services, BlueStar Solutions turned the existing SAP-based environment into a unified, usable information system, thus enabling Autodesk to maximize its business investment and rationalize its internal processes.

Specialist or Function-Focused ASPs

Specialist ASPs provide applications that serve a specific professional or business activity, such as customer relationship management, human resources, financials, sales force automation, messaging, and Web site-related services. Specialist ASPs focus on understanding, developing, streamlining, and managing selected areas of expertise.

Salesforce.com

Salesforce.com provides enterprise software and specializes in the multiple aspects of online CRM. The target customer group is enterprises in any industry, including large customers such as Texas Instruments, Time Warner Communications, and Thomas Cook. Its current operational scope is U.S.-wide and international (Europe, Asia, Japan). Operations capitalize on value chain partnerships with ISVs and Web service providers. These partnerships are essential to provide customers with complementary software products and services that add value to Salesforce's integrated and customizable solutions. Salesforce's goal is to be anywhere, anytime. To this end, it works strategically to understand customer issues and solve them quickly, as critical factors enabling clients to build their own lasting customer relationships. It has built up a knowledge base of solutions that have resolved customer needs. Therefore, organizations that use Salesforce are able to more quickly and efficiently control existing solutions to help solve present and future problems as they arise, maximizing the ASP investment (Salesforce.com, 2001b).

In 2000 Putnam Lovell was an investment banking firm that had skyrocketed in just eighteen months and discovered that its informal record-keeping system, which lacked a central database to track relationships and sales process execution, was no longer adequate. In short, it was failing to coordinate activities or share information among departments or individuals. Putnam investigated CRM vendors. It decided to go for an ASP with a deep functional (process) knowledge and experience, a full range of services, and customization, to support its desired level of internal CRM-related business process performance, including a strong Web-based application availability that would permit "anytime, anywhere" access and would guarantee global-scale expertise and speed in implementation, among its mission-critical requirements (Salesforce.com, 2001b). Salesforce fit Putnam Lovell's needs.

Salesforce's application solution had optimal business process-focused features arising from in-depth functional expertise in the CRM process and underlying challenges that allowed quick implementation and efficient utilization of the new application, resulting in Putnam rapidly meeting "80 percent of the firm's needs at 20 percent of the cost," as acknowledged by Rodric O'Connor, Putnam's vice president of technology (Salesforce.com, 2001b). This was possible because of the high level of responsiveness developed by this ASP and achieved through implementing CRM solutions over a wide and increasing user base, which enabled Salesforce to understand its customer's needs and to implement the application quickly. The solution was up and running within sixty days of the ASP's selection. There was no hardware installation, software download, or IT setup or maintenance costs and concerns for Putnam, because Salesforce had a strong application configuration methodology that created customizable applications at the customer's end, which met Putnam's time-to-market needs (Salesforce.com, 2001b).

The solution began paying off immediately. Putnam Lovell sales and marketing employees were able to start tracking their daily calls and logging deal progress from the office, hotels, or airports. Management was delighted to notice that the company was on target with its main goal, which was to make its revenue earners more efficient and productive. With the help of Salesforce.com's experienced ASP management team, Putnam Lovell is now "a more successful enterprise. It gives us a more coherent culture and makes us more competitive," said chief executive officer Donald Putnam. Salesforce's application solution was also a financial success. "Salesforce.com is cheap and very powerful," said Putnam. "It has been bottom-line profitable for us within six months. I just don't see how you can help but make money using this product" (ASPnews, 2001a).

Success here came from this ASP being able to apply expertise in a well-defined area, CRM, which previously required continuous manual customization by the users and wasted time. Manual customization was no longer needed after the implementation of Salesforce's integrated CRM, which enabled Putnam's staff to finally devote energies to their regular activities.

Salesforce.com also had the right function-focused model and approach for another customer. Access to a powerful solution at a variable cost, the solution's ability to grow with the business, and fast implementation due to internal cost and turnaround time considerations were major requirements needing prompt action at Neoforma, an e-business service provider. When Neoforma won a ten-year contract in early 2000 to create and run an e-marketplace for medical supply giant Novation, it urgently needed a powerful application that would let its scattered national sales force gather and track leads from

2,000 Novation-affiliated hospitals. Neoforma turned to Salesforce.com to manage all contacts with prospective customers, evaluate prospective customers, assess the effectiveness of various sales strategies, and design better training programs for new sales representatives. Neoforma selected Salesforce.com's ASP CRM application package because of the variable cost schedule it offered relative to purchasing its own Oracle or Siebel CRM system (Boyd, 2001) and because of the speed in implementation this ASP guaranteed.

Salesforce.com's solution was rapidly delivered at a variable cost and as a predictable expense—$2,500 per month for fifty initial users—and required no up-front capital investment and minimal technical equipment—a Web browser. This was possible because of the availability of IT experts at Salesforce with deep knowledge of the required applications and in-depth functional expertise in the selected CRM-related process, which the new application was specifically asked to support. This solution freed Neoforma from up-front costs—at least $750,000—and from a lengthy installation and training process, which would have taken six months to complete through an in-house deployment. Neoforma's management had been skeptical as to what they could get for the low price charged by Salesforce. However, they were pleasantly surprised with the excellent results of this integrated, easily accessible ASP-based CRM solution, and made no short-term plans to change it by buying and implementing an in-house system (Boyd, 2001). Salesforce provided its customer with an integrated CRM application suite that made its solution quickly, efficiently, and cost-effectively available for immediate utilization (Salesforce.com, 2001b).

In short, Salesforce.com had the right solution to match and address the client's set of challenges—a good strategic and operational fit. The ASP provided access to the required specialist expertise at a variable cost and a scalable solution to meet future needs, and was also focused and flexible enough to guarantee and sustain a predictable price.

Exult

Exult offers eHR, a comprehensive, Web-enabled integrated service supporting HR departments of Global 500 corporations. Its operational scope covers the United States and has global ramifications to support the geographically extended needs of its customers. It works closely with clients on the design and redesign of their HR processes, and then provides transition and change management solutions to manage the migration of existing systems into new, Web-enabled operational infrastructures. By applying the Internet to HR processes, it enhances relationships and communications between employer and employees. Exult's operations rely upon mission-critical value chain partnerships with consulting and management companies such as the Saratoga Institute, McKinsey and Company, and the Corporate Leadership Council to ensure the objectivity of its information and analysis and provide a high level of specialist ASP service. Through partners, Exult benchmarks the performance of its clients' actual operations and sets specific targets for service quality improvement and internal cost reduction, delivering excellence in business processes and operational efficiency at the same time (Exult, 2001a).

In 2000, Bank of America, a large bank, was exploring the outsourcing of its entire HR operations because of the problems involved in finding qualified IT staff to carry out these functions internally. Because the HR-related business function was rated mission critical within Bank of America, and a value-adding one to its overall business mission, it looked for a strong ASP-customer alliance partnership, not just a customer-vendor relationship, and a single provider that would have deep functional (process) knowledge and experience of the complex HR-driven challenges within a large company. Exult was selected for the purpose. This ASP had a customer-centric focus on its customers' needs and worked closely with management to redesign Bank of America's HR processes, with the aid of its strategic value chain partnerships, which resulted in a totally reengineered HR function whose thrust was Exult's bulletproof application delivery and management process. Later, Bank of America was to become closely associated with Exult: Bank of America not only owned 5.5 percent of its ASP in 2001, but also got preferred status as a financial service provider on Exult's HR Web portal, following a $1.1 billion deal made in 2000 (Boyd, 2001).

After the ASP solution was implemented, employees from Exult and Bank of America were able to coordinate planning and implementation of all their HR programs. The bank and its 150,000 employees got improved technology access and HR expertise and streamlined both their internal HR and non-HR tasks, a major accomplishment for Bank of America. As a result of a strong partnership, the most important requirement for Bank of America, Exult was now able to manage all of Bank of America's payroll, benefits administration, employee records, call center, and IT functions within the HR department, as well as asset management, accounts payable, and travel and expense transaction processing functions. This was also the result of Exult's focus on mission-critical integration and customization skills, which seamlessly combined the bank's old information systems environment into its technology platform (Exult, 2001a).

Exult was also asked to manage some relationships with third-party vendors, assuming a trusted partner role with the bank. Another important benefit to the bank was its access to a powerful solution at a variable cost, due to the availability of IT experts at Exult with deep knowledge of the required applications, which resulted in cost savings. Bank of America estimated it has saved and will save 10 percent per year of the costs of administering its HR department internally (Exult, 2001a). This experience illustrates the working strategic and operational fit between Bank of America's specific functional needs, managing a large employee base, and Exult's specialized skills in handling HR-driven challenges.

United Messaging

United Messaging is 100 percent focused on Web-delivered messaging functions and concentrates on the messaging needs of businesses of any size in any industry. A profile of this ASP is presented in Chapter 2 (United Messaging, 2001a).

In 2000, Centocor was a leading biopharmaceutical company that created, acquired, and marketed therapies developed primarily through monoclonal antibody technology. The company faced huge internal challenges in managing its existing IT systems, particularly because of an unreliable messaging system, which threatened to jeopardize its mission-critical need to stay connected on a twenty-four-hour basis with its worldwide health care industry clients. It realized it urgently needed to migrate to Microsoft Exchange yet did not want to experience the burden and complexities associated with building and maintaining the internal resources necessary to make the change. Centocor was looking for an ASP with deep functional knowledge and experience to support a smooth migration to a full-scale e-mail system, a single point of contact to manage the variety of tasks its limited internal IT staff could not handle, and a full range of services and customization, to help the company integrate the messaging system into an overall seamless workflow adapted to its needs (United Messaging, 2001a; Sun Microsystems, 2001b).

United Messaging was the perfect match, according to Centocor's chief information officer, Jim Maguire. The ASP provided a complete, end-to-end proprietary migration solution (Mailgration) for 1,500 users, including a full range of services such as monitoring, help-desk support, and consulting services to extend messaging management into the future, which also met Centocor's desire for scalability, and which completely solved Centocor's problem. This was possible because United Messaging had a defined ASP core competency focus in the messaging business process, a full-service approach, relied in-house on some of the best IT experts with in-depth ASP functional expertise in the business process underlying messaging solutions, and focused their expertise in the complex technology and hosting capabilities to provide the optimal level of performance (United Messaging, 2001a).

The mix of world-class people, processes, and technologies proved a good operational match between Centocor and United Messaging. The result for Centocor was the ability to get "a positive view of the IT department, which did not exist when they could not manage e-mail. We can finally move forward to extend the system and truly add value to our internal customers," Maguire said, adding, "we could not have got where we are without United Messaging" (Sun Microsystems, 2001b).

These comments identify the successful strategic and operational fit between United Messaging's capabilities and its client's requirements. This fit was possible because United Messaging's model was robust as well as flexible enough to meet Centocor's specific messaging business requirements, associated with fast time to market, ongoing connectivity, and smooth transitioning considerations.

Employease.com

Employease.com provides HRM applications, which it has developed and markets itself, as well as a suite of related services for managing HR departments in companies with up to 3,000 employees. A more detailed profile is given in Chapter 2 (Employease.com, 2001).

In late 2000, STI Knowledge, Inc., was a provider of help desk, call center, and knowledge center products, services, and certification that was using a homegrown information system to manage a variety of aspects of its growing business. However, the internal system had limited applications and capabilities, and lacked the HR, employee benefit, and payroll tracking features necessary to address its expanding workforce-driven business complexities. Its main challenge was to minimize and gradually eliminate the use of book-based methods for payroll and benefit management functions, which had resulted in an administrative nightmare. The company was looking for a robust online reporting and tracking system that would provide better, faster access to information across departments. STI required an ASP with deep functional knowledge and experience in HR, offering access to a powerful solution at a variable cost, a full range of services to complement the HR application process-driven functions, customization to match the application to its specific HR needs, and a single point of contact to enable STI to remain focused on its strategic goals (Employease.com, 2001).

Because over 1,000 customers were already using Employease, STI had no doubt it was a proven solution. Results fulfilled all of STI's expectations. Employease provided STI with an easy to implement, learn, and use new HR application suite, managed by Employease in a secure environment, which reduced STI's employee turnover from 30 percent to 10 percent. This was possible because of Employease's customer-centric approach to its client's business, which produced an affordable, yet complete, solution. STI reported this improvement was primarily due to the launch of new training, benefit, and compensation programs developed by Employease for its HR department and arising from an optimal balance between significant customization and internal business objectives (Employease.com, 2001).

Among the eleven new employee-related programs was the Help Desk Professional Compensation Program—directly powered by the ASP and especially tailored to STI's needs—something that would have been impossible for STI to develop on its own without overloading its administrative resources and distracting managers from their regular work. Prior to the relationship with Employease, the internal

benefits process cycle would typically last eight weeks; it was reduced to ten days with the ASP solution by the end of 2000. Data
flowed automatically throughout the company, changes were made
online, and plans were approved in three hours. This was the result of
Employease's in-depth functional expertise in the HR business processes and of the numerous implementations that strengthened its
specialization approach (Business2.com, 2001). This experience illustrates how targeted customer services are most successful in narrowly focused and straightforward functional areas, such as HRM.

Vertical-Market ASPs

Vertical-market ASPs tailor solutions to the needs of one or a few
selected specific industries or industry sectors, such as banking,
health care, education, engineering, financial services, and professional services.

Portera

Portera provides integrated Web-based PSA applications and services for the professional services industry worldwide. A more detailed profile is given in Chapter 2 (Portera, 2001).
   In 2000, Fluid specialized in creating e-business solutions for customers in a wide range of industries. Each solution entailed a long,
complex project requiring the coordinated effort of multiple skills at
multiple locations. Managing resources for these projects, and at the
same time capturing mission-critical data quickly and efficiently,
were Fluid's biggest challenges. Fluid needed a comprehensive ASP
solution including a full range of services, one that would also grow
with its business, a strong ASP-customer alliance partnership, proven
experience in professional services industry-specific challenges, and
a single point of contact for its widely dispersed customers and their
own users—Fluid could not manage this all internally. Fluid selected
Portera because of the depth and breadth of its Serviceport application management system, its scalability, and its full-service approach
(Sun Microsystems, 2001b; Portera, 2001).
   Portera provided Fluid with a totally Web-based, integrated application management suite, arising from this ASP's expertise in the
complex technology and hosting capabilities needed—a major skill
in Portera's vertical-market ASP model. Also, its bulletproof applica-

tion delivery and management process enabled this ASP to design a solution that would quickly increase Fluid's staff productivity. Early results reportedly showed over 50 percent resource and time-and-expense management efficiency improvements, and consistently high performance of a system accessible remotely by users from anywhere. As Fluid's director of project management, Kent Deverell, acknowledged, Portera's skills enabled it to work out problems proactively rather than reactively—what Fluid had historically done.

Because of its long track record with professional services companies, Portera met Fluid's requirement for an experienced ASP management team, which had the deep ASP value chain expertise that enabled Portera to transfer its lessons learned to its Serviceport system. In addition, Portera met Fluid's requirement for a single point of contact, an interface available to manage all its expected and unexpected issues. Just a few months after implementing Portera's ASP solution, Fluid declared it a success. "Its resource management powers are outstanding. Issues are easy to track. We have a real time picture of time and expenses," Kent Deverell said (Sun Microsystems, 2001b). Beyond assuming total responsibility, Portera's people were "receptive to feedback. The really great thing is that when we make a suggestion for enhancing Serviceport, they will if it makes sense" (Sun Microsystems, 2001b). Receptiveness to feedback was the result of a high level of customer responsiveness built into Portera's ASP model.

W3Health

W3Health serves the health care industry. Its core offering is a Web-based customized reporting and analysis solution that delivers robust decision-making application support to health care enterprises. It is designed to help health care organizations control costs and improve the quality of the care they deliver. In this industry, although cost effectiveness is a priority, the ability to deliver high-quality care is even more important. W3Health is active across the United States. It is committed to meeting the complete range of customer requirements in this sector, and its full-service operational scope is reflected in value chain partnerships with leading application and technology providers in the health care industry. Among them are national consulting firm Managed Care Resources, Internet-based communications channel HealthTrio, health care software vendor

Confer Software, and analytic tool developer Symmetry Health Data Systems, Inc. They enable this ASP to deliver an innovative Web-based comprehensive solution that is rapidly accessible, usable, and manageable (W3Health, 2001).

In early 2001, Yale-New Haven Physician Hospital Organization (PHO), delivered health care services to more than 200,000 members and employed over 1,000 physicians. It needed an integrated system not only to analyze data from multiple participants in the health care market, such as individual physicians, medical directors, and senior company executives, but also to make fast, informed decisions. The primary challenge for this health care organization was to unify and harmonize disparate information coming from diverse sources in different formats. It was looking for a full range of services to fully implement and remotely manage the selected application, customization to adapt the application to its internal business needs, deep industry knowledge to satisfy its internal harmonization and centralization requirements, and access to a powerful solution at a variable cost to avoid the burden of high and increasing overhead IT costs. It selected W3Health's W3 Distributed Reporting System (DRS) to outsource its entire data management, application hosting, and maintenance functions (W3Health, 2001).

W3Health's W3-based solution enabled this health care organization to deploy a new reporting and analysis application to a wide base of users, which proved easy to access, use, and manage, while also reducing its total cost of ownership and maximizing use of the application. With W3, the Yale-New Haven PHO was now able not only to extract, clean, integrate, build, and load data, add clinical intelligence throughout its systems, and host and maintain applications, but also to receive analytic consulting services and seamlessly connect disparate entities. This was possible because W3Health had an in-depth understanding of specific health care industry challenges and had a strong application configuration methodology, enhanced by the Web, which accelerated the application implementation. Tucker Leary, executive director of PHO, was enthusiastic about the results: "The W3 system is an ideal way for us to analyze data from the multiple payors in our market" (W3Health, 2001).

A major benefit was Yale-New Haven's ability to view all its managed care participants in one consolidated environment, arising from W3Health's clearly defined market focus and core competency and an optimal balance between customization and internal business objectives, which made customization features easy to add without disrupting the ASP's cost structure. These factors enabled Yale-New Haven PHO to speed the decision-making process and improve the quality of the information that it provided to its users. Before the W3 system, it took PHO data specialists months to prepare reports because they had to compile records manually from insurance company databases. They could now gather the same information across all databases using W3 DRS in a matter of minutes, which was possible because of W3Health's long-term focus on mission-critical integration and customization skills, which made W3 a single, comprehensive, consolidated system (W3Health, 2001).

W3Health has demonstrated an intimate knowledge of specific target industry needs. Analysis and reporting software such as W3 DRS is particularly important in an ASP model, says Bill Dering, analyst at C.E. Unterberg, Towbin (Boyd, 2001). This experience illustrates the extent of operational fit found in successful vertical-market ASPs.

Surebridge

Formerly Panoptic, Surebridge is a vertical-market-oriented enterprise ASP. It is listed in the vertical-market category as an example of this model's strategic fit with customers' industry-specific business challenges and market requirements.

Surebridge offers a broad variety of enterprise applications—CRM/e-business, HR, e-procurement, financial, and PSA—targeted to midmarket, high-growth companies in a few selected industries, such as Internet services firm Context Integration Inc. and pharmaceutical manufacturer Paratek Pharmaceuticals. Its operational focus is both national, through its offices in the United States, and international, through its value chain partners, among which are Cisco, Citrix, Microsoft, and Compaq. Surebridge keeps in-house the application configuration process that is developed prior to the solution delivery to end users, including customization and integration. It also maintains centralized operations through its application (Vignette, Siebel, and PeopleSoft) and technology value chain partners, and thus operates a full-service model overall. Its vertical focus reflects the commitment to thoroughly understanding customers' business challenges and how they use technology. Surebridge aims to offer a one-stop-shopping model, which delivers complete, quality-driven services through a single point of contact, and focuses on the client's customers (Surebridge, 2001b), which is Surebridge's key to delivering a total, fulfilling customer service.

In late 1999, Robinson Nugent was a fast-growing designer and manufacturer of high-technology electronic connectors, sockets, and custom cable assemblies with global operations. It needed the hosting of a specific application suite, the financial, distribution, and manufacturing ERP software modules, via the Web, to be available across its global enterprise, to more than 150 users. In addition, it needed its problem resolved rapidly. It had identified PeopleSoft as the best software vendor for its purposes. It wanted an ASP to run a broad application portfolio and integrate it with existing internal support systems. It needed significant customization of the selected complex ERP application to adapt it to its individual business objectives and optimize its software investment. It was also looking for global-scale expertise, deep industry knowledge and experience, and a full range of services to effectively manage the ERP application. Surebridge was selected, as its solution appeared to be the best match for Robinson's requirements, given Surebridge's full-service approach arising from its directly managed data center and mission-critical infrastructure, enhanced by closely controlled value chain partnerships that enabled global-scale coverage of the implemented solution for Robinson, and the experienced ASP management team required to implement and run a complex PeopleSoft-based ERP (Surebridge, 2001c).

Surebridge managed to complete an eleven-module implementation for Robinson in half the time and at one-third to one-half of the cost quoted by Surebridge's competition, which dramatically surpassed Robinson's expectations. This was possible not only because Surebridge tightly controlled its value chain partners, but also because it retained full control over its strong application configuration methodology. In addition to implementing and hosting the PeopleSoft suite and transferring the client's old technology platform to an Oracle NT platform, Surebridge provided significant customization and a full range of services. These services included the creation of a customer portal to assist Robinson in providing its customers with direct access to order status, to availability, shipment quantity, and timing, and to Robinson's supply chain for accurate and timely information (Surebridge, 2001c).

The immediate results for Robinson Nugent were increased customer satisfaction and loyalty. Robinson had also required and obtained a strong ASP-customer alliance partnership, in which both Robinson and Surebridge closely worked to meet the needs of Robinson's customers (Bernard, 2001b; "Surebridge Ranked," 2001; Surebridge, 2001c).

Surebridge's clearly defined vertical-market focus enabled it to understand underlying industry challenges and how Robinson's clients used technology, and so to deliver a high-quality, focused application and access to a powerful solution at a variable cost. This experience illustrates how the working strategic and operational match between Robinson's requirements and Surebridge's capabilities was both industry focused and robust enough by design and infrastructure to meet a wide range of requirements, reflecting not only a customer's goals but also the ultimate needs of a customer's customers.

LearningStation.com

LearningStation.com exclusively serves the education/training industry, providing technology solutions to meet academic requirements and delivering content through personalized Web-based educational desktops. A more detailed profile is given in Chapter 2 (LearningStation.com, 2001a).

In 1999, the Lowcountry Day School of Pawley's Island, South Carolina, presented challenges typical for a school with 200 students: limited funds, lack of IT resources, diversity of staff expertise and needs, and the desire to offer up-to-date educational tools to its students and teachers. There was also a lack of on-site technical support staff. In essence, this school needed access to a broad application portfolio, deep industry knowledge and expertise to understand its specific requirements, a full range of services to complement the Web-based application solution, and some degree of customization. LearningStation.com was selected to upgrade the school's educational services. This ASP equipped the school with a networked desktop PC environment designed for educators, administrators, and students, and tailored this solution to the specific needs of the school's programs (LearningStation.com, 2001a).

This was possible because of the highly customized applications included by LearningStation in the application suite, arising from its in-depth understanding of the educational challenges tied to a small school's resources. These capabilities enabled this ASP to provide the resources needed, without overloading the school's network environment with redundant content or information, and so enabling all Low Country School users to immediately use the applications effectively (LearningStation.com, 2001a). LearningStation also met Low Country's desire for system scalability by implementing a top-class application suite that could become as comprehensive as needed (LearningStation.com, 2001a).

Low Country quickly realized the benefits of state-of-the-art equipment and availability of the required applications at a variable cost. The school's performance is now far ahead of where it was before, when no adequate technology platform was available, PCs on hand were antiquated and unreliable, and lack of technology-related funding seemed to offer no hope for improvement. The school's applications now run on an integrated platform on updated PCs at the school, linked by high-speed line to LearningStation's servers, and the system is also accessible via private log-in from remote locations. In addition, a range of services, such as training and ongoing technical support, were provided to ensure smooth operations at Low Country (ASP Industry Consortium, 2001c), reflecting LearningStation's core competency in the education market. This is a good example of an effective strategic and operational fit between a clearly focused vertical-market ASP and its customer's business requirements, due in no small part to the customer's small size and well-defined business.

TriZetto Group

TriZetto is a fast-growing health care technology company, whose vertical-market ASP division provides services to any businesses and end users within the health care market. It has over 150 customers, representing over 70 million patient-related data entries. A more detailed profile is presented in Chapter 2 (TriZetto Group, 2001a).

In 2000, Maxicare Health Plans was a managed health care company serving Indiana and California residents that had realized it needed to replace its antiquated administrative systems, which were hindering business growth. Considering the high costs of in-house implementation and the risks of selecting, installing, and managing the required technologies on its own, Maxicare was looking for a strong ASP-customer alliance with an ASP that had a deep industry-specific knowledge and experience of its challenges, and that would act as a single point of contact to alleviate the burden of internal IT system management. According to Susan Blais, Maxicare chief operating officer and executive vice president, it was also important that their ASP understood "the many nuances of our business" (Fortune.com, 2001), and would provide significant customization. TriZetto met Maxicare's needs, because the ASP had a high level of focus on mission-critical integration and customization skills coupled with clearly defined vertical-market ASP focus, expertise, and health care industry knowledge, as well as a full-service approach, to be able to provide a single point of accountability for a breadth of application solutions, supported by a full range of services. Also, because of its bulletproof application delivery and management process supported by robust infrastructure elements, it was able to act as a strong partner to Maxicare and to provide a comprehensive application solution (TriZetto Group, 2001a).

TriZetto was able to meet all the requirements thanks to the availability of IT experts with deep knowledge of the required applications that enable TriZetto to bundle the best supporting technology and application management processes and to provide complete and industry-specific tailored solutions. A planned eighteen-month project working with TriZetto immediately brought benefits to Maxicare. A major one was the development of a HealthWeb unit, which provided an Internet platform and access to a variety of e-business applications. Another was the ability to access through TriZetto a powerful software module called HealtheWare, which gave Maxicare a number of applications to manage its resources information management processes, and significant enhancements in productivity, such as the increase in the number of claims paid in a day and much higher accuracy on payment-related processes (TriZetto Group, 2001a).

Maxicare's relationship with TriZetto was also coordinated from the beginning to provide scalability for future requirements, such as new systems to enroll members and pay claims, and new applications for medical management, physician credential management, and financial management. TriZetto's strong application configuration methodology was able to meet this requirement and, according to the terms of the agreement, would also provide additional technologies for information gathering, analysis, reporting, and data warehousing (Fortune. com, 2001).

ASP Aggregators or AASPs

An AASP is a group of ASPs, which may have diverse models themselves. ASP aggregators are designed to integrate software-based application offerings from multiple entities and provide a single sign-on access and unified billing and administration tools.

The specific AASP models that have been implemented so far are defined and empowered by large networks of partnerships, which enable ASP aggregators to function on a larger operational scale than business, enterprise, specialist, and vertical-market ASPs and also give their customers more flexibility. The AASP model gives customers the freedom to shift from one ASP to another without breaking or modifying existing contracts. This characteristic seems to indicate that ASP aggregators sensed an opportunity to fill market gaps in the ASP industry in the early stages of its life cycle, when customers were perceiving the relationship with an ASP vendor as too binding and restrictive.

ASP aggregators are more complex than the other four ASP models, the higher complexity arising from the aggregation of numerous ASP providers and other service providers in the ASP value chain under a single organization. Also, the AASP is more versatile than the other models, which is evident in the offering of ASP outsourcing solutions for access, management, integration, and support for Web-enabled applications from any source. In addition, the ASP aggregator model is characterized by a commitment to higher system performance and higher cost effectiveness than the other four ASP models, with solution offerings that are designed to be less expensive, more flexible, and much more powerful, in terms of guaranteed performance, security, and reliability. Typically, this is achieved by utilizing small or start-up ASPs and ASP value chain enablers that provide their specialized, core-competency contribution, which ultimately helps keep costs low.

Jamcracker

Jamcracker gives companies multiple IT and ASP services through a single source. It supports multiple application and service vendors in each service category (Jamcracker, 2001b). A more detailed profile is given in Chapter 2.

In late 2000, B2BWorks was an online marketing services company that had over 500 Web sites, more than 100 million page views, and thousands of business executives on its network. Adding to this complexity was the diversity of company operations, which had created enormous challenges to its sales force. It was looking for a comprehensive SFA system that required deep functional (process) knowledge and experience to implement and significant customization to adapt the new system to its internal needs, to enable its staff to better manage internal changes, to benefit from a versatile and effective tool, and to support the company's rapid growth. It also desired global-scale expertise, a full range of services to support the new application, a single point of contact to safely outsource the entire SFA function and related technical complexity, and scalability. Jamcracker had the right package for B2BWorks and rapidly solved this client's most critical challenges (Jamcracker, 2001b).

Jamcracker equipped B2BWorks with a full UpShot-based SFA system, which bundled together a variety of Web-based services. This made it possible to implement a comprehensive SFA system with global-scale features in three weeks. Jamcracker employs best-of-breed partners in all areas of the ASP delivery mechanism, such as industry leaders Siemens for on-site support, McAfee for antivirus and security tools, and established ASPs, including enterprise ASP Surebridge for its PeopleSoft HRM and Siebel CRM solutions, vertical-market ASP Portera for its PSA solutions, and specialist ASP Employease for its HRM and benefits administration suite. These enable Jamcracker's customers to choose among a variety of services through a single sign-on access via the Web.

Jamcracker's wide range of ASP expertise, including in-depth functional expertise in the business processes underlying the SFA application B2BWorks needed, was the main factor behind speed in implementation and access to a powerful solution at a variable cost. According to B2B's chief technology officer Bob Zimmerman, this solution "does everything we wanted to do. It provides all of the sales productivity tools we need, and it's easily accessible whether our salespeople are in the office or on the road." In addition, executives can now check accounts without being disruptive or intrusive to their sales force. "That's something we could never do with our old system," Zimmerman acknowledged (Jamcracker, 2001b), highlighting the versatility of a top-class application suite B2B could not have afforded to get on its own.

Finally, what really made the deal a fulfilling experience for B2BWorks was the single point of contact and accountability provided by Jamcracker, which gave B2B the benefit of round-the-clock outstanding customer support. B2BWorks recognized these outstanding capabilities. "With Jamcracker I have an entire team supporting my sales staff, and I am getting world-class support. For us, it's just an unbeatable package," said Zimmerman (Jamcracker, 2001b).

iFuel

iFuel is a fast-growing AASP that enables ISVs and NSPs to deliver their applications through either direct or indirect channels, and also partners with them to serve individual business customers of varying size. A more detailed profile is presented in Chapter 2 (iFuel, 2001).

In late 2000, the Really Useful Group Ltd. (RUG) was an established international entertainment company actively involved in theater and concert production, recording, merchandising, music publishing, and television and video publishing throughout the world. The group also co-owned and managed thirteen theaters in London. The company's main challenge was the ability to seamlessly connect in a single network disparate, geographically dispersed business divisions within the group. RUG was looking for a flexible ASP provider of a broad range of applications, with global-scale expertise, a full range of services to manage a multitude of core applications, and an experienced management team, which would guarantee RUG the ability to access the applications securely from anywhere in the world with no business disruption.

iFuel's extended menu of offerings matched RUG's requirements with Integration, a proprietary methodology reflecting its focus on mission-critical integration skills. iFuel's AASP model is characterized by a commitment to offering a one-stop solution and a single point of contact, and was designed to provide greater contractual flexibility than individual ASPs, in order to avoid high switching costs in case of service additions or changes along the way. iFuel provided RUG with the needed flexibility and its employees with secure, ubiquitous access to a broad range of key productivity applications, including Microsoft Office and Exchange, Forest and Trees, and Vision (iFuel, 2001).

Security and worldwide instantaneous access were possible because of iFuel's deep ASP value chain expertise, which enabled it to create secure data environments, and a defined ASP core competency focus, which enabled iFuel to integrate new applications with the existing application environment. As a result, iFuel significantly simplified RUG's IT infrastructure and provided its management with a predictable variable cost schedule. iFuel's strong application configuration methodology enabled RUG to access applications from anywhere in the world securely, thanks to a two-factor authentication process, twenty-four-hour remote support, and data backup and virus protection. In addition, iFuel assumed total responsibility for the entire back-end infrastructure, ranging from server hardware to communications and system management.

iFuel also guaranteed RUG a minimum 30 percent of extra capacity, thanks to its wide-scale integrated ASP operating system, supported by leading NSPs and ISVs, which assumed full responsibility for their ASP value chain tasks, and which in turn enabled iFuel to commit to total responsibility toward RUG, which was able to instantly scale up the number and kind of applications and related service and customer support as new users were added to the system (iFuel, 2001), without halting or disrupting its business activities or engaging in a new implementation process. This successful experience indicates that the strategic and operational fit between a challenged global business such as RUG and a robust AASP such as iFuel worked well.

Summary

Table 3.1 summarizes and highlights the customer requirement areas the five ASP models have fulfilled as shown in the description of successful experiences. Table 3.1 highlights the match between the list of requirements analyzed in the first part of chapter and the model types analyzed in the second part, giving emphasis to the specific ASPs that met the requirements, reflecting the contingency approach that has structured this book.

TABLE 3.1. Winning Strategic and Operational Fit

Customer Requirements	ASP Models					
	Business	Enterprise	Specialist	Vertical Market	Aggregators
Broad range of applications/ application portfolios	FutureLink TeleComputing	Corio QCS		Surebridge LearningStation	iFuel
Full range of services	TeleComputing FutureLink Mi8	USi QCS BlueStar	Salesforce.com United Messaging Employease	Portera W3Health Surebridge LearningStation TriZetto	Jamcracker iFuel
Customization		Corio USi QCS Oracle BlueStar	Salesforce.com United Messaging Employease	W3Health Surebridge LearningStation TriZetto	Jamcracker
Total responsibility	TeleComputing	USi Oracle BlueStar		Portera	iFuel
Strong ASP-customer alliance partnership	Interliant	USi QCS BlueStar	Exult	Portera Surebridge TriZetto	
Experienced ASP management team	FutureLink Interliant Mi8	Corio QCS BlueStar	Salesforce.com United Messaging	Portera Surebridge	iFuel

Criteria				
Single point of contact		USi QCS	United Messaging Employease	Portera TriZetto	Jamcracker
Access to a powerful solution at a variable cost	FutureLink Interliant Mi8	Corio BlueStar	Salesforce.com United Messaging Exult Employease	W3Health Surebridge	Jamcracker iFuel
Global-scale expertise		Oracle	Salesforce.com	Surebridge	Jamcracker iFuel
Ability to grow with business or scalability	TeleComputing Interliant Mi8	Corio Oracle	Salesforce.com United Messaging	Portera LearningStation TriZetto	Jamcracker
Speed in implementation	TeleComputing FutureLink Mi8	Corio Oracle BlueStar	Salesforce.com		Jamcracker
Deep industry knowledge and experience				Portera W3Health Surebridge LearningStation TriZetto	
Deep functional (process) knowledge and experience			Salesforce.com Exult United Messaging Employease		Jamcracker

CONCLUSION

This chapter has provided an analysis of the unique mix of resources and competencies, combined with a situation-based approach to understanding customer requirements, required of an ASP to win credibility, build a solid customer base, and sustain and grow its business. Successful ASPs were found among all the categories of delivery models that were discussed in Chapter 2. The mix of working strategic and operational fits indicates that all five models, when they effectively focus on fulfilling specific customer requirements, work well.

The crucial element underlying optimal strategic and operational fit for diverse customer needs is strong focus, not just on technology and internal goals, but also on effective management of internal capabilities, on filling internal gaps, and on building and sustaining competitive advantages in fulfilling customer requirements. Adequate focus on these factors has enabled the contingency-driven ASPs to meet or exceed clients' critical requirements. Successful ASPs were found to be those who do not just rely on the rental delivery mechanism itself but also concentrate on the quality of the applications and the individualized service that customers and their end users receive.

By focusing on services, providing comprehensive, business-oriented service-level agreements and customer support, the ASPs discussed have appealed to their customers' desire for more than just access to a software application on a rental basis. Although the successful ASPs analyzed in this chapter have been almost an exception in a transitioning period, they signal that the ASP delivery model works, and that there are at least a few identifiable good ways to implement it.

To sustain the ASP delivery model, it is necessary to extend the superior performance of a few into a generalized practice, which involves a significant industry-wide shift in strategic focus, from a generic "if you build it, they will come" approach (Toigo, 2001) to the creation of distinct, compelling market positions, attracting substantial numbers of customers and developing strong business value propositions, adequately supported by a robust infrastructure and technology platform and by a deep understanding of both the ASP value chain and the target customer group.

The following chapter identifies the best practices initiatives that foresighted ASPs, ASP partners, and the ASP Industry Consortium have put in place to improve individual ASPs' chances of survival and to broaden ASP market acceptance in general.

Chapter 4

Emerging Best Practices

INTRODUCTION

This chapter identifies success factors that can help ASP managers to develop and grow their businesses. It also systematically reviews for ASP customers and stakeholders, such as potential ASP partners, the success factors they should consider.

After discussing the importance of best practices and their impact on the future of the ASP industry, this chapter reviews the best practices observed in existing ASPs, and then briefly discusses specific best practice development at Microsoft, which is part of a larger ASP-bound initiative it is promoting. At an industry-wide level, the chapter presents the ASP Industry Consortium's best-practice focus and analyzes in more detail its best-practice initiatives involving developing customer confidence and trust. The discussion then provides a summary of the best practices identified through the analyses in Chapters 1 through 4. These provide a basis for building customer confidence and trust in ASPs for the future.

The conclusion is that future progress within the ASP industry depends on continuous focus on and improvement of best practices, at all levels of the ASP environment, as they are important to the education of customers, partners, and investors about the positive value of application service provision and ultimately to its sustainability and development.

THE IMPORTANCE OF BUILDING BEST PRACTICES

This chapter follows the conceptualization of best practices in the IT sector. Best practices are the most successful solutions or problem-solving methods developed by a specific organization or industry

(Laudon and Laudon, 2001). They are a natural progression in any nascent industry. In general, in new industries, firms must do their job right first—deliver consistent and repeatable service—and then based on their successes (those documented in Chapter 3, for example) and failures (those discussed in Chapter 2, for example), gradually develop a formal and informal set of best practices. In particular for the ASP industry, best practices are a vital requirement to manage the transition through its growth phase, given the many dynamic factors in the ASP market, including the following (ASPIC-WIPO, 2001):

- The enormous market potential, which has attracted hundreds of companies that have reinvented themselves as ASPs or joined other entities, often rapidly forming ASPs that in many instances lack experience with the technical complexities involved in managing the wide and diverse range of services delivered.
- The customer's quest for assurance that an ASP has a deep understanding of the customer's business and industry. Many new entrants in the ASP arena have shown little experience and expertise in industries outside their own.
- The still unknown effects of using multiple ASPs for process management. The ASPs often are competitors among themselves. For example, compatibility problems with hardware and software often occur.
- The ASP industry's lack of stringent regulations. Many other industries are already heavily regulated by outside agencies or are self-regulated.
- The issues of performance, security breach, and accountability for value chain partners, which are plaguing the industry.
- The rudimentary stage of privacy regulations, coupled with the fact that ASPs in the meantime have access to consumer information, proprietary enterprise information, and a multitude of other data.

A brief listing of these and other industry dynamics is a necessary step to understanding the challenges that lie ahead for the ASP market. For example, end user awareness and adoption of ASP services was lower than expected in 2000 and 2001, as noted in Chapter 2.

ASPs need to attract more users, in order to expand their market presence and at the same time deal with these dynamics, whose positive and negative effects make the ASP landscape both complex and interesting for the future. The recognition that winning customer confidence and trust is possible, through education of ASP stakeholders and through proactively working to turn industry dynamics into opportunities to grow, prompted the following analysis of the role of best practices. The positive impact of systematically identifying initiatives in the ASP market is expected to help win that confidence and trust. As in any fast-changing industry in the early stage of its life cycle, the ASP market lacks homogeneity in the type and size of its participants, which necessarily makes this analysis a contingent one.

An attempt at management and customer education that helps serve as a basis for best practice development is found, for example, in the creation of "beware checklists" for customers to use when evaluating a prospective ASP alliance. Such checklists have been put together by industry analysts (Borck, 2001; Hunter, 2001; Mears, 2001b; Wohl, 2001; Anthes, 2000; CIO.com, 2000; Flanagan, 2000b), early adopters, and leading ASPs. They are available in many formats, and typically recommend some or all of the following:

- Assess your company's reasons for using an ASP. Weigh potential trade-offs between in-house and ASP-managed deployments. Decide which applications make the most sense to host.
- Look carefully at the ASP's business strengths. Gather data about potential ASPs—their size, reputation, market experience, the partnerships they have forged, and existing customer base. Get references. Select an ASP that has good prospects of long-term viability.
- Evaluate architecture. Assess the flexibility and scalability of the ASP's back-end infrastructure. Can the ASP facilitate rapid, tight integration? Check the ASP's usage of technology such as XML and Java.
- Perform a data center analysis. Find out whether the ASP has its own data center or outsources it to a third-party provider. Evaluate the infrastructure on which your solution will run. Consolidating all managed services within the walls of a single ASP benefits manageability.

- Demand recovery and backup plans. Ask for specifics, including the method of archiving and retrieving data, off-site storage and backup, and alternate power and disaster recovery.
- Ask for evidence of the capabilities and certifications of the ASP's technical support operations and employees. Ask for its hiring and training practices. What strategies does it have for retaining its technical people—and their knowledge of the end users' needs?
- Evaluate security. As your systems will reside on the Internet, determine your candidate ASP's security track record. It should have strict practices already in place and a willingness to strengthen measures to meet the expectations of your customers and business partners. You and your ASP should create specific plans to minimize losses in the event of a breach.
- Service and support are crucial. Make sure your ASP provides dedicated management and twenty-four-hour help desks, and look into its geographic coverage in your area. Can the ASP provide a customer advocate and a technical liaison to your account?
- Determine scalability features. What plans are in place to add computer and network capacity, and how quickly can the ASP provide it?
- Check pricing. Hidden costs can await the unsuspecting user. Ask again and again: do network connections or integration cost extra? What are the costs of transitioning the solution in-house at a later date?
- Ask what level of system availability is guaranteed, and how it is measured. Read the fine print. What penalties does the ASP accept if it fails to meet the goals? Put down SLAs and penalties in writing before proceeding.

The main drive underlying such checklists is to advise prospective customers to exercise extreme care in selecting an ASP and to alert ASP managers to customer expectations and concerns. Care and concern are justified since so many ASPs have not fulfilled their promises and so many have entered the market without sound business fundamentals and a deep understanding of the ASP delivery model. In addition, ASPs are going out of business every day, as they go bankrupt or are acquired by wealthier players. These checklists are undeniably useful. However, the negative implications are easy to see. The "caveat emptor" focus of such customer lists may distort the ASP concept. The result may be a threatening and discouraging message for potential customers and partners and alienating, instead of educating, the targeted ASP stakeholders.

Another critical matter affecting the future of the industry is technical and nontechnical developments in the sector, whose implications are discussed in Chapter 5. A vital nontechnical element that depends on technical adequacy is customer confidence. Winning consumer confidence is especially difficult in light of the questions in the "beware checklists." The need to win customer confidence is common to the global business world, for example, where geographic distance and cultural, language, and legal differences represent a great challenge to building consumer confidence. However, because ASPs are increasingly regarded as the future of computing, as they transcend borders with efficiency and effectiveness (ASP Industry Consortium, 2001d), it is even more important to initiate and channel efforts to enable the industry to develop in the future.

An important step in building confidence and trust is the development of best practices by sensible existing market players and building policies to improve the ASP delivery model. Drivers for establishing ASP standards arise from various sources. One source is large companies that are potential or actual ASP customers, whose primary concern involves security for their internal data and mission-critical information. A second driving force is savvy ASPs, which have recognized that to be successful they must adopt standards that make their services as reliable as those of a telephone company (Bendor-Samuel and Goolsby, 2000). Those discussed in this chapter are, not coincidentally, the successful ASPs examined in Chapter 3. A third driving force consists of leading ASP partners. A fourth is the ASP Industry Consortium. These parties all have in common a best-practice focus and signal the positive relationship between successful efforts and customer and stakeholder confidence.

Given the rapid changes in IT and its management, resolving customer challenges is a daunting, though most rewarding, task. The best way an ASP can meet clients' needs and reduce its internal operating costs is to minimize errors and provide a predictable customer experience (Hunter, 2001). Being a long-term successful ASP is likely to be the result of having a best-practice focus in the management of all its operations.

BEST PRACTICES DEVELOPED FROM EXISTING INDEPENDENT ASP EXPERIENCES

This section describes useful best-practice strategies developed by existing successful ASPs. Most have received industry-level recognition and certifications for their best-practice efforts.

TeleComputing

Business ASP TeleComputing has been increasing its adoption rate among European and U.S. customers thanks to an internally developed system framework, TECOS, built on Compaq server-based technology, designed to manage its internal IT costs and complexity, while improving accessibility, reliability, and security for its customers worldwide. TECOS seamlessly integrates applications with technology architecture and infrastructure and is a key factor in fulfilling application delivery to customers, made possible by the strategic business relationships this ASP has developed with Microsoft for software, Compaq for server technology, and Citrix and Exodus for infrastructure. The underlying system framework enables TeleComputing to automate many of its application management-related services and brought this ASP four best-practice awards for its exceptional performance in just a few months in 2001 (TeleComputing, 2001a).

A significant part of TeleComputing's success stems from the set of carefully selected strategic partnerships it has built to effectively manage and control all the crucial aspects in the application delivery process, which are all oriented to ensure consistent and effective performance delivered to end users. In August 2001, for example, TeleComputing entered into a strategic alliance with Safeguard, which provided management support and operations services, and its technology management practice subsidiary Aligne, Inc. to help its customers deploy and manage the Microsoft .Net framework (XML protocol-based Web service) with speed and ease. For its part, Safeguard chose TeleComputing to capitalize on the opportunities tied to the ASP's integrated TECOS system to manage and deliver the .Net

Instant Infrastructure to its ISV customers and accelerate their entry into the ASP market. Microsoft and Summit Strategies rated this alliance as the most important factor for building a competitive advantage in the XML-based Web service arena (TeleComputing, 2001a).

In March 2001, TeleComputing received the Best Practice Award for Service Level Management, during an ASP Summit in Rome, Italy, for excellence in service, outstanding service performance, quality of service, and security and system accessibility to its clients (TeleComputing, 2001d).

Interliant

Interliant developed and launched in July 2001 a real-time performance monitoring and reporting process designed to allow its customers to track actual application performance against the negotiated SLAs, a major ASP best practice. The reporting tool is Web-based and allows clients to access performance measures for their IT systems managed by Interliant. The process also enables this ASP to monitor all aspects of its application service management from both inside and outside the data center, ensuring that all components perform at optimal levels. In addition, Interliant utilizes customization tools for the performance monitoring and reporting process to tailor data for use by engineers, managers, and executives. The performance tracking and reporting mechanism gives additional visibility and accountability to every system managed by Interliant and empowers customers to monitor their mission-critical systems, measure their performance, and ensure that they are maximizing their ASP investment (ITAA, 2001b).

Interliant also developed and launched in August 2001 an additional security device for its customers' data. A remote monitored firewall, a twenty-four-hour offering, provides Interliant customers with backup support and expertise to ensure the security of their critical system resources and data. This best practice complements internal defenses to ensure the highest degree of protection against malicious intruders. The service offers a significant value addition for companies already using Interliant's security-driven solutions. Interliant security professionals can audit the customer's site to identify and check all installed network security devices. The remote monitored firewall provides companies an additional layer of monitoring expertise that is not subject to internal customer demands and is 100 percent focused on security (ITAA, 2001c; Interliant, 2001a).

Corio

Corio developed Intelligent Enterprise, a suite of enterprise applications that fully integrates software applications, technology, and services, designed to deliver maximized e-business capabilities, which provides a framework for all its application delivery, management, and support solutions. Each business function across the customer's organization is integrated with the others through a world-class application. Since 1999, Corio has been seeking the best ways to assemble the best possible Internet-based application and technology components. Corio's vision entailed a strong standard availability or uptime, as well as a system that extends the standard core functions by building customization features. Corio worked closely with leading partners, such as BroadVision for software and Sun Microsystems for hardware and infrastructure services. The result is the intelligent integrated suite, which allowed Corio to win large customers, which comprised the bulk of its customer base at the end of 2000 (Fonseca and Jones, 2001).

Given a strong focus on high-quality service, Corio sought and obtained SunTone certification; it was among the first ASPs to receive this certification for best-practice business efforts. Certification is awarded in three areas: service provider services, hosted applications, and integrator services. Sun Microsystems' SunTone program is one of the service provider industry's first collaborative efforts to define and audit infrastructure, operational practices, hardware, applications, and overall service delivery to help ensure industry-leading performance, security, and availability. SunTone certification gives customers of Web-enabled services a valuable way to identify suppliers that meet defined high standards (Corio, 2001b; Sun Microsystems, 2001b). Through SunTone, ASPs can receive standard-setter status in the ASP industry, which is a key to maximizing their market opportunities.

USinternetworking (USi)

USi has become a market leader because of its strong enterprise ASP model. It ranked first in the IDC list of top ten ASPs of 2000 (Whalen et al., 2001). What made it so strong, in addition to other factors, was its network of effective partnerships for the management and control of critical infrastructure components, such as that developed with OrderTrust, a new type of ISP, to host infrastructure for making transactions. Another strategic partnership lay behind USi's expansion of its data center capacity in Europe to efficiently meet the international needs of its U.S.-based multinational corporations. CityReach International (CRI), a builder and operator of data centers, hosts its data center in Dublin, Ireland (USi, 2001). OrderTrust and CRI were selected by USi because they shared its key commitment to setting standards that enabled USi to deliver consistent application service to end users ("USinternetworking Expands," 2001; Ladley, 2000; USi, 2001).

Another example of USi's best-practice focus is the development and marketing of extensive educational services, which tailor a training curriculum to individual customer requirements, to cover the entire scope of USi-managed services through both on-site and Web-based instruction. This service enabled USi to share and transfer knowledge to its customers' end users, creating a high level of customer confidence and trust (USi, 2001).

USi, which received SunTone certification, also obtained Microsoft Gold Certified ASP Partner recognition. It is the only ASP that had both certifications by mid-2001. The Microsoft Gold certification is awarded to ASPs that offer SLAs directly to end-user customers and fulfill those agreements. Microsoft examines all aspects of an ASP's business process and operational infrastructure before certifying the robustness of its overall capability to deliver application services. This certification program examines ASPs in ten core IT capabilities and appraises their service readiness, competency, and capacity for hosting Microsoft and Microsoft's partners' solutions (USi, 2001). This recognition has positively affected USi's name and should be a key factor in its future growth, since the Microsoft Gold validation aims to help raise customers' awareness and consideration for the ASP delivery model (McCabe, 2001) and acts as a guarantee of the highest service level an ASP can offer today.

Qwest Cyber.Solutions (QCS)

QCS developed a high-standard three-level SLA approach that allows customers to pay for the performance guarantee and system availability they need, ranging from 99 percent to 99.99 percent application availability. Unlike most SLAs' average lower standards (99.4 for successful ASPs) (Gilmore, 2001c), QCS SLAs offer some of the highest performance guarantees in the industry and are comprehensive, as they also address response time, disaster recovery, and storage utilization issues (Mears, 2001e). QCS can thus be flexible and cost effective and has enabled its customers to remain focused on their business objectives without being locked into service levels that do not reflect their strategic intent and business scope (Qwest Cyber.Solutions, 2001a).

QCS has been partnering with ADP, the leading provider of HR services, to provide a best-practice payroll solution to its customers, by combining QCS's resource-planning ASP services with ADP's payroll expertise with large companies. The partnership ensures that customers can capitalize on their technical capabilities and expertise and receive full-service, robust, and high-quality solutions. These companies decided to partner because they shared the same commitment to guaranteeing customers the freedom to focus on their core business (Investquest, 2000; Qwest Cyber.Solutions, 2001a). QCS is another Microsoft Gold Certified ASP Partner.

Surebridge

Surebridge's success is due to a commitment to delivering the highest quality solutions, which it achieved through a proprietary methodology called eMethodology, designed to meet the complex challenges of midlevel, fast-growing companies. This custom tailoring process optimizes every aspect of the application services for a particular company. A critical element of eMethodology, and a core competency, involves developing, documenting, and maintaining internally the application configuration or framework process prior to delivery to end users. It is based on five steps that streamline the search for and selection of application solutions that truly meet the needs of each specific business: performance management (comprehensive monitoring, optimization, and upgrades); security management (for system and data integrity through a secure, stable, and lasting environment); configuration management (to ensure customers' applications are updated and fully utilized); and user and issue management (for the early detection and resolution of system problems) (Surebridge, 2001d).

Also, as an expression of its customer-centric business approach, Surebridge regularly surveys its customers to find out whether they are pleased with the service, to ensure ongoing high-level performance in all its business processes, and to keep its personnel's compensation tied to performance. If customers are satisfied, so are Surebridge and its employees. The survey asks customers to rate Surebridge against all the vendors they use, and also asks questions designed to determine how well it completed projects on time and how customers judged the quality of work (Bernard, 2001b), a major best practice. Surebridge's best-practice orientation is also evident in the design and content of its Web site, which offers White Books on useful topics and easy-to-access information on CRM. These are effective and efficient ways to maintain fruitful ongoing, fulfilling relationships with clients and to proactively respond to market requirements and build customer confidence today and tomorrow (Surebridge, 2001a).

United Messaging

United Messaging became the leader in delivering high-performance messaging solutions by building its services on the technologies that were standard in each industry. For example, United Messaging's Mailgration process for migrating existing customer messaging systems to its ASP-based delivery, which includes system analysis, integration, and consulting services that it developed internally, is also the result of United Messaging using high-quality, high-performance technologies, acquired through leading partners such as Sun Microsystems and Microsoft (United Messaging, 2001b).

In addition, by adopting standard-setting technologies and partners, United Messaging was able to commit to exacting SLAs with customers, which it was then able to fulfill. For example, by partnering with Sun Microsystems and obtaining SunTone certification, this ASP has never had unplanned server outages and was able to create a strong reputation with clients. Because Sun Microsystems is a leader in its area of expertise, it acts as a guarantee for United Messaging's customers. United Messaging rates this alliance as a key factor for winning customer confidence (United Messaging, 2001b).

Exult

Exult became a leader in offering comprehensive, Web-enabled integrated HR services for Global 500 corporations thanks to a strategic consultation and analysis process it developed internally. To enhance efficiencies and implement HR best practices, Exult performs a thorough assessment of the clients' existing internal HR processes. Exult also uses comparative HR studies obtained through strategic partnerships with leading HR research companies (such as McKinsey and Co. and the Corporate Leadership Council). After performing the benchmark study of existing operations, it sets targets for service quality improvement and cost reductions. Exult designs or redesigns clients' HR processes and helps them transition their HR procedures into Exult's application delivery. Exult's HR centers of expertise can support the major categories of HR processes since these centers of expertise are responsible for the entire solutions from beginning to end (Exult, 2001b).

Salesforce.com

Salesforce.com has been increasing its market share in providing CRM software and has won large customers, such as software developer Adobe and media giant Time Warner Communications, thanks to an internally developed process that guarantees ease and speed of implementation, requires little or no support at the customer's end, and delivers affordable prices relative to established CRM software vendors. Salesforce.com's ASP process for delivering CRM—one of the most critical software applications, in this ASP's view, as it can help an enterprise make and save money—is based on multiuser design: just a single CRM application suite and a single database run on a Web site, which deliver simplified, just-in-time applications to end users, require minimal training, assistance, and support, and which each customer can configure, customize, and access by using its own computing infrastructure. This multiuser process translates into ease of access and lower total costs of implementing Salesforce.com's CRM applications (Salesforce.com, 2001a).

Microsoft thought the process and methodology were promising and was working with Salesforce.com in 2001 to make it part of its .Net initiative, which means users can access Salesforce.com from their Microsoft applications. Thanks to its lean model, Salesforce.com was also named "Cool Company of 2001" by *Fortune* magazine in June. This annual honor designates technology companies that effectively blend new ideas with effective management, financial health, and an unlimited possibility for growth (Salesforce.com, 2001a). *Fortune* applauded Salesforce.com's efforts to create an effective application delivery model that makes CRM software quick to implement, customize, access, and benefit from, and allows sales, customer support, and marketing staff to collaborate and benefit from new solutions to current needs as they arise.

Portera

Portera has become the leading provider of Web-based application services for the professional service industry, which enabled it to win large customers such as Siemens, the New Zealand government, Microsoft, and Booz-Allen and Hamilton, thanks to a supporting application delivery process that the ASP has developed and effectively manages. The process is 100 percent Web enabled, and utilizes Java (a programming language developed by Sun Microsystems, designed to run on any computer or computing device, regardless of specific microprocessor or operating system) (Laudon and Laudon, 2001) to enable Portera to write applications and their customization features once and then run them anytime, anywhere, on an as-needed basis through delivering only the software applications needed for a particular task. In addition, end users access their remotely managed applications through a simple Web browser (Portera, 2001; Sun Microsystems, 2001b).

This process has produced, for example, Portera's ServicePort, a versatile application management system developed to allow application customization features for each client, ranging from large organizations that need to support a complex, distributed workforce to small-company individual projects, which provides them with a single point of access for diverse business functions, such as project collaboration, internal reporting, client communications, and document sharing. ServicePort's online forum for sharing schedules, ideas, developments, reports, and plans between Portera and its customers ensures instantaneous access to problem-solving teams and builds on lessons learned. Portera is a Sun partner, not only for Java but also for the underlying server capability that guarantees high-quality SLAs, and the partnership has become a critical success factor for Portera in winning large customers, whose confidence in the process was difficult to achieve previously (Portera, 2001).

TriZetto Group

TriZetto's vertical-market ASP division has gained a leading position in the health care industry thanks to an early focus on Web-based applications. In April 2000, this ASP entered into an agreement with New Era of Networks Inc. to customize and speed integration of its application-based solutions, whose associated benefits—faster time to market, little or no training needed, and the desired level of performance arising from customization and integration—were passed on to customers. Previously, TriZetto had to individually rework every application purchased from third-party vendors (and their updates as well) to enable integration with its ASP system. This ASP continued its core specialization in fully integrated, customized solutions by announcing in early 2001 its next generation of services, called ASP bundles. These are integrated prepackaged health care application solutions consisting of a core software application surrounded by specialized complementary applications. TriZetto has taken the best-of-class core applications and enriched them with pre-integrated customization features, thus creating fast, cost-effective solutions implemented in half the standard time that ensure high reliability and cover the full spectrum of the health care industry's business needs (TriZetto Group, 2001b).

TriZetto developed its ASP bundled offerings with a "transformation" team-based methodology. TriZetto's transformation staff works with each client to assemble a portfolio of applications specifically targeted to the client's desired performance. The first step is the strategic service line, where business strategies are defined. The second is the enablement service line, where solutions are identified. The final step is the management service line, which offers solution management tools. This methodology, among other benefits, enables systems implementation time to be reduced by up to 50 percent. The bundled solutions also come with performance guarantees that ensure high levels of reliability and significant savings over assembling comparable, nonpackaged applications. Also, TriZetto entered a partnership with health care software vendor Erisco, whose Facets software is the leader in the health care administration business, specifically to deliver a powerful, flexible depth and breadth of applications that would enable scalability. TriZetto was able to effectively manage more than 70 million individuals' data in 2001 (TriZetto Group, 2001b; Goldman, 2000).

LearningStation.com

LearningStation.com is focused exclusively on the school industry and its educational requirements and challenges. It developed an entirely Windows-based ASP and pioneered efforts to wire desktops throughout the United States for educational purposes. To produce an integrated, unified ASP value chain, LearningStation merged with its network provider, Computer Network Power, which had previously been market leader Citrix's operating partner for network management. LearningStation saw the huge potential in a unified relationship with Computer Network Power to benefit from the talent this company had acquired by working for Citrix. Such an enhanced ASP business model and application delivery mechanism, implemented over a large and growing customer base, was the key factor behind LearningStation's winning the ASPire Award for Delivery in November 2000. This award was established by the ASP Industry Consortium to identify and promote best practices and so documents the effectiveness of LearningStation's efforts (LearningStation.com, 2001b).

To be considered for the ASPire award, consortium members must submit case studies of application deployment illustrating best practices in at least one of four categories: delivery, integration, management/operations, and enablement (Wainewright, 2000a). The first yearly awards were given in late 2000, and recognized member companies that promoted excellence in the ASP industry (ASP Industry Consortium, 2001e).

Jamcracker

Jamcracker has focused on keeping its customers' most important organizational asset, its people, productive and effective. This is the foundation for its core application delivery and service model, which is entirely based on high-level responsiveness to customers, continuous support to end users, and a proactive application monitoring tool for early detection of problems in customers' outsourced systems. The last is not a standard service and is provided only by the leading ASPs. Jamcracker utilizes a multitude of providers to deliver services such as the proactive monitoring tool. To effectively manage its providers, it has developed an operating process designed to make it easy to add or replace service providers according to the needs and business objectives of its diverse customers. This process, or unified platform as Jamcracker calls it, provides access to software and services that are already integrated through a single sign-on on its Web site. This preintegration process ensures Jamcracker can make a very broad variety of services available to its customers, who can rely on Jamcracker as their only point of contact (Jamcracker, 2001a).

Jamcracker's unified platform is enabled by industry-standard security and infrastructure technologies that deliver high levels of service and allow this AASP to also offer an industry-leading directory server for user management, including reporting and organization chart capability, which enables scalability. Another significant result is a service center available to customers for help, whose staff delivers extremely fast responses, usually in less than a minute. The service center process consists of four steps. First, the problem is diagnosed upon customer contact. Second, some questions are answered right away, and those that cannot be answered immediately are dispatched to a second line of support. Third, at this upper level, Jamcracker provides the necessary support to ensure the problem is managed to resolution. Finally, continuous follow-up tracking of problem status, performance, application usage, and system monitoring is incorporated into the overall process (Jamcracker, 2001a).

These stories document a strong link between success and having a best-practice orientation, which these ASP companies share with their partners and whose benefits have been transferred to their customers. Through robust, proprietary core business methodologies that are driven by a commitment to high quality, through additional services that fulfill present and future customer needs, and through tightly managed effective partnerships that ensure optimal application performance for each specific customer requirement, these ASPs have set standards in the industry and have been rewarded for their outstanding efforts. Individually, and as benchmark models that were achieved as a result of their best-practice focus, these ASPs appear to be well positioned to remain successful.

MICROSOFT'S BEST-PRACTICE GUIDELINES FOR ASPs

This section discusses the guidelines Microsoft has developed for ASPs in three mission-critical performance areas: capacity, contingency, and security management. The rationale underlying its set of ASP guidelines is that Microsoft wants ASP to survive its challenges and grow. Microsoft has an enormous interest in ASP. It has created an ASP operation that delivers its applications to small businesses, bCentral, but its main strategic thrust lies in partnerships with a large number of ASPs to deliver its software (Parizo, 2001b). In October 2000, Microsoft released three books that discuss and give practical examples of best practices for ASPs in the areas of capacity, contingency, and security management. They can be considered part of a broader initiative, or framework, which focuses on best practices, principles, and business models that provide comprehensive management and technical guidance for achieving mission-critical system reliability, availability, supportability, and manageability. The framework deals with two concepts: service solutions and IT service management. Service solutions include the capabilities or business functions that IT provides to its customers, among which are ASPs.

The three books address best practices relevant to service provision, technical infrastructure, billing processes, and service-level management. Planning and managing capacity, contingencies, and security represents a significant cost for ASPs, yet the inability to recover from problem situations is even more costly if the ASP cannot meet customer requirements. The success of an ASP, in Microsoft's view, depends on thoroughly satisfying customers by delivering solutions that perform per agreement in terms of:

- *quality*—delivery to the customer of the agreed quality as identified in the SLA;
- *speed*—timely management of resources to meet solution requirements as identified in the SLA; and
- *value* (measured by low cost)—optimized and predictable cost.

Proactive management of capacity, contingencies, and security ensures a balance between the customer expectations of quality, speed, and value. The following sections analyze the details of best practices in these three areas in Microsoft's study (Microsoft Enterprise Services, 2001).

Capacity Management for ASPs

ASPs that do not always have sufficient capacity to serve all of their customers according to the agreed service levels will frustrate them with slow response times, timeouts and errors, and broken applications. Customers will likely turn to other ASPs that can meet their requirements. To prevent this, ASPs must build a computer infrastructure that can handle not only average levels of demand, but also peak levels and beyond. Capacity management is the process of measuring an ASP's ability to deliver solutions to its customers at an acceptable speed. It ensures that optimum use is made of existing resources and that upgrades are completed in the most cost-effective and timely manner. The process continuously seeks to optimize existing and future resource demands. When performed correctly, capacity management makes it possible to estimate how much computing hardware is necessary to handle demand.

Capacity management can help an ASP's staff proactively design future infrastructure improvements to handle increased customer demand. To the extent that capacity management tools are automated and general enough to be applied to multiple applications, ASPs will reduce dependency on human intervention, increase customer satisfaction, and increase the financial viability of the ASP model. Strategies and specific action steps need to be provided for best-practice capacity management, such as identification of capacity-limiting resources, management of resources, and robust logging. An integrated capacity provisioning architecture is offered in Microsoft's book that integrates all capacity management components in an optimal system. Also, a fictional case study is included, which summarizes best-practice activities and proposed strategies in a quasi-real-life setting. In essence, capacity management is a facilitating process ASPs can use to differentiate themselves from competitors when approaching potential customers.

Contingency Management for ASPs

Microsoft's ASP guidelines address contingency planning to maintain business continuity. Contingency management involves being prepared for unforeseen events that could disrupt services and focuses on the IT services an ASP needs to support its customers. Running IT operations successfully is a prerequisite to achieving business success. Its main objective is to ensure that the required IT technical and services facilities (computer systems, networks, applications, telecommunications, technical support, and help desk) can be recovered according to the business performance guarantee defined in the SLA. Contingency management is important for ASPs as they constantly face risks, from a single incident in one department to major incidents that affect multiple clients or the clients' own customers.

Contingency management uses risk management principles to identify threats to service, such as equipment failure or fire. Introducing countermeasures, such as an alternative data center, can eliminate vulnerable areas of the service design and limit the impact of a threat. In the event of a major problem, contingency plans for service continuity must provide the facilities, knowledge, and procedures for a full recovery of service at an alternative location. Contingency management can help the staff plan for contingencies and adequately implement countermeasures, and can deliver business benefits such as credibility, potential lower insurance costs, and strengthened business relationships. Strategies are provided for problem prevention and minimization, such as rigorous testing of the contingency procedures, proper problem prevention with scheduled maintenance and backup, and accurate process documentation. A fictional case study is included in Microsoft's book that summarizes the proposed contingency management activities and underlying strategies. Contingency management is a necessary part of the overall business continuity process and is dependent upon information derived through this process.

Security Management for ASPs

The third section of Microsoft's ASP guidelines focuses on security in processing and storing information. For IT, information is the core of its existence. Anything that threatens the information or its secure processing will directly endanger the performance of the ASP. Whether it concerns the confidentiality, integrity, or timeliness of the information, or the availability of processing functions or confidentiality, threats have to be neutralized by security. Security management is the process of managing a defined level of security and also the process of managing security breaches when they occur. Security planning and management is important for ASPs, as it enables being ready for attacks by malicious entities in such a way that those attacks can be handled without fear for business continuity. The goal of security management is to ensure continuity, protect information, and help minimize damage from security breaches. Microsoft's guidelines for managing security breaches include:

- a clear security policy that is actively implemented and monitored;
- a security organization with clear responsibilities and tasks, guidelines, reporting procedures, and measures that are properly matched to the needs of customers;
- physical security measures, such as the physical separation from the computer room;
- technical security measures that provide security in the ASP's computer systems and network; and
- procedural security measures describing how the ASP staff is required to act in specific cases.

For each service or application outsourcing function, the ASP must define the proper security policy, such as the requirements it must follow and what needs to be protected. Microsoft provides detailed best practices for ASP security management, such as single sign-on, support for Internet Standard Authentication Protocol, public key infrastructure (encryption, digital signature), and VPN systems. In addition, policies are recommended that act as a two-way channel to communicate existing security problems and procedures at any time. In summary, the best practices described in Microsoft's study show how an ASP can make sure the security objective is met. All elements need to be in balance to ensure a security level that meets the requirements of the ASP's customers.

ASP INDUSTRY CONSORTIUM'S BEST-PRACTICE GUIDELINES

This section describes a best-practice initiative formulated by the ASP Industry Consortium in the area of dispute avoidance and resolution for ASP market stakeholders: ASPs, ASP customers, suppliers/business partners, and investors. This initiative was developed in an effort to build customer trust.

The consortium is concerned with the establishment, promotion, and dissemination of standards. In this organization's view, standards are objective benchmarks for customers to use in evaluating ASP providers. The overall goals of the ASP Industry Consortium (2001e) are to:

- educate the marketplace;
- develop common definitions for the industry;
- promote best practices;
- foster open standards and guidelines;
- sponsor research in the industry; and
- serve as a forum for discussion about the industry.

As a major first step in its standard establishment and promoting efforts, in late 2000 the ASP Industry Consortium formed a Best Practices Committee, whose main objective was to ensure effective delivery of ASP services. In commercial relationships of all kinds, disputes arise; the ASP marketplace is not immune. Particularly in an international relationship, the commercial and legal risks can increase significantly, as does the potential for conflict due to different legal requirements and commercial cultures, as well as language barriers. As noted by former consortium chairman Gruen-Kennedy, "Cyberspace has no borders, yet the world still operates under a system of cultural and historic borders"; a process is therefore required to address business disputes, especially ones involving cross-border relationships (ASP Industry Consortium, 2001d). Recognizing this reality, the consortium sought to develop guidelines that would provide greater certainty about business and legal obligations for the ASP model.

The main concern is that an ASP's liability exposure may be multiplied by the one-to-many delivery model characteristic. The ASP Industry Consortium asked the World Intellectual Property Organization (WIPO) to prepare a set of dispute avoidance and resolution guidelines specifically tailored to reflect ASP business models. WIPO's Arbitration and Mediation Center is a recognized leading dispute resolution provider for Internet and IT disputes involving intellectual property (ASP Industry Consortium, 2001e). The strategy first involved defining the relationships between the value chain partners that make up an ASP, and then creating procedures for handling conflicts. In May 2001, the ASP Industry Consortium and WIPO jointly published a comprehensive set of recommendations and guidelines for enacting global dispute avoidance and resolution procedures (ASPIC-WIPO, 2001). This section summarizes information from this primary source. The best-practice report on dispute avoidance and resolution aims to provide:

- stakeholders in the ASP industry with an insight into the use and possible benefits of conflict management procedures;
- ASPs and their partners with practical and applicable information that will enable them to introduce conflict management procedures within their organizations and into their contracts, and take advantage of conflict management processes when disputes arise; and
- lawyers, judges, arbitrators, and other dispute resolution experts not familiar with the ASP industry with an insight into the structure, relationships, and likely areas of dispute in the ASP value chain.

As of early 2002, there had not been many reported disputes involving ASPs, because of the following issues:

- The ASP business model was still evolving.
- Small and medium-sized enterprises may not have had the resources (financial or otherwise) to pursue a dispute.
- Larger enterprises have a higher threshold of tolerance for poor technology performance. Also, they are less dependent on ASP services for mission-critical functions.
- The financial loss suffered by customers or end users that have had problems with ASPs has not been sufficient to justify pursuing formal dispute resolution, regardless of the forum.
- ASPs and their customers have sought to avoid dispute resolution processes because of the cloud this may cast on the prospects of future funding, and because of their general adverse effects on business and marketing activities.
- Many ASPs have taken additional precautions and measures in service delivery and customer care. Planning for this enables ASPs to avoid the major costs and consequences of unexpected service delivery and customer care-related problems.

However, as the ASP market grows, the number of disputes will rise, especially as a result of the increasing failure rate of providers in meeting service commitments. In addition, disputes over issues such as data ownership, data transfer, and software ownership may materialize due to the significant consolidation in the industry that was taking place in 2001. The objective of publishing dispute avoidance and resolution guidelines was first to make sure the various stakeholders in the ASP industry know and accept the fact that there will be challenges as the ASP business model continues to evolve. At the same time, the goal was to clarify that individual ASPs must not let these challenges stand in their way. Instead, they must address these challenges quickly, efficiently, and in a manner that maximizes the likelihood of preserving business relationships while minimizing business disruption.

Although directed primarily at ASPs, dispute avoidance guidelines are also relevant for all the other stakeholders in the ASP industry. Recommended best practices require ASPs to:

- adopt and promote operational excellence in the planning and management of infrastructure, connectivity, security, applications, implementation, and support;
- be proactive in determining service-level compliance problems by deploying systems that can isolate the cause of a problem and the associated vendor that owns the problem component, and through comprehensive and meaningful reporting of service-level compliance issues to customers;
- provide timely and responsive problem resolution, proactive support services, and efficient information management by establishing customer-care policies and comprehensive help desk facilities;
- negotiate and implement fair, balanced, comprehensive, and clearly drafted service-level agreements, which set out the respective rights and obligations of the parties and ensure that each party fully comprehends the legal and technical implications of the contractual commitments;
- implement technical, administrative, and operational mechanisms that enable proactive relationship management; and
- acquire proper insurance coverage as part of an overall risk reduction plan and work with experienced professionals to obtain the best, most efficient insurance protection available.

The ASPIC-WIPO report discusses alternative dispute resolution methods, ranging from the least formal, such as negotiation, settlement counsel, and mediation, to the most formal—litigation. It also provides guidelines in the form of "suitability screening matrices" to assist parties in choosing the most appropriate dispute resolution technique to use in light of the business model, the contractual relationship, the amount in controversy, and the identity of the parties. ASPIC and WIPO recommend including a dispute resolution clause when the other terms and conditions of the agreement are negotiated. Once a dispute has arisen, it may be hard for the parties to agree about anything, let alone the procedures about how to resolve their dispute. Instead, a dispute resolution clause provides both parties with a degree of certainty regarding how problems will be resolved and can expedite the dispute resolution process. However, it is still possible to decide on a resolution process after a dispute has arisen if the parties' relationship is good enough to allow an agreement without significant delay, expense, or acrimony.

As important as quick cost-effective dispute resolution mechanisms can be, the most important step involves the best practices that ASPs implement to avoid conflict and business disruption in the first place. The main expected benefit is to help ASP stakeholders address potential contract disputes before they arise. Operating under the premise that dispute avoidance is the best remedy, the guidelines aim to maximize the likelihood that the parties' relationship will be preserved. Because disputes may be unavoidable in some cases, however, procedures must exist for dealing with multiple disputes involving multiple parties, some or all of which may be located in different legal jurisdictions. In addition, because no direct contractual relationship exists between an ASP's partners and its customers, procedures can overcome the lack of contractual link.

In addition to the organizational and operational benefits that can be realized benefits involving customer confidence and trust are expected to result from a public commitment by an ASP to the adoption, implementation, and promotion of best practices. Thus, ASP Industry Consortium members are encouraged to adopt the legally nonbinding ASPresolve Pledge, a commitment to minimize disputes by the use of best practices. The pledge is intended to be a badge of honor within the ASP industry, affirming to customers and partners an intent to build long-term, profitable, and constructive business relationships, and to deliver reliable and consistent service. ASPIC-WIPO's "Dispute Avoidance and Resolution" report is a living document, to be periodically updated.

The ASP Industry Consortium's decision to begin policing itself has an important message. As the model evolves and more vendors flood the market, self-policing or some sort of accreditation will not just be increasingly important, but might even become necessary to prompt companies to adopt the ASP outsourcing concept. The consortium hopes to give potential and existing customers greater confidence in ASP outsourcers. Although the group cannot mandate guidelines, as customers become increasingly savvy about their outsourcing needs, voluntary adherence to proposed guidelines is being recognized by industry analysts as increasingly important for ASPs' credibility and growth (Borck, 2000).

WINNING CUSTOMER CONFIDENCE AND TRUST

The major conclusion from the analysis so far is an appreciation that customer and partner education is one of the necessary conditions to ensure a future for the ASP business market. Another necessary condition is for ASPs to have a sound business model that incorporates best-practice focus as a primary managerial drive, which is necessary to approach the ASP businesses, the ASP value chain partners, and the end users with education and future growth in mind. The analysis in this chapter has identified important efforts and the best practices guidelines developed from them that are particularly conducive to a more confident and trusting consumer environment:

1. The development of an appropriate internally developed computer information system framework designed to manage internal IT costs and complexity and improve system accessibility, reliability, and security for customers, such as that of business ASP TeleComputing, also resulting from the set of carefully selected effective strategic partnerships. Doing this enables the ASP to automate application management-related services and effectively manage and control all the crucial aspects of the ASP process. The result is consistent outstanding performance delivered to end users, excellence in service, which is also formally recognized and rewarded, and security and system accessibility to the ASP's clients.

2. The development of a real-time performance monitoring and reporting process designed to allow the ASP's customers to track actual application performance against the negotiated SLAs, such as that at business ASP Interliant. Doing this also enables the ASP itself to monitor all aspects of its application service management from both inside and outside the data center, ensuring that all components perform at optimal levels. Also, by utilizing customization tools for the performance monitoring and reporting mechanism, the ASP can deliver additional visibility and accountability to every system managed, and empowers customers to monitor their mission-critical systems and directly measure their performance. The result is customers who are able to maximize their ASP investment.

3. The development of a twenty-four-hour remote monitored firewall device that enhances security for customers' data by providing backup support and expertise, as was done by Interliant. This enables the ASP to complement internal defenses to ensure the highest degree of protection against malicious intruders. Also, the customer site can be audited remotely to identify and check all installed network security devices. Doing so enables the ASP to avoid the likelihood that some problems may escape customers' control in their internal systems. The result is an additional layer of monitoring expertise that is not subject to internal customer demand and is 100 percent focused on security.

4. The development of an "intelligent" suite of enterprise applications and services, designed to deliver maximized e-business capabilities, which provides a framework for all application delivery, management, and support solutions to customers, as was done at enterprise ASP Corio. By working closely with market leaders in respective fields, it is possible to assemble the best application and technology components. Doing so enables the ASP to achieve a strong application performance as well as deliver customization features, and also achieve certifications that validate its high-quality service. The result is an integrated intelligent suite that always performs at optimal levels, which enables the ASP to address the complex needs of large customers and to achieve standard-setter status in the ASP marketplace, key to maximizing market opportunities.

5. The development of a network of effective partnerships with ASP value chain enablers for the management and control of critical infrastructure components, such as the hosting of infrastructure and

data center management, as was done by enterprise ASP USinternet-working. By carefully selecting partners that share its commitment to standard-setting goals, the ASP is able to effectively control the infra-structure elements that enable consistent application service to be delivered to the end users. The result is a robust and integrated Internet-empowered business that gives the ASP a strong reputation with clients, because it shows customers a commitment to quality, which acts as a guarantee for the adequate treatment of their mission-critical processes.

6. The development and marketing of extensive educational ser-vices, which tailor a training curriculum to individual customers' re-quirements, and which cover the entire scope of the ASP-managed service, as was done at USinternetworking. By offering a customized training solution at all levels in the customer's organization, through both on-site and Web-based instruction, the ASP enables the sharing and transfer of knowledge to customers' end users. The result is a high level of customer confidence and trust in the outsourced applica-tion delivery mechanism.

7. The development and marketing of a high-standard three-level SLA approach that allows customers to pay for the performance guarantee and system availability they need, as done at enterprise ASP QCS. Doing this enables the ASP's customers to choose from among some of the highest levels of performance guarantees, up to comprehensive, top-service levels, which also address response time, disaster recovery, and storage utilization issues, and also enables the ASP to be flexible and cost effective while delivering the service that had been previously agreed to. Also, entering into a partnership alli-ance with the leading provider of HR services, as was done by QCS, enables the ASP to capitalize on its partner's expertise so customers can receive full-service, robust, and high-quality solutions. The result for customers is the freedom to focus on their business objectives without being locked into service elements that do not reflect their strategic intent and business scope.

8. The development of custom tailoring application delivery meth-odologies that are especially designed to meet the needs of specific target customer groups and that optimize every aspect of the applica-tion service for a particular company, as was done at vertical-market enterprise ASP Surebridge. By developing, documenting, and main-taining the application delivery methodology internally, and building

it on a few key steps, the ASP is able to streamline the search for application solutions that truly meet the needs of each business. The result is the delivery of comprehensive, effective solutions.

9. The development of a customer-centric approach that is closely tied to feedback from clients' experience, for instance in the use of regular customer surveys to find out whether customers are satisfied with the service they are receiving, and whose input also reflects the ASP's staff performance and compensation, as was done at Surebridge. In addition, the creation of Web sites that are easy to access and use by potential and actual customers in terms of both design and content and where useful information is stored and publicly accessible results in a customer-driven ASP model that succeeds in maintaining ongoing, fulfilling relationships with clients, and in proactively responding to market requirements and building customer confidence.

10. The utilization of high-quality, high-performance technologies appropriate for individual customers, acquired through leading ASP value chain partners, which represent the standards in each underlying industry (such as Sun Microsystems), as was done at specialist ASP United Messaging. Doing this enables the ASP to build, for example, a process for migrating existing customer systems to the ASP-based delivery framework, which includes system analysis, integration, and consulting services, and also enables it to commit to exacting SLAs with customers, and then deliver the required service levels, for example, avoiding unplanned server outage issues. The result of capitalizing on leading partners' expertise is the display of a high-level quality focus in the ASP's operations and core business processes, which acts as a guarantee for customers as it creates a strong ASP reputation, and is a key strategic factor for addressing their concerns over the migration and outsourcing of their mission-critical data.

11. The development of a strategic consultation and analysis process, which performs a thorough assessment of the clients' existing internal processes, uses comparative studies obtained through strategic partners, produces a benchmark study, and finally sets targets for process quality improvement and cost reductions, as was done at specialist ASP Exult. Doing this enables the ASP to design or redesign clients' processes and helps them successfully transition to ASP-based systems. The result is a series of centers of expertise available

to customers that can support the major categories of selected business processes to systematically understand and address the needs of clients and their employees, and which are fully responsible for the entire solutions from beginning to end.

12. The development of a multiuser ASP process design that delivers simplified, just-in-time applications that each customer can configure, customize, and access by using its own infrastructure and resources, which guarantees ease and speed of implementation, requires little or no training, assistance, and support at the customer's end, and delivers faster, more affordable outsourced application services, as was done at specialist ASP Salesforce.com. Doing this enables the ASP to create an effective application model that is rewarded for blending new ideas with effective management and financial health. Also, doing this allows the ASP's customer sales, customer support, and marketing staff to collaborate continuously with the ASP, and mutually benefit from the ASP solutions. The result is new, focused, effective solutions to current needs as they arise.

13. The development of a 100 percent Web-enabled, standard communication language-supported process that enables the ASP to write applications and their customization features once and then run them anytime, anywhere, on an as-needed basis to a wide range of clients, by delivering only the software applications needed for a particular task, as was done at vertical-market ASP Portera. Doing this enables customers to access remotely managed applications through a simple Web browser and quickly share schedules, ideas, reports, and development information with their ASP. The result is a versatile application management system developed to allow customization features for each client.

14. The acquisition of integration capabilities, through effective partnerships and an early focus on Web-based application solutions, to customize and speed integration of solutions, as was done at vertical-market ASP TriZetto. Doing this enables the ASP to avoid reworking every application purchased from software vendors (including updates). The result is the ability to deliver fully integrated solutions and to transfer the associated benefits—faster time to market, little or no training needed to access the applications, and the desired level of performance arising from customization and integration—to customers.

15. The development of integrated prepackaged application solutions that complement core software applications, or customized bundled services, to be able to rapidly implement and solve industry-specific challenges, as was also done at TriZetto. Doing this is the result of a dedicated transformation team assembling a portfolio of applications targeted to each client's desired application performance, which is possible after the definition of specific customer business strategies, the identification of solutions, and the offering of solution management tools, and thanks to alliance partnerships specifically developed to enhance flexibility and scalability. Doing this enables the ASP to deliver best-of-class solutions that are implemented in half the standard time, ensure high reliability, and also cover the full spectrum of the target industry's business needs. The result is the delivery of a powerful, flexible depth and breadth of applications that are scalable and the ability for the ASP to efficiently manage huge amounts of data.

16. The development of exclusive relationships with one or two application and technology partners with wide expertise and background in leading IT sectors, to effectively tighten and integrate the underlying ASP value chain and operate a unified, integrated delivery process, as was done at vertical-market ASP LearningStation with its network provider, formerly partner of market leader Citrix. Doing so enables the ASP to benefit from the talent of focused alliance partners, and the result is an enhanced business model, whose application delivery mechanism can be effectively and consistently implemented over a large and growing customer base, and which is recognized for best practices by entities such as the ASP Industry Consortium.

17. The development of an operating process designed to make it easy to add or replace value chain service providers according to the needs and business objectives of each customer, such as at ASP aggregator Jamcracker. Doing so enables the ASP to provide customers with access to software and services that are already integrated through a single sign-on on the ASP's Web site, and also produces nonstandard, extended services such as a proactive application monitoring tool for the early detection of problems in the customers' outsourced systems, such as that developed by Jamcracker. The result of this operating process is the availability of a very broad variety of services for customers, who only need to have a single point of contact with the AASP, a high-quality level of services, such as an indus-

try-leading directory server for user management, and long-term benefits such as scalability.

18. The development of a service center option always available to customers, based on a multiple-step customer response process at the ASP's end, designed to immediately diagnose the problem upon customer contact and resolve it in minutes (or to transfer the matter to another level of support until the problem is managed and solved), as was done at Jamcracker. Doing this enables the ASP to provide a high level of responsiveness to customers. This, coupled with ongoing follow-up tracking of problem status, performance, and application usage and system monitoring, minimizes the likelihood of unplanned system failure. The result is optimal customer service, and productivity and effectiveness at the customer end.

19. The development, implementation, and diffusion of codes of conduct, guidelines, and best practices, as was done at Microsoft. Doing this enables individual ASPs and the entire industry to use and implement best practices and to minimize the likelihood of unwanted, challenging issues for both the ASP and the customer, such as those deriving from less than adequate ASP capacity management, contingency management, and security management.

20. The creation of third-party validation or certification, such as Sun Microsystems SunTone and Microsoft's Gold Certified ASP Partner awards. ASP businesses displaying a certification shows that they accept external oversight and operate in compliance with the code of practice established by the certifying third party. Certification aims to help raise customers' awareness and support for the ASP delivery model, and validates the certified ASPs' ability to guarantee the best possible service. The seal of approval gives customers a valuable way for identifying suppliers that meet defined high standards. The result for the ASP is increased market potential.

21. The use of balanced, impartial, quick, and cost-effective procedures for problem and dispute resolution, such as those promoted and developed by the ASP Industry Consortium in cooperation with WIPO. In most cases, consumer confidence is predicated on the belief that disputes will be settled fairly and rapidly. Using effective problem and dispute resolution methods enables the ASP and its customers to cooperate on their business goals, and may become the only way for ASPs to prompt companies to adopt the ASP outsourcing concept.

Continuous focus and improvements in these areas are essential to ASP growth, combined with IT industry-wide efforts toward the promulgation of laws regulating online (Internet or private network-based) commercial activities that balance the rights of consumers and the concerns of online service providers (ASPIC-WIPO, 2001).

CONCLUSION

This chapter has provided insights into significant best practices that can help ASPs plan and effectively manage, and ultimately help minimize and avoid, problems over the long run. Although it is easy to understand the desirability of disseminating best practices to managers, customers, and other ASP stakeholders, it is too early to project their potential benefits for the ASP market. Although it is evident that evolving standards are increasingly being addressed by individual companies and associations, ASPs still must balance individual customer demands and varying market-dictated requirements with their own need for standards. One case in point is the market need for customization that can conflict with the core one-to-many ASP model characteristic, which relies on application standardization. Therefore, in the future, successful ASPs are likely to be those which provide the best services to their customers, while also adhering to best practices. The future of ASPs is still uncertain, since many factors will influence their form, their best practices, their role in the application market, and their growth and profitability.

Chapter 5

The Future of ASPs

INTRODUCTION

The objective of this concluding chapter is to explore the longer-term prospects for the ASP marketplace and present some insights into expected future models, which may be:

- existing ASP models (adapted and modified where necessary) that survive the current industry shakeout and emerge from expected consolidation, or
- other models, which might include competitors from other IT sectors and today's ASP partners and business enablers whose different models (new or combinations of their existing models) become predominant ways of application service provision.

The chapter also presents conclusions drawn from this analysis.

FUTURE MODELS: OVERVIEW

This section examines the outlook for the ASP industry and competitive marketplace and discusses the kinds of application service provider models that are expected to be in use in the next two years.

The research and analysis in Chapters 1 through 4 has documented the viability of the core ASP delivery concept, through identifying and studying successful models. In this final chapter, current application service provider business models and alternative models for application service delivery and management are developed and examined in order to identify possible future approaches to, and players in, the ASP market. Since the preliminary results of the ASP Industry Consortium's first global tracking study indicate the ASP market will reach a level of relative maturity in three to five years from 2001 (Newcomb, 2001b), this analysis examines possible future developments within this time frame. While the ASP model's sustainability is not in question, its actual delivery will likely change during the coming years, and this chapter aims to provide an insight into the possible directions the market will take.

In spite of the shakeout that was to produce significant consolidation in 2001/2002, research results indicate there are still bright prospects for the ASP model's ability to change the course of IT and how end users will employ technology in the future, and many good reasons to suggest application service providers can prosper (Wainewright, 2001c). The current economic slowdowns are negatively affecting ASPs as there are other providers in most IT industries. In the long run, however, corporate belt tightening is expected to raise the average businessperson's awareness of the ASP industry, and the inherent benefits of application outsourcing will eventually lead to increased ASP revenues (Bernard, 2001a). As ASP services become more pervasive, customers can leverage for their own benefit the leading ASPs' best practices.

A continuing debate among ASPs and market analysts involves which models will survive. Some analysts contend that the harvesting of today's low-quality providers is a necessary part of industry evolution, and is actually good for the industry, as the strong ones that remain will be able to lead the industry to its full potential (Bradbury, 2001; Knight, 2001; Mears, 2001f). According to Gartner Group vice president Peter Dueck, there will be opportunities for a large number of existing savvy ASPs as a result of the expected market consolidation (Gartner Group, 2001b). However, in a long-term perspective, IDC predicts the market leaders will be those service providers that are able to adapt to business needs. According to IDC senior analyst Amy Mizoras, today's ASPs need to prove they are here to stay "by providing quality services and allowing their customers to recognize a high return on investment" ("Ebusiness," 2001).

The emergence of ASP aggregators indicates that more or different models are needed to accommodate customer requirements that are not adequately satisfied today, as noted in Chapter 2, and signals that some current models may not be suitable over the long run. ASP winners in 2001, and those that will appear on the market next, need to do more to grow and keep their customer base. IDC analyst Meredith

Whalen (Gilmore, 2001c) observed that the next generation of winners must go beyond today's recipe for success. They should strive to offer unique value-added elements. Some elements involve expansions to existing services, such as:

- *Service-level agreements:* Rather than trying to provide more application performance availability or uptime (for example, from the industry average, 99.4 percent, to a more expensive 99.6 percent or better), ASPs should consider offering SLAs for the "last mile" of their clients' internal environment (for example, the desktop).
- *Security:* In spite of the fact that security at ASP facilities is already better than most clients can achieve in-house, it remains an often-cited adoption inhibitor. Security insurance policy offerings could help convince potential customers to adopt ASPs and give another value-added service enhancing their profitability.
- *Customer support:* Because customer support is already a standard offering, ASPs should leverage alternative methodologies to achieve cost-effective and enhanced service. Using the Internet and e-mail for some types of customer support could reduce expensive call handling and increase the effectiveness of their service.

Although the analyzed successful ASPs have seemed almost an exception, they signal that the basic ASP model works, and that there are several good ways, as identified in Chapter 3, to implement it. However, to sustain the model, it is necessary to extend the superior performance of a few into a generalized practice, which requires resolving the most cumbersome issues the ASP industry has faced. In this respect, before it is too late ASPs must be able to show, among other things (Borck, 2001; Gerwig, 2001; Toigo, 2001):

- the creation of a defined customer and application focus to reach strong market positions;
- high-level system security and integrity for remotely stored data and end user support; and
- automation of external processes with new Internet-based tools that result in more effective integration.

To gain a broader perspective, it is necessary to move from generic to specific discussion, and analyze both existing models' long-term prospects and possible alternative methods of application delivery and management. As a first step, the following section analyzes the future prospects for the five main ASP models. Possible alternative methods, which are discussed later in the chapter, include some that are already operating in other IT sectors but are yet to be implemented by ASPs.

THE FUTURE OF EXISTING ASP MODELS

The focus of this section is the long-term viability of existing models, on the grounds that several ASP players in all five models have been successful and are willing to adapt, change, and grow within the market and have developed some forms of best practices. For this reason, it is worth exploring whether, why, and how they may be among future industry participants.

Analytical Framework

The discussion of each model aims to highlight the strengths that may be conducive to long-term survival and success; the weaknesses that may undermine future prospects; and the market opportunities and threats that, as analysts indicated, will determine future ASP models. The following analysis of models provides in a sequence:

1. a summary of the model's characteristics;
2. highlights of how each model is successful and what it should continue to do;
3. highlights of what each model has done poorly to date and should stop doing; and
4. alternative strategies each model should implement to become stronger and endure, the future strategic profile and future success formula, as well as summary of future prospects.

The goal is to recognize the contribution of specific characteristics that differentiate, for good or bad, one model from the others in terms of future viability. In an effort to avoid generalizations and to keep this analysis focused, the discussion only briefly pinpoints, where applicable, elements in common for all models that are expected to shape possible future models' profiles.

Business ASPs

The business ASPs that have proved successful have had a broad range of application offerings, provided speed in implementation (such as FutureLink), gave access at a variable cost to a large portfolio of application-based solutions supported by robust technology (such as TeleComputing), and supplied valuable management team and experience (such as Interpath). These strengths, in many cases stemming from a full-service focus, were found in the large, most established business ASPs in the market through 2001. Most of these strengths are common to the other ASP models. For these strengths to ensure success in the future, they must be nurtured and maintained as true core competencies and hard-to-match internal resources to differentiate business ASPs in the ASP market. In order to achieve differentiation, they have to be associated with, and enhanced by, additional strategic elements for success.

A major weakness of business ASPs is related to the one-size-fits-all generic approach. This approach will very likely no longer meet market requirements in the future. As analysts have observed (Lepeak, 2001; Tally, 2001; Bucholtz, 2001a), simply delivering someone else's software to a customer does not necessarily create a long-term sustainable business model. The majority of business ASPs, which have had a horizontal customer market and a limited-service focus, have neglected to provide for diversified, additional services. Therefore, they appear to be not sustainable over the long run, since they failed to address primary market and business requirements.

Business ASPs, more than other models, have been predicated on the original one-to-many concept, whereby an ASP concentrates on application management and relies on partners for other components of the ASP value chain. To provide a one-to-many service while offering a variety of applications for different needs, business ASPs had to supply prepackaged, standard applications, in most cases not designed to run on the Internet, and provided limited additional services and customer support. However, most information systems require at least 10 percent customization to adapt to current business processes (Davison, 2001). Therefore, application customization has been inadequate. Only a few business ASPs have been able to deliver a satisfactory range of services including the necessary degree of customization.

One service that has been neglected or ignored by business ASPs involves integration capabilities, enabling customers' old systems to smoothly communicate with new, upgraded, Web-based systems and sparing customers from separately keying data into both old and new systems. Customer applications cannot be left unconnected to the remaining applications' environment. Businesses need a smooth data flow across their organization. The majority of business ASPs have shifted the integration process outside their application delivery and have relied for that process on partner providers, for example systems integrators, to ensure that new software solutions interface seamlessly with a customer's existing information systems. The result for the majority of business ASPs has been the inability to control in-house the full interactivity of applications and the failure to eliminate the time-consuming, costly rewrites needed to make applications effectively work at the customers' end. To survive and succeed in the future, they must provide the integration to make their applications functional.

Offering Web-based and Web-enabled software applications and additional services, including customization and integration, appears to be a life-or-death strategic element for future success, largely because other ASP models are gaining a stronger foothold in these areas. That is why Herb Hribar at Interliant focused early on the service side as a strong market requirement (Wright, 2001). He turned the company into a true full-service ASP, offering data integration and application customization for full application performance and usability. Other ASPs that early on had only offered business administration applications have increased their offerings and strengthened their related service focus by acquiring small, specialized IT services firms with expertise in implementing high-end ERP and e-commerce applications and with development competencies. Acquisition and diversification strategies pursued by leading business ASPs to supplement and expand their offerings were an identified trend in 2001 (Total Telecom, 2001).

Business ASPs should make sure to focus enough attention on integration capabilities and discontinue their existing practices, if any, which have led them to perform poorly in this area. By modifying their integration-related strategies, they can improve their strategic profile.

Therefore, business ASPs will need to turn into truly service-oriented application providers. Only a handful of existing business ASPs have a true full-service orientation and so an adequately robust model. Integration creates efficiencies at both ends. It is achieved by enhancing communication across multiple applications for a single customer and among multiple customers across a single application. That in turn leads to lower unit operating costs (Laudon and Laudon, 2001) and expanded service offerings.

John Whiteside, chief executive officer of enterprise ASP netASPx, confirms the importance of a dramatic improvement in the strategic formula for success of business ASPs—such as an adequate degree of customization and providing for effective system integration—in his claim that, unless this happens, they will soon disappear completely (Dering, 2001a). Business ASPs should work to increase their core competencies, as successful ones have done. For instance, TeleComputing has developed an internal process framework that enables it to reduce its costs and deliver high-performance, complete solutions while at the same time ensuring fast implementation and security/data integrity issues (Imp@ct-it, 2001; TeleComputing, 2001c).

However, the need to partner for critical aspects of the ASP delivery mechanism typical of limited-service business ASPs could be a main barrier to success, unless the partnerships are adequately planned for and constantly monitored for performance, quality, and security. In order to be successful, it is therefore essential that existing business ASPs maximize their market opportunities by focusing attention on the quality of their value chain partners.

Some savvy business ASPs are exploring these new strategies, especially those related to security. Security is the main challenge for most ASPs, especially business ASPs, as the majority of them have not had adequate resources to control security in-house and have either neglected this element or shifted it to the wrong partners, as discussed in Chapter 2. ASPs that have not adequately accounted for security are very likely to go out of business, unless they focus very strongly on it.

A successful alternative strategy, as indicated by some analysts (Chamberlin, 2001; Gibbons, 2001; Mateyaschuk, 2000), involves business ASPs becoming leaner by becoming more vertical. That entails being more focused both in customer selection and application offerings by marketing to fewer customer groups and selecting fewer applications. As Marty Gruhn, Summit Strategies vice president, says, "you cannot be a jack-of-all-trades and master of none" (Parizo, 2001a). Some business ASPs have already found their way out of seemingly limitless model that diffused internal energies and resources among too many applications and too many customer sectors, and opted for a more narrowly defined target market. For instance, FutureLink has abandoned its core-service business ASP model to improve its chances of survival and moved toward professional services, thus showing an interest in a clear vertical-market focus.

Becoming more focused, more vertical, also involves discontinuing stand-alone, mostly inefficient, application-related practices. In addition, it involves partnering and working with organizations that have substantial brand recognition and established sales channels to reach target markets that have not yet used ASPs. The idea is that key partnerships, to offer fewer business applications in more effective ways, through more efficient channels, will make business ASPs accessible by potential clients (Russell, 2001). Communications companies are among the best potential partners for business ASPs, according to a June 2001 report from Zanthus ("Play the ASP," 2001). By having solid partner programs that make business ASP offerings more visible in the market, some business ASPs might still be viable in the long run.

The success formula for business ASPs involves having a stronger, clearer diversification-oriented market focus, emphasizing effective value-adding technology and application partnerships and becoming more vertical. As the Web-based market matures and applications are all designed to be run on the Web, business ASPs that do not offer add-on services, especially customization and integration capabilities, appear to be becoming a redundant element in the delivery chain from software vendors to end users and therefore are unlikely to remain in the marketplace. Business ASPs that simply handle the delivery and management of applications developed by software vendors are likely to become an unnecessary third party, with scarce prospects for survival and future growth. This scenario especially involves small ASPs, which are most likely to disappear in the short term or eventually be acquired by larger, more established market players that find in them a ready-made source for business applications.

On the other hand, Microsoft claims that there will always be a need for an "intelligent client"—a computer running Windows ("Gathering Steam," 2001)—and that business ASPs will continue to be useful as a way of managing applications on a customer's behalf. Microsoft's ASP strategy focuses on the conviction that ASPs' general core competencies, delivering and managing applications on behalf of customers and end users, are a hard-to-match strength in themselves that gives them a chance for survival. This may be a possibility, yet in order to increase their prospects of survival they must significantly improve their knowledge of the selected applications and develop core competencies out of them.

Business ASPs appear to be among the weakest enterprises in the ASP continuum and to have low chances of survival unless they change in the strategic directions recommended. They appear in urgent need of drastic improvement of their approaches to the applications and the entire ASP value chain in order to remain in the marketplace and grow. Only one of the most successful ASPs of 2000 (Whalen et al., 2001) was a business ASP—Interliant, discussed in Chapters 2 and 3. This limited-success history was reconfirmed in 2001. Market information available through ASPnews, a leading source, confirms the scarcity of business ASPs among the market leaders. In the ASPnews monthly review of the top twenty ASPs (ASPnews, 2001c) approximately one of every ten most successful ASPs was a business ASP. Thus there is only a remote possibility that the ranks of successful ASPs in the future may include more than a few business ASPs, the exceptions being the successful ones that were identified and studied in this book.

Enterprise ASPs

Most existing enterprise ASPs, like business ASPs, have been horizontally oriented, targeting large customers in all industry segments, such as QCS, or serving one customer size only, such as growing medium-sized customers in selected industries, or midmarket companies across industries, such as Corio. Others have only been offering application solutions based on one kind of software, for example

SAP-based ERP, such as BlueStar Solutions, and only targeting customers that need that particular application and related management services. However, enterprise ASPs such as Surebridge, which targets midsize companies, or Agilera, which serves fast-growth ones, have shown a defined vertical-market strategy by serving a few industries only. Individual enterprise ASPs vary widely in terms of target customers.

In operational terms, enterprise ASPs have been either limited-service oriented, such as QCS and Corio, or full-service oriented, such as USi. The enterprise ASP model involves many variations of customer-driven and operational strategies.

Several enterprise ASPs have proved successful, such as Corio, BlueStar Solutions, and Interpath, described in Chapter 3. They offer a wide range of services, such as a degree of application customization, integration, and global expertise, and provide scalability. They give a single point of contact to their customers. They are able to control all the crucial aspects of delivery, either by implementing mission-critical elements internally or by partnering for them. They have developed objectively measurable processes, tested and improved over a large, typically demanding user base, which has helped them gain significant learning experiences and economies of scale, and ultimately enabled enterprise ASPs to optimize their cost structures and application implementation time while also keeping the application performance levels high.

As noted for business ASPs, the service side of application service provision is almost more important than the core application management competency itself. Enterprise ASPs are better positioned than business ASPs in terms of service orientation. However, this strength must be nurtured and sustained as other players in the market have a very strong service focus. Increasingly, leading enterprise ASPs such as USi, Corio, and QCS see traditional outsourcers such as IBM and EDS as their primary competitors, as the latter are known to be strong at bundling services and delivering them to customers. On the other hand, it is also significant that traditional outsourcers' services are more expensive and that they do not offer the same fast implementation time ASPs can offer (Gartner Group, 2001b). A strength of successful enterprise models arises from the process efficiencies they are able to pass on to customers (Parizo, 2001c), a hard-to-match core competency. Thus enterprise ASPs should capitalize on their process-driven differences and should sustain the service-driven approach.

A major weakness was the failure to meet major customer and market needs, stemming from a lack of narrowly defined customer focus, which translated into too-broad application offerings that depleted internal resources and led to limited services. Most enterprise ASPs have offered a broad array of applications yet could not supply truly full service packages to customers. The need for support services involves, for example, training provided to customers' end users. In general, the amount of training provided has been inadequate.

Enterprise ASPs must work toward recognizing their customers' most critical requirements. They should strive to enhance their business opportunities in the future by providing the kind of customer service approach adopted by successful enterprise ASPs. USi, for example, has developed and marketed a customized training curriculum tailored to individual customer requirements, designed to cover the entire scope of their services for all organizational levels, through both on-site and Web-based instruction. That has allowed USi to gain a high level of customer confidence and trust.

Another identified weakness involves the level of customization that enterprise ASPs can provide without disrupting their cost structure. As noted in Chapter 2, although enterprise ASPs have shown a much stronger focus on customization than business ASPs, the degree of customization most business enterprise ASPs have been able to provide was found insufficient to really match complex customer needs. On the other hand, providing too much customization works against the general ASP model's one-to-many characteristic and is likely to deplete an enterprise ASP's resources, if the ASP devotes significant time and staff resources to each customer's customization features.

An alternative strategy involves understanding exactly how much customization is needed to ensure customer satisfaction while keeping costs at a sustainable level. In 2001, for example, Corio adopted this strategy to try to understand how much standard performance could be made adequately flexible to provide additional customization (Fonseca and Jones, 2001). At the same time, the company attempted to continue to balance the standardization required by its integrated Intelligent application suite.

Another main weakness arises from horizontal customer-driven strategies and application offerings that are too broad, which results in a lack of focused market approach. Choosing to offer many enterprise applications to many, or to any, customer sectors, in an effort to cover as many market niches as possible, often results in a dispersion of internal resources and in the risk of losing business focus. Success may be achieved by reducing the number of application offerings and the number of targeted customer sectors; in other words, becoming more vertical-market focused.

Enterprise ASPs that focused early on these strengths and offered these capabilities have shown they have recognized the importance of their customers' business objectives and challenges. Surebridge and USi, for example, have both built their models around top-level customer service. These enterprise ASPs have crafted, implemented, and operated true full-service models, which have been able to function as efficiently as utility companies providing power to very large numbers of customers, because they have tightly controlled all the ASP value chain components. Full-service enterprise ASPs such as Surebridge and USi, for these reasons, seem the most promising among enterprise ASP models for long-term viability (Bernard, 2001b), and are a benchmark for all enterprise ASPs wishing to stay in business.

Surebridge is also a particularly interesting enterprise ASP with bright prospects because of its vertical-market orientation. By forming, or sustaining, defined target customer and industry sectors, enterprise ASPs may be able to abandon the markets in which they are weaker than ASP models. According to Summit Strategies vice president Marty Gruhn, a strategic element of success is knowing "where they're going to go when the music stops" (Parizo, 2001a). Where to go when market opportunities shrink and competition from more focused ASPs becomes stronger seems tied to increasing vertical-market orientation, by narrowing their customer group target to their best opportunities for growth.

Future success, therefore, involves the ability to provide a wide range of services, especially the ability to address customer support issues, such as training, as well as round-the-clock customer service such as help desks and call centers accessible from anywhere in the world through multiple channels: voice, e-mail, and Web access. Mitch Kristofferson, Corio's vice president of marketing, claims that the single most important factor for long-term stability of enterprise

ASPs is offering a one-stop-shop experience (Mears, 2001f), in which a service-driven approach is essential. It involves continuing to effectively control complex managed or extended services throughout the ASP value chain. This control is tied to the continued ability to reduce internal costs and application implementation time while also keeping high the quality of the application-based solution and services and ensuring an optimal degree of customization. Finally, it involves adopting a more defined vertical approach in the customer selection process and in the reduction of application offerings to match the actual and expected needs of target customer groups.

Successful enterprise ASPs appear to have good chances to remain in the market and grow because of their size and high market recognition. QCS's chief executive, John Charters, believes enterprise ASPs' future prospects are directly associated with longer market recognition and growing brand name. Companies are looking for credible, well-financed service providers, and successful enterprise ASPs such as QCS are the best positioned in this respect (Bucholtz, 2001b). This view is echoed by USi's chief executive officer, Andrew Stern, who believes that size—meaning a large, established ASP, which has had sufficient customers to test its capabilities and get enough revenues to sustain the business—is a guarantee of reliability for customers (Parizo, 2001c) and greatly enhances an enterprise ASP's prospects of future success.

In contrast, some venture capitalists questioned enterprise ASPs' ability to remain in the industry beyond 2004. For instance, Bill Gurley, analyst at venture capitalist Benchmark Capital, argues that companies such as Corio are mere "service bureaus." Because the applications they host are not always specifically written for the Internet, Gurley believes their ASP business model is not efficient—therefore, not sustainable—over the long run. This is why his company is not investing in enterprise ASPs, but is betting on ASPs such as the specialist ASP Employease, which has built its HRM application entirely for the Internet ("Gathering Steam," 2001). In essence, what venture capitalists such as Gurley suggest is that companies such as Corio are likely to succumb because they do not have a strong competitive edge in terms of valuable internally generated processes and know-how.

Enterprise ASPs appear to have a medium chance of survival, provided they change in ways consistent with the strategic analysis provided in this chapter, and in particular providing they work to become more vertical. The good prospects for enterprise ASPs are substantiated by the actual market composition in 2000 and 2001. This shows that enterprise ASPs experienced growing acceptance by the large customer market segment. Most of the best ASPs of 2000 offered enterprise applications (Rosenthal, 2001). Growing acceptance of enterprise ASPs was also confirmed by the preliminary results of the ASP Industry Consortium's first global ASP tracking study, released in 2001 (Newcomb, 2001b).

Their success is further corroborated by the results of the IDC study of ASP market leaders in 2000 (Whalen et al., 2001), in which 50 percent of the top ten ASPs were enterprise ASPs, and by the 2001 ASPnews' monthly reviews of leading ASPs (ASPnews, 2001b), in which, on average, nine out of twenty in the top twenty ASP list were enterprise ASPs.

Specialist or Function-Focused ASPs

Specialist ASPs have been growing in the ASP market. They differ from business and enterprise ASPs because they specialize in one or a few selected business functions and provide the software application, management, and related support and services required to completely manage the areas they choose to serve. Specialist ASPs offer application solutions to diverse customers across diverse industries. Many specialist ASPs have developed their own software, which enables them to better understand and manage the targeted functions and deliver end-to-end application solutions based on a software they thoroughly know. In terms of customer target, specialist ASPs have been both horizontal, when their main focus is the application offered, and vertical, when they choose to address the needs of either large companies (e.g., Exult) or SMEs only (e.g., NetLedger). Those which selected only SMEs as their main customer target, such as Employease, reckoned these companies cannot afford to buy brand software and so will benefit from turning to ASPs.

Most specialist ASPs have been limited-service oriented, using only a few selected technology and software partners to fill the internal gaps in their value chain. What they typically have maintained in-house is a team of experts who recognize and understand the requirements of their specialist customer and end user base, and who are therefore able to provide tailored solutions.

Successful specialist ASPs have delivered expertise on one or more business functions, have offered a full range of function-supporting services, and have given their customers a single point of contact and a one-stop shopping experience. Most have achieved these core competencies as a result of direct development of the supporting application software, which they were then able to offer as a full, complete service. The benefits passed on to their customers were, among others, cost-effective access to powerful solutions, achieved as a result of efficiencies inherent in the direct development of the software. The benefits arise from specialization, which has given these ASPs deep insight and the necessary expertise to thoroughly oversee business functions. Other main benefits come from strong alliance partnerships, such as the ones achieved by Exult with its clients, discussed in Chapter 3, which enabled customers to safely shift entire functional activities outside their facilities. Successful specialist ASPs, such as Employease and United Messaging, have become trusted third parties to their customers, and much more than specialists in application implementation and management.

The main specialist ASP characteristic is the ability to work around a business process and offer the streamlined process to a variety of users. For some successful specialist ASPs, this focus has been the major strength and should be a continued strategy for future success. For others that were not as successful, focusing on the business process first and then applying the process to diverse customers in diverse industries has not been a successful strategy. As the enterprise ASP analysis also shows, having a too-broad customer base in too many industries may not be the best strategic course of action. Therefore, specialist ASPs would benefit from focusing on fewer industries or industry sectors, to maintain their specialization.

A major strength in the specialist ASP model is building and retaining in-house a team of experts, which has become one of the most important core competencies and is expected to be a major success factor in the future. This is also an interesting example of a focused internal resource utilization strategy that shifts activities rated as non-core competencies outside the firm, which can effectively concentrate on application development and management. This important strength should be nurtured and maintained in the specialist ASP model because it will enable differentiation from other models, in particular ASP aggregators and business ASPs, whose strategic analysis has indicated an inadequate focus in this respect.

Another major characteristic of the specialist ASP model involves developing all or part of the software. In most cases, this strategy has been successful. In some cases it has not paid off, and some analysts ("Gathering Steam," 2001; Kerstetter, 2001) believe both activities, software development and ASP functional expertise, cannot be financially sustained over the long run. These analysts have pointed out that software-development costs and the marketing muscle needed to promote a new offering are so enormous that they may destroy specialist ASPs, since these ASPs write their own code.

In addition, private software with inferior brand recognition may be a barrier to specialist ASPs' future success. The problem is that most customers, regardless of their size and business complexity, are still making buying decisions mainly based on brand name before looking for an application provider, as noted in Chapter 2. Specialist ASPs that develop their own software may go out of business if their software is perceived as not comparable to established software vendors' products. An issue for specialist ASPs is therefore whether software development is to be considered a strength or a weakness, and whether they should continue to develop their own software.

In contrast, some specialist ASPs have demonstrated that focusing on both software development and offering it has paid off. Salesforce.com is a useful example of successfully blending software development with the ASP model because of benefits such as reduced costs, fast implementation, and high performance. Salesforce's chairman, Mark Benioff, states that the company has gained a crucial strength in the current ASP marketplace, and will have a strong competitive advantage in the future, because of the synergies resulting from understanding the software, which enhances customization and integration capabilities and the ability to streamline the specific functions on which the software is deployed ("Gathering Steam," 2001).

Salesforce.com's success substantiates the positive opportunities associated with a strategy that assigns value to both elements: the software development and the application service. Success can be maintained, if the ASP has enough resources for software-related research and development and can avoid taking resources away from their value chain and delivery mechanism.

The strength in Employease's model lies in effectively acting as a service company, not as a software company, as noted in Chapter 2. This has enabled the company to overcome the issues noted by market analysts and to focus on software development and ASP value chain-related activities. The service focus appears to be successful and should be adopted by specialist ASPs that can sustain it and benefit from it. All other strategies that do not adequately focus on service should be discontinued.

A major weakness identified in existing specialist ASPs is the fact that these companies are fairly new companies, usually not older than five years (Kerstetter, 2001). A major problem connected to their young age is the lack of profitability for most through 2001. By focusing on alternative strategies, specialist ASPs may be able to overcome the weaknesses associated with their young business models.

Finally, a noted weakness concerns the specialist ASP's focus on the business process first and customer needs second. Customers' needs may not be adequately recognized and understood and therefore will not be effectively incorporated in the ASP application. Specialist ASPs should focus their attention on the customers' needs at least as much as, or even more than, they focus on business processes. They should adopt the vertical-market ASPs' customer-driven approach.

A major alternative strategy involves deepening specialization strengths. This can be achieved, for example, by analyzing in advance what customers may need next and being ready, before the competitors are, to address market challenges and meet customer requirements.

At the same time, specialist ASPs should also better target their marketing message by carefully selecting the right audience. For instance, they should avoid the marketing strategy adopted by business ASP Mi8, which addressed their advertising communication to the very people whose jobs could be eliminated by Mi8's proposed business automation services (Bernard, 2001c). According to Salesforce. com's Ann Burgraff, vice president of marketing, the right strategy is not "a shotgun approach," not a generalized mass-market approach that confuses recipients. Instead, specialist ASP models should maintain a contingency-based strategic approach, by carefully crafting their message to hit the people that are actually looking for their solutions (Bernard, 2001a).

Such focused strategies should include not only involving chief information officers, who are typically directly involved in IT upgrades and have substantial decision-making power (Gartner Group, 2001b), but also soliciting the interest of department heads and corporate headquarters, by showing them the strategic importance of business-process maximization through their specialist outsourced resources.

The formula for success for specialist ASPs involves the ability to create and retain a team of in-house experts, balancing service with software development, actively working to address what customers may need next, and maintaining a narrow customer focus.

Specialist ASPs seem to have a better chance of survival and future success than business ASPs. This is confirmed by the interest shown by venture capitalists in savvy specialist ASP players. Because this model is younger than enterprise and business ASPs, it has learned from early failures, by focusing on specific functions and by avoiding a generalized approach. In spite of this advantage, ASP market composition in 2000 and 2001 suggested that specialist ASPs did not effectively learn from others' experiences. Although there were twice as many specialist ASPs as enterprise ASPs, few positioned among the leading ASPs (Whalen et al., 2001; ASPnews, 2001c), with an average of only two to three specialist ASPs in the top twenty in 2001, and none in the IDC top ten in 2000, relative to the much higher percentage of enterprise ASPs. This indicates that specialist ASPs have lower prospects of future success than enterprise ASPs.

Altogether, specialist ASPs have reasonable prospects for future success and a decent chance of survival and growth, providing they improve in the recommended directions and become profitable soon enough to sustain their core competencies. Because of their narrow focus, niche market approach, and the significant learning curves for other ASPs in their area of specialization, the specialist ASPs may remain ahead of competitor models in the next three to five years.

Vertical-Market ASPs

Vertical-market ASPs' primary business is the choice of applications to meet the requirements of selected industries. Similar to full-service enterprise ASPs and specialist ASPs, they are committed to offering a full range of services. Like specialist ASPs, vertical-market ASPs also focus on implementing and managing software applications that support entire business processes. However, their specific goal is to address industry-specific challenges.

Vertical-market ASPs' application offerings may range from a single software application used to manage one function in one industry to a variety of applications, either acquired from software vendors or developed as their own software, delivered as a service.

Successful vertical-market ASPs have demonstrated the ability to provide a full range of services for selected industry participants, a single point of contact, price competitiveness stemming from the efficiencies arising from thoroughly knowing the industry-specific challenges and priorities, and particularly deep knowledge of and experience in the business segments they have targeted, in essence providing strong, positive alliance partnerships for customers. They deliver additional customization and more comprehensive services than business and enterprise ASPs. Differentiation within a narrow focus has enabled vertical-market ASPs to further customize solutions. Vertical-market ASPs have been successful in this market differentiation strategy and should continue it.

In addition, the strategies underlying vertical-market models are the opposite of specialist ASPs, which offer streamlined function to a variety of users. The vertical-market ASPs, in contrast, work to understand specific customer requirements. They seem best positioned to understand and fulfill future market requirements, because so far they have worked toward understanding the customer's challenges first.

Some vertical-market ASPs risk losing focus because they cover many industries. Because their strength is deep knowledge of an industry's challenges, they would benefit from streamlining their markets by reducing the number of industries they cover.

Strategic opportunities appear bright in a few vertical markets for applications that meet very specific, targeted needs, such as health care, education, financial services, and construction (Bucholtz, 2001a). In particular, the health care industry offers a major opportunity for growth. The U.S. Health Insurance Portability and Accountability Act (HIPAA), a set of standards for health care transactions, privacy protection, and security that was released in July 2001, offers a set of challenges to the market and a strategic opportunity for vertical-market ASPs.

In general, thoroughly focusing on a single industry can result in significant business advantages. TriZetto, which has concentrated on the health care industry, was ranked second among the top ten ASPs of 2000 (Whalen et al., 2001). Focused strategies, in which one to three industries are selected by an ASP, appear to be crucial for the future of ASPs in general, given the fact that more software vendors are beginning to offer ASP-based services directly, and existing ASPs may be forced to find market opportunities elsewhere, such as in specific industry niches. Stacie Kilgore, Forrester Research analyst, claims that if ASPs cannot or do not want to develop software, they must build specific industry expertise, or they are going to be "the companies formerly known as ASPs" (Peitsch, 2001). Vertical-market ASPs, therefore, appear to be very well placed for future success.

Vertical-market ASPs were often cited in 2001 as the best positioned to be among the ASP models of the future (Parizo, 2001a; Chamberlin, 2001; Toigo, 2001; Panker, 2001). Traver Gruen-Kennedy, former ASP Industry Consortium chairman and founder, also observed that the ASP market is moving toward a vertical market (Peitsch, 2001). Large, established enterprise ASPs, such as Corio, have expanded their activities with a vertical focus. To Summit Strategies analyst Laurie McCabe, vertical-market ASPs are even expected to promote and increase customer adoption of the ASP delivery model and thus significantly affect the industry's future growth overall. Because they have the industry expertise and relationships to win target customers, they can grow higher-margin businesses more quickly. Their expertise and connections better enable vertical-market ASPs to offer industry-specific applications with complementary services, market their offering throughout value chains, and develop solutions with fewer technical and sales barriers than other approaches ("Vertical Service Providers," 2001).

Vertical-market ASPs therefore appear to be in a much better position than business and enterprise ASPs, because the former have a narrower-focus customer selection process and a leaner suite of application offerings. Vertical-market ASPs also appear to be better positioned than specialist ASPs, because they focus on their customers' needs before turning to the application-based solution, which is the reverse of specialist ASPs' typical process.

In addition, a promising element is the fact that vertical application service providers that offer module applications for specific use and bundle services, such as TriZetto and Portera, provide a unique set of comprehensive solutions that would be cost prohibitive for in-house development, even for large customers. These factors give them a higher probability of success than other models (Bernard, 2001d; Toigo, 2001), and the brightest future overall. In summary, most analysts' views and market indicators validate the expected growth and long-term existence of vertical market ASPs that have, or develop, the strategic profile needed for success. Because some industries are highly volatile or are subject to intense, changing regulations, using an ASP that deeply knows one's industry may well become a natural choice for many, if not all, companies looking to outsource their IT systems.

ASP Aggregators or AASPs

The ASP aggregator models to date have offered access, management, integration, and support for Web-enabled applications from any source. These solutions are designed to be less expensive, more flexible, and much more powerful, in terms of guaranteed performance, security, and reliability, than any provided by single ASPs. Successful AASPs have shown that their core competencies and primary strengths were a fuller range of services, a comprehensive single point of contact for customers, global coverage, and the ability to scale the application to customer growth. Examples include Jamcracker and iFuel, whose profiles were presented in Chapters 2 and 3.

The partnership of leading ASP aggregators with individual ASPs with different models is a significant AASP strength. Even established ASP players, such as enterprise ASP Surebridge, specialist ASP Employease, and vertical-market ASP Portera, have partnered with AASPs. The AASPs have gained the efficiencies deriving from their single ASP partners' successful models.

A major strength also lies in the ability of ASP aggregators in the market through 2001 to recognize that market and customer requirements existed that had not thoroughly been fulfilled by the other four models. For example, customers are reluctant to sign contracts that may lock them into an individual ASP provider for years. Successful AASPs realized that an effective way to meet customers' desire to change ASP vendors was through the ASP aggregator model.

Individual ASPs have used the AASP partnership as another channel to reach out to market segments they were unable to reach individually, which makes the ASP aggregator a model demanded not only by customers but also by some of the other ASP models to survive. The AASP model has facilitated the meeting of ASP suppliers and clients. Although this element can be considered a source of strength and competitive advantage, in the future it may become a weakness.

Individual ASPs may no longer require an AASP to reach clients in the future as they become stronger and improve their own customer channel strategies. Therefore, they may deprive the AASP of partnership. AASPs should take this possibility into account and forge partnerships with dedicated ASP partners that have fewer opportunities to pursue their goals on an individual basis. AASPs should enter into strategic alliances with ASPs and ASP value chain partners that do not have an interest in competing directly as ASPs.

A main weakness in the model is the likelihood that as the market matures and the strongest ASP models expand, customers also may no longer have a need for ASP aggregators. As more comprehensive ASP models develop, customers will be able to find the same or equivalent services in individual ASPs and likely stop using ASP aggregators.

In theory, AASPs are capable of fulfilling any business-to-business and business-to-consumer demand, and this appears to be an important element of the formula for their success in the future. Even more, ASP aggregators are expected to dictate future developments within the ASP market (Gilmore, 2000a). If aggregators can develop a strong presence in the ASP market, they may help accelerate the development of market software protocols. Such standards could enable AASPs to more easily integrate software packages. In addition, by offering a solution specifically designed to allow a broad "mix and match" of IT choices, aggregators may gain long-term success due to their strong presence and their customers' large base. In turn, this success could help discourage weaker models' survival. Looking forward, however, ASP aggregators appear to be becoming unnecessary and are likely to be supplanted by savvy competitors implementing models that develop or effectively partner for missing ASP value chain components, without joining an ASP aggregator.

Some AASPs have experienced mixed results, as noted in Chapter 2. Some ASP aggregators, such as Agiliti, discarded the AASP model in 2001, turning to a different area of ASP value chain expertise such as providing infrastructure. This is an important strategic indicator that the AASP model is likely not fit for the long run, at least in its present form. Its complexity, because each provider may have a different business model, is the primary element that ASP aggregators must streamline to sustain adequate performance.

Jamcracker initiated significant changes, by announcing in late July 2001 the formalization of two technology partnerships that it hoped would take its business to a wider level. With this new strategy, Jamcracker displayed the intention to go beyond the ASP aggregator world toward the broader realm of hosted IT management (Newcomb, 2001d), to enable its clients to get from Jamcracker all the required elements to run a comprehensive IT operation. Agiliti's distancing from the ASP aggregator world and Jamcracker's substantial modifications are an interesting trend that demonstrates the need for a radical restructuring of the AASP model.

Managers of leading ASPs claim that ASP aggregators are at disadvantage relative to other ASP models, because AASPs do not truly specialize in the applications they deliver. Because ASP aggregators rely upon the expertise of single ASPs and technology partners, the ASP aggregators are not driven to develop core competencies internally. ASP aggregators, says Corio's marketing vice president Mitch Kristofferson, do not develop the multilayer ASP value chain expertise that enterprise ASPs, in contrast, carefully work to either develop internally or acquire. John Charters, enterprise ASP Qwest Cyber.Solution's chief executive officer, shares this view. Although the other ASP models may offer fewer applications than an aggregator, they are experts in those offerings, Charter says. He also points out that Jamcracker has offered a mass of Web-based applications, some of which were useless or did not meet its clients' real needs (Ledford, 2000).

The single most important element for a company considering the ASP aggregator model in the future, is ultimately where its expertise lies and how large the market is. As Agiliti's vice president of marketing, Feisal Moshleh, claims, the aggregator model makes the most sense for companies that are already core service experts. "Service companies are the service experts. Single-application service providers will have a heavy time trying to expand" (Ledford, 2000). Therefore, the success formula for AASPs involves a substantial streamlining of the complexity inherent in networks of partnerships, significant modifications to the business scope (such as those made by Jamcracker) and carefully examining market composition and competition from other models and focusing on underserved niches.

Future prospects for the ASP aggregator model are low, probably the lowest of the ASP models thus far discussed. The illustrated factors confirm the perceived need of a radical change in strategy. If a few ASP models are here to stay, there may be no space in the ASP arena for AASPs. As the market matures, the ASP Industry Consortium may act as a global-scale aggregator and eliminate the AASPs that were implemented through 2001.

Summary

Among the most probable survivors are expected to be vertical-market ASPs, focused vertical-market-oriented enterprise ASPs, lean specialist ASPs, full-service business ASPs, and eventually restructured ASP aggregators. In general, ASPs that offer diversified business lines, whatever their application offerings, and smaller focused players that have consolidated their offerings into vertical-market-oriented solutions may have a strategic place in the future market. However, are these models the only possible future methods of software application delivery and management? The following sections first discuss the search for further ASP models and then explore each of them in detail.

THE SEARCH FOR OTHER MODELS

A word of caution about today's ASPs was expressed by Audrey Aupfel, vice president and research director at Gartner Group, who warned that just because an ASP is well known today does not mean it will be successful tomorrow (Ledford, 2000). Others claimed that in ten years the ASP industry will be unrecognizable. Even the acronym ASP may no longer be used (Dering, 2001b; Mizoras, 2001; Paul, 2001b). This insight has prompted a search for other forms of application delivery and management that may become predominant in the future. Models have been identified that may compete in the ASP market in three to five years or even eliminate current leading ASP evolutions. Potential future ASP players may be among the current ASP value chain enablers. Also, existing delivery methods that are not called ASP but have similar characteristics may become prevalent in the future. New models may emerge with characteristics different from the existing general ASP model. Finally, the general model known today may be replaced by ASP customers that become ASP competitors. Signs of these developments already exist.

Success is achievable as long as both the technical and operational aspects of the ASP model and its supporting strategies are taken into account. The secret for success is not unique to the ASP industry: it is called maintaining competitive edge. Tower Group's Richard Beidl defines as winners those ASPs which "create a solution that is difficult or expensive to replicate, and who improve, rather than complicate, the value chain" (Kersnar, 2001).

This does not prevent other players from entering the market. In fact, it stimulates their entry. Competition can come not only from current market participants, but from providers that cannot strictly be defined as ASPs. For example, some are IT market participants that are increasingly adopting the ASP model, such as traditional outsourcing companies. Others are some of the ASP enablers and partners discussed in Chapter 2, such as telecommunication companies and ISVs. Others are new models, such as the master ASP, having characteristics different from the models analyzed in this book. Still others are large private companies that are importing the ASP model into their own structure and doing ASP in-house.

Research has identified future marketplace participants coming especially from the following areas of competition:

- Storage service providers
- Telecommunication companies
- Hosting providers
    —Hosting service providers
    —Systems integrators
- Hardware vendors
- Independent software vendors
- Traditional outsourcing companies
- CyberCarriers
- Master ASP
- In-house ASP

Storage Service Providers

Storage service providers offer hosting and access to storage devices and technology. They bundle services, software, and the storage devices formerly sold directly or through other vendors' channels, as noted in Chapter 2. Storage service provider companies offer data-storage services as a utility using an ASP approach (Lepeak, 2001). Because of reduced business opportunities following the dot-com collapse in 2000, storage service providers have been adding new activities to increase their revenue. For instance, in 2001 Storage Network started offering software and services to support or supplant the infrastructure of large companies and telecommunication companies. Storage Network's chief executive officer, Peter Bell, recognized customers are looking for high service levels, operational automation, and integration of old systems with new systems, and only a company that delivers all of that will be among the market winners. Therefore, it is fundamental for storage service providers to diversify. According to EMC's CEO, Joe Tucci, the original storage service model is gone forever (Komiega, 2001), and it is now a life-or-death issue for storage service providers such as EMC to test other markets.

Telecommunication Companies

Telecommunication companies provide the physical links between applications and end users by supplying the physical connection between applications and clients, as noted in Chapter 2. Because guaranteed performance, or uptime, is still a challenge for ASPs with limited scope, other players in the network provider area may fill these market gaps. Telecommunication companies are good candidates and can compete effectively within the ASP market. Actually, according to analysts (Sperling, 2001), they will be forced into the ASP market—with their long-distance service rates falling, they probably will not have a choice—and will likely emerge as the big winners. Telecommunication firms are deemed the best equipped providers for the ASP business, even though many have ignored it so far as a direct venture.

They have the best connections to the customer and all the billing equipment and processes to track usage and deliver a utility-like service. A major difference is that it will be data they are carrying over their lines instead of voice. An example of an expected long-term winner in this category is British Telecommunications (BT). Its subsidiary BT Ignite is an ASP, but this makes up only a small part of its total activities, which include value-added IP and data services, content hosting, systems integration, and media distribution. According to David Furniss, vice president of BT Ignite's e-business division, there is no doubt that in the long term, ASPs will be the owners of networks, on the grounds that "an ASP without a network only provides a limited benefit when providing the network [from a third party]." On the contrary, BT Ignite benefits from all parts of service provision, and this makes it a viable business model. In addition, Furniss predicts that, with the exception of a few very specialized "boutique" ASPs serving highly targeted vertical markets, an ASP will be viable as a bolt-on service to an existing telecommunication business, rather than a stand-alone business in itself (Rubens, 2001).

Hosting Providers

Hosting Service Providers

Hosting service providers supply all the services and the infrastructure necessary for the deployment of a Web site or Web presence and for management of data center facilities, as noted in Chapter 2. The limited-service ASP companies are threatened by the entry of specialists in hosting services, such as Verio and Exodus. Because they rent both the application and the line, they are expected to adapt quickly to the ASP market and impact it (Imp@ct-it, 2001). Moreover, analysts indicate that in the future, not only will every business application be Web-enabled, it will also be designed and provided as a service rather than an application to be supported. Further technology advancements will enable bandwidth to support a remote pervasive continuous connectivity with a Web site, and hosting providers may become the backbone of the operating system of the future (Bolding, 2001). For example, hosting provider Qwest is already offering the entire necessary infrastructure and services that will allow ASPs and companies to build a new generation of distributed applications (Qwest Communications, 2001). For Qwest, entry into the ASP market is an easy prospect, already indirectly realized through its subsidiary, QCS, an enterprise ASP.

In general, leading hosting service providers are expected to partner or merge with ASPs that have proprietary software development solutions, and to create a powerful vertically integrated combination of core competencies that will appeal to a broad range of consumer and corporate users (Bolding, 2001).

Systems Integrators

Systems integrators carry out technical integration work to ensure that new software solutions integrate seamlessly with a customer's existing information systems. They supply applications implementation, maintenance, and outsourcing business, as noted in Chapter 2. As the Internet escalates competition in an effort to satisfy integration demand, the ability to integrate multiple applications appears to be a key capability, and systems integrators qualify as the service providers that will have the most powerful impact on the future industry. Forrester Research's Stacie Kilgore even sees a convergence between systems integrators and ASPs, as customers increasingly are seeking solutions that combine the custom fit of integrators with the efficiencies of ASPs. An example of this line blurring is KPMG, whose systems integrator division is now increasingly offering ASP-like prebuilt implementations of enterprise applications instead of custom development (Kilgore, 2000). In addition, Gartner Group's Audrey Apfel predicts that the struggle for a long-term position in the ASP market will be among systems integrators themselves (Paul, 2001b).

Hardware Vendors

Hardware vendors provide the computing and networking hardware that resides in the data center, as noted in Chapter 2. Some hardware providers are likely to win significant portions of the future ASP market. In fact, although PCs are not going to go away, the dependence on constant improvement in PC power will decrease as a result of having a third party manage upgrades. Hardware vendors were invading the ASP market in 2001 and also working to set up strategic alliances with ASPs. Hardware vendors such as Sun Microsystems have been among the most aggressive established companies pursuing the ASP opportunity by offering to supply ASPs with the necessary supporting technology infrastructure (Sun Microsystems, 2001a). The alliances and base value chain networks provided for an ASP can prove an invaluable background and resource base for a hardware company to move directly into ASP core activities as the demand for ASPs grows (Imp@ct-it, 2001).

For example, in January 2001, IBM and telecommunication giant AT&T started jointly offering the ASP Enablement Suite, a new solution for the ASP market that provides powerful server hardware and a secure infrastructure to meet the needs of ASPs, and also includes comarketing and ASP development programs (AT&T, 2001). By partnering with a range of ASPs, IBM has actually been in the ASP market indirectly for some time. Moreover, as USi's chief executive officer, Andrew Stern, predicts, IBM is going to be an ASP because it is in the same business. According to Stern, IBM is expected to deliver ASP-like services in the future in direct competition with current ASP models (Parizo, 2001c). Therefore, the likelihood that IBM may become a future successful ASP is quite high.

Independent Software Vendors

ISVs create the software or content that an ASP customer wishes to access and use, as noted in Chapter 2. Established ISVs that have not yet entered the ASP market represent a threat to many current business and enterprise ASPs, which rely on software developers to do their application implementation and remote management. Software development companies entering the ASP market may stop providing ASPs with the necessary software. A threat exists also for specialist ASPs that have developed their own software but have not built a strong brand name. Established software developers in the market could eliminate young software firms whose only revenue channel is ASP.

Looking forward, both back-office and ERP vendors such as SAP and front-office vendors such as Siebel and PeopleSoft may enter the ASP market directly. Simply put, this is just another license sale for such vendors. The ASP market is nothing but an extra or enhanced distribution channel for ISVs. The sale is going to the ASP rather than to the enterprise's customer, which ISVs would serve directly.

However, for these vendors to become ASPs themselves, as in the case of Oracle, it is necessary to shift focus from sale to rental, from software to services. Packaged ERP applications have proved difficult to transition to the ASP environment—as J. D. Edwards' unsuccessful attempt, discussed in Chapter 2, indicates. Another major factor that could hurt future growth prospects for limited-service ASP models is Microsoft's decision to massively tap the ASP market directly. Beyond its ASP bCentral for small business customers, Microsoft has more than enough capital to create the largest single ASP ever developed, and Microsoft Network gives it a ready vast customer base. The company has analyzed the market and worked out alliances with leading ASPs such as USi and Corio. It has recognized the potential of an ASP as a revenue channel.

In a perfect ASP world, no software will be purchased and installed in a client environment. All applications will be centralized in the ASP and secure, thus preventing data piracy and hacking, creating a favorable environment for the continuous development and growth of software applications, Microsoft's core business.

Traditional Outsourcing Companies

Outsourcing companies provide the management of applications and the delivery of application functionality, and their services often involve extensive and lengthy engagements, ranging from the custom development of applications to on-site participation by consultants, developers, and others within the outsourcing company (Gilmore, 2001a). Analysts at META Group (Davison, 2001) have indicated that large, traditional outsourcing vendors that have so far failed to build on ASP offerings will develop ASP solutions when the market becomes more stable and profitable. META Group believes that by 2003 close to 80 percent of technology service providers, including IBM Global Services, EDS, and the top worldwide consulting companies will offer variable pricing, hosting, and management services typical of ASPs. Some are conducting test marketing, and will eventually launch full-scale offerings. Others are already heavily involved in the ASP market. For example, Andersen Consulting was a major force in introducing ERP SAP software.

According to an IDC study from December 2000 (Gilmore, 2001a), these service providers, called application management service providers (AMSPs), were already delivering extended ASP services and dominating the application outsourcing market. AMSP companies were showing longer track records than ASPs and had more experience, considerable brand recognition, and more resources than most ASPs. For these reasons, they could increase their domination in the ASP market by 2006. Given today's consolidation in the ASP industry and AMSP companies' larger resources, AMSPs may acquire or partner for the ASP capabilities they lack internally, and enter this IT niche more easily, cheaply, and faster than developing ASP divisions themselves, representing a threat to ASPs. Gartner Group's Dataquest even observed that some ASPs, such as Corio and Exult, were even partnering with these traditional outsourcing consultants in 2001. Corio and Exult were actively promoting the capabilities of PriceWaterhouseCoopers (PWC) in their marketing messages. Dataquest noted that PWC, in contrast, was not promoting Corio and Exult in its marketplace communications at all, and suggested that ASPs should immediately distance themselves from outsourcing providers and reinforce in their marketing message the customer benefits of avoiding expensive outsourcing companies (Gartner Group, 2001b).

CyberCarriers

The results of a study conducted by management and technology consultant Booz-Allen and Hamilton (2001) indicate that a new generation of service providers will emerge and create an end-to-end provider model that will completely supplant ASPs. This new generation of providers, CyberCarriers, supplying integrated network, application, and outsourcing services, will offer customers improved reliability, scalability, and security, plus access to broadband-driven heavy data. CyberCarriers are expected to be the result of the merging of application hosting and data/voice transport companies, prompted by lower transport costs and the commoditization of Internet hosting facilities. They will be able to offer reliable Internet-related services, including transport, data and applications hosting, managed services, and outsourcing of traditional enterprise IT infrastructure and services. Their main advantage derives from the expected ability to control all the elements along the ASP value chain, from the location where the application is stored to the location where the end user accesses the information. This will enable CyberCarriers to offer integrated solutions to their customers with guaranteed end-to-end service (Booz-Allen and Hamilton, 2001).

Booz-Allen cites IBM's $5 billion deal with Qwest in 2001 to create twenty-eight super data centers as an early example of the trend.

Similar deals have taken place between SAP and BT, and among Compaq, Cable and Wireless, and Intel. Improved reliability of data centers is what will drive customer trust toward CyberCarriers. Today, the viability of existing ASP delivery models is highly dependent on the breadth and quality of data center–based storing and hosting services. Although some ASPs have built their own data centers, such as USi, most partner with third-party service providers, which underlie the application rental service ASPs typically offer. Because mission-critical tasks are shifted outside the ASP, and only a few can closely control them, the average end-to-end performance connected to the data center is rated as equal to the weakest service levels provided by any of an ASP's value chain suppliers. In contrast, CyberCarriers are expected to be able not only to deliver 99.999 percent availability, but also to provide 100 percent security and near-instantaneous application responsiveness (Whittle, 2001).

Because they are also expected to deliver cutting-edge applications in their ASP-like model, Booz-Allen and Hamilton (2001) strongly believe that the emergence of the CyberCarrier model will pose an end to ASPs. According to vice president Barry Jaruzelski, "It's one thing for a small organization to use hosted applications, but quite another for a big company" (Whittle, 2001). CyberCarriers will be large and robust enough for corporate customers to let them successfully host enterprise applications and other services (Booz-Allen and Hamilton, 2001).

Master ASP

According to senior ASP market analyst Phil Wainewright, a new form of ASP, the master ASP, is emerging that is shaping a next generation of application-enabled Internet. The master ASP underlying concept is to avoid attempting to maintain a direct relationship with every individual customer. The master ASP is predicated on operating applications in large-scale facilities for delivery to end customers and users via partner channels, and in this way is designed to achieve economies of scale based on very large volume rather than on individual solutions. The master ASP is viewed as bound to take a wholesale role in the ASP value chain, meaning it is expected not to have or need direct contact with the customer. This is the main factor that differentiates the master ASP from all other ASP models, which have implemented a direct, retail type of relationship with customers.

In particular, the master ASP is the opposite of the AASP, which acts as the only point of contact with the customer, while individual ASPs and ASP-value chain enablers physically delivered the application and related services. The partners supporting the master ASP are those who will actually manage the entire communication and implementation process with the customers and handle the retail-level processes. Partners in the master ASP model are expected to configure the appropriate specific functionality for delivery to customers, either tailored to a specific vertical market or customized to an individual client. Master ASP partners may be able to market the available offerings as if they were their own, and add complementary functions or services. They may also have the option of providing frontline support and customer service elements, such as first-level help desk, billing, and account management (Wainewright, 2001a).

The master ASP will develop because it is enabled by the most recent developments in software technology, module- or component-based software, associated with the traditional multilevel partner relationships that compose the ASP value chain. Using component-based software architecture, the master ASP can separate different layers of functionality in an application, and then delegate the configuration and management of certain layers to partners. The master ASP model is viewed as able to successfully mix the advantages of general ASP delivery with the foremost customer needs. It seems able to offer the economies of scale of a shared infrastructure that delivers functionality on a one-to-many basis, one of the basic associated benefits being cost reductions for end users. At the same time, it appears capable of maintaining a one-to-one tailoring and customization approach through the relationship with individual partners that are in charge of the final solutions.

Some emerging forms of master ASPs can be seen in the evolution of the enterprise ASP models. An example is BlueStar Solutions, formerly eOnline, whose systems integrator partners are now getting complete freedom to configure the business logic of the enterprise applications it offers, while BlueStar remains firmly in control of the underlying application system architecture. Other master ASP models are also emerging among Internet-enabled service providers. An example is Rivio, which provides a complete business administration platform for small clients. In the future, the evolutions of the master ASP model may also give rise to providers that host a portfolio of on-line functions without packaging them into finished applications. It will be up to partners to assemble the available components into useful business service functions (Wainewright, 2001a).

In-House ASP

Another factor to consider, to take into account as many potential directions as possible, is the likelihood of business companies performing ASP-like functions in-house in the future. In other words, businesses may create their own ASP inside their organization, using their own IT staff and capital resources. In late 2001, market activities signaled that this opportunity had not been ignored by some companies, which had adopted the general ASP concept, or a few elements of it, as an internally managed function. For instance, Fairmont Hotels and Resorts Inc. was reportedly acting as its own ASP to provide service to its properties in Canada and the United States (Brewin, 2001), after having invested most of its forecasted yearly IT budget ($30 to $40 million) to develop its own ASP and Internet service provider services.

Fairmont acquired commercial software, such as SQL database software from Microsoft, through ASP licenses, and also installed its own high-speed network covering its North American operations. This move was a nontraditional approach to the management of IT requirements in the lodging industry and, according to Fairmont's vice president of technology, Tim Aubrey, greatly helped keep the company's IT budget under control. Other reported benefits included increased value for the chain's properties, with each of the 20,000 rooms now equipped with high-speed broadband access, resulting in significant lowering of room wiring costs. The decision to manage IT in-house depended on Fairmont's focus on internal IT expertise, ranging from network management to in-house application development, as a competitive advantage for the company when serving guests and making affiliate agreements with other companies. A long-term benefit was expected to be turning a high-cost service, guest-room phone connections, into a profit center (Brewin, 2001).

Although this experience was not overly popular in 2001, as research results do not indicate a significant sample of equivalent experiences, it signals some important elements. On the one hand, the experience of a company that has imported some elements of the application service delivery model (such as the purchase of software through ASP licenses) to provide services to itself adds value to the ASP model as an effective application management and delivery solution. On the other hand, Fairmont's experience cannot be defined as a full-scale ASP model implementation, since it lacks some of the elements of basic ASP service, according to the definition given in Chapter 1. ASP is an external subscription fee-based service.

By leveraging some of the elements of the ASP model, Fairmont was able to see a short-term return on investment arising from optimized and streamlined IT capital disbursements. However, by rejecting a variable cost schedule associated with the "per user, per seat" mode that characterizes ASP service, and by developing an internal system only to support its own operations. Fairmont may or may not experience significant gains. In summary, whether the move would bring long-term benefits to Fairmont was unclear in 2001, yet in the future ASPs may be threatened by potential customers that decide to become their own ASP vendors.

Summary

This section has provided a brief summary of the possible evolution of the ASP market, whether it is improvement steps by current ASPs or new models. Future ASP models might be existing categories of service providers that were not started as ASPs but are now testing the market with offerings that are fit for the ASP delivery approach. The predicted changes in application development, distribution via new channels, and utilization by end users are expected to produce change in the ASP market and the relationships among today's participants, whose effects are still hard to fully envisage at this time.

CONCLUSION

This is based on the certainty that there is a future for ASPs in some form and has documented alternatives to current ASP models for the delivery and management of mission-critical computing applications. Prospects indicate that life will be good for ASPs three to five years into the future and for existing players at that time, because the global market is expected to mature and stabilize. When this happens, the hype that characterized the market from 1999 through mid-2000 and the market disillusionment and customer distrust that overwhelmed ASP players in late 2000 and 2001 are likely to be just a memory. As one analyst has observed, the future looks considerably more promising for those who accept that years from now the worldwide ASP industry will be totally different from what it is today (Paul, 2001b).

When the ASP market stabilizes, it will be possible to appreciate the shift from services and software to full business solutions. Most analysts view the focused ASP models as bound to enjoy a continued existence. This also applies to existing models that were identified as most likely to survive the market consolidation in 2001-2002. ASPs destined to survive are those which successfully differentiate themselves with value-added offerings such as consulting, integration, and customization services, with performance guarantees, and with end-to-end robustness that provides a full-service solution and also an effective single point of contact for their customers. Vertical-market ASPs and specialist ASPs that have clear market targets and hard-to-match solutions and that fulfill customer requirements, and enterprise ASPs that effectively capitalize on the advantages of integration and customization capabilities, are the models that appear most likely to remain and prosper in the future.

There are early indications that the most promise for the future global ASP industry lies in effective alignments between today's best-practice ASPs and other service providers that complement the ASP value chain. Such alignments are expected to produce some of the strongest models for application service provision in the post-shakeout market (Lepeak, 2001). In addition, given the results of field research and the analysis of existing models, other strong models are expected to result from the combination of best-practice enterprise ASP functions with the vertical-market customer selection process, probably the best match among current ASP models. Actually, market growth through 2005 is expected to be most rapid for vertical-market ASPs in financial services, government, and health care—industries that are sensitive to large project capital costs, and will quickly take advantage of ASP offerings (Davison, 2001).

Research results reveal a broad consensus that future ASP developments depend on today's decisions, including strong partnership strategies and defining core competencies ("Reshaping IT," 2001; Flanagan, 2000b). Corporate decision makers have realized that successfully "e-enabling" their companies requires more than having the best technologies or the fastest implementation times. It requires working with suppliers that have a deep understanding of their specific business and can help the customer reinvent business processes to capitalize on the digital economy. It requires ASP players to be able to help customers change their organizational and business processes today to win tomorrow. Ultimately, it requires educating customers on the value of application service provision. These are the keys to ASP vendor success in the future (Gruhn, 2001). In addition, ASPs that survive the current stage of development and grow must incorporate in their business structure the customer's experience, which successful vertical-market ASPs such as Surebridge and Portera have already started doing.

Of course, technological improvements will also contribute to the expected evolution of the global ASP market. As broadband technology developments continue, and as Internet usage and e-commerce accelerate, the ASP concept is expected to become extremely appealing. Many businesses and individuals are in need of an ASP solution due to the fact that they lack the capital required for IT investments and must focus their core competencies on their strategic initiatives, and not on technology improvement, maintenance, and upgrades. As the ASP market matures and the best practices noted in today's multinational environment have the desired effect, the ASP solutions of the future will be a strong value-adding service to businesses and to their end users.

ASP Industry Consortium founder and former chairman Traver Gruen-Kennedy best summarizes the future ASP outlook as bright and an opportunity not to be missed: "We need to stop thinking about applications as something that you buy in a box and start thinking about applications as something that is a capability of doing something" (Peitsch, 2001). This statement values the revolutionary approach developed by pioneering ASPs in providing software application-related services in a new, effective, and efficient way in general, and attributes the most value to unique, creative strategies that fully match customer and market requirements in particular, because these strategies will take the ASP concept into the future and will enable the industry to grow and prosper.

References

Agilera (2001). Services. <www.agilera.com>, accessed September 23, 2004.

Allen, P. (2001a). "ASPs Hit by Job Insecurity," *Network News,* May 3.

Allen P. (2001b). "Cool Reception to Unrealistic Promises Keeps the Freeze on ASP Model," *Network News,* April 11. <www.Web.lexis-nexis.com/universe>, accessed September 23, 2004.

AMR Research Inc. (2000). "AMR Research Predicts the Enterprise Application Service Provider Market Will Reach $4.7 Billion by 2004," July 24. <www.amrresearch.com/pressroom/files/00831.asp>, accessed May 31, 2001.

Anthes, G.H. (2000). "Avoiding ASP Angst." *Computerworld,* October 16. <www.computerworld.com/managementtopics/outsourcing/story/0,10801,52410,00.html>, accessed September 23, 2004.

Arlen, G. (2000). "Great Aspirations, or Last Gasp?" *Newsbytes,* December 4.

ASP Industry Consortium (2000). "Research and Trends Within the ASP Industry," November, <www.aspindustry.org/ev-presentationFall00.cfm>, accessed October 17, 2004.

ASP Industry Consortium (2001a). "A Buyer's Guide to Application Service Provisioning," no date. <www.aspindustry.org/ASPBuyersGuide.pdf>, accessed October 17, 2004.

ASP Industry Consortium (2001b). "ASP Industry Consortium Releases Fourth Quarterly Tracking Studies," *ASP Street,* February 1. <www.aspstreet.com/pr/a.taf/idpr,16891>, accessed September 23, 2004.

ASP Industry Consortium (2001c). End-User Resources. <www.aspindustry.org>, accessed October 17, 2004.

ASP Industry Consortium (2001d). End-User Resources – Learning Station. <www.aspindustry.org/ASpire2000-LearningStation.cfm>, accessed October 17, 2004.

ASP Industry Consortium (2001e). News. <www.allaboutasp.org/builder.asp?cname=pr-18May01.htm>, accessed October 17, 2004.

ASP Industry Consortium (2001f). Site Resources. <www.allaboutasp.org>, accessed October 17, 2004.

ASP Industry Consortium and World Intellectual Property Organization Arbitration and Mediation Center (ASPIC-WIPO) (2001). "Dispute Avoidance and Resolution Best Practices for the Application Services Provider Industry," May. <arbiterwipo.int/asp/report/pdf/report.pdf>, accessed October 17, 2004.

ASPInsights (2001). "Second Generation ASPs – Part III," March 15. <www.aspinsights.com/docs/white_books>, accessed October 9, 2004.

ASPnews (2001a). ASP Case Studies. <www.aspnews.com>, accessed October 9, 2004.

ASPnews (2001b). "June ASPnews Top 20," June 6. <www.aspnews.com/top50/article.php/11307_860951> accessed October 7, 2004.

ASPnews (2001c). ASP Directory – ASP types. <www.aspnews.com/directory/article/0,4231_384921,00.html>, accessed October 7, 2004.

ASPscope (2001a). "EU Data Laws Behind the Times," April 10. <www.aspscope.cpm/articles/1229.htm>, accessed October 7, 2004.

ASPscope (2001b). "Survey Results Show ASPs on the Move," April 10. <www.aspscope.com/article/2026.htm>, accessed October 7, 2004.

ASPstreet (2001). ASP Directory. <www.aspstreet.com/directory>, accessed October 7, 2004.

AT&T (2001). "AT&T, IBM, and Lotus Create ASP Enablement Suite," January 16. <www.att.com/press/item/0,1354,3608,00.html>, accessed October 7, 2004.

Aun, F. and Sperling, E. (2000). "ASPs Profitable? Not Even Close," *ZDNet.com*, October 24. <www.zdnet.com/enterprise/stories/main/0,10228,2644186,00.html>, accessed October 7, 2004.

Bendor-Samuel, P. and Goolsby, K. (2000). "Evaluating Excellence: A Report on Emerging Standards of Quality for ASPs," *Outsourcing Center*, February. <www.outsourcing_research.com/banners/outsourcing_center/evaluatingexcellence.pdf>, accessed October 7, 2004.

Bernard, A. (2001a). "Bad Economy Not Paying Off for ASPs," *ASPnews*, August 31. <www.aspnews.com/trends/article.php/877201>, accessed October 7, 2004.

Bernard, A. (2001b). "Discover the Secret of Surebridge's Success," *ASPnews*, March 5. <www.aspnews.com/strategies/article.php/704381>, accessed October 7, 2004.

Bernard, A. (2001c). "Marketing Is Everything," *ASPnews*, August 1. <www.aspnews.com/trends/article.php/858351>, accessed October 7, 2004.

Bernard, A. (2001d). "Net-Native and Loving It," *ASPnews*, June 21. <www.aspnews.com/trends/article.php/789291>, accessed October 7, 2004.

BlueStar Solutions (2001). Service Offerings. <www.bluestarsolutions.com>, accessed October 7, 2004.

Bolding, J. (2001). "Service Providers As the Operating Systems of the Future," *NetworkWorldFusion*, June 11. <www.nwfusion.com/newsletters/asp/2001/00872844.html>, accessed October 12, 2004.

Bonasera, J. (2000). "AMR Research Predicts the Enterprise Application Service Provider Market Will Reach $4.7 Billion by 2004," *AMR Research*, August 31. <www.amrresearch.com/Content/View.asp?pmillid=13391&docid=970>, accessed September 23, 2004.

Booz-Allen and Hamilton (2001). "CyberCarriers Enablers of the Networked Economy," April 6. <www.lucent.com/livelink/129191_Whitebook.pdf>, accessed October 12, 2004.

Borck, J.R. (2000). "Customers Can Really Find Happiness with the Application Service Provider Model," *InfoWorld*, December 11, p. 66.

Borck, J.R. (2001). "Selecting a Good ASP Is Daunting but If You Find the Right Factors, the Benefits Are Great," *InfoWorld*, March 19, p. 62.

Boyd, J. (2001). "Not Dead Yet – Think ASPs Make No Sense? Think Again," *Internet Week*, issue 857, April 16, p. 1.

Bradbury, D. (2001). "What Does It Take to Be a Good ASP?" *Computer Weekly*, March 15. <www.computerweekly.com/articles/article.asp?liArticleID=27067

&liArticleTypeID=20&liCategoryID=2&liChannelID=16&liFlavourID=1&s Search=&nPage=1#>, accessed October 12, 2004.

Brewin, B. (2001). "Hotel Chain Becomes Its Own Service Provider," *Computerworld,* volume 35, issue 32, October 15, p. 10.

Bucholtz, C. (2001a). "ASPs: Where They Are, Where They're Going – A Q&A with Connectria CEO Richard Waidmann," *VARBusiness,* April 20. <www. varbusiness.com/showArticle.jhtml?articleID=18814520>, accessed October 12, 2004.

Bucholtz, C. (2001b). "The Fate of Pure-Play ASPs – A Q&A with Qwest Cyber. Solutions CEO John Charters," *VARBusiness,* April 23. <www.varbusiness.com/ showArticle.jhtml?articleID=18823328>, accessed October 12, 2004.

Burrows, P. (2000). "Technology on Tap," *Business Week,* issue 3686, June 19, p. 74.

Business2.com (2001). Successes. Employease Case Study. <www.business2.com/ whatworks/entry/1,1981,2556,FF.htm>, accessed October 8, 2004.

Chamberlin, T. (2001). "Secrets of Survivoirs," *VARBusiness,* April 13. <www. varbusiness.com/showArticle.jhtml?articleID=18813885>, accessed October 12, 2004.

Christensen, C.M. (1997). *The Innovator's Dilemma.* Boston, MA: Harvard Business Press.

CIO.com (2000). "The Value of Opting for an ASP," October 1. <www.cio.com/ sponsors/1000_asp/index.html>, September 23, 2004.

CIO.com (2001). "Caution: ASPs Ahead," January. <www.cio.com/archive/011501/ et_predictions_content.html>, accessed October 12, 2004.

Cirillo, R. (2001). "An ASP by Any Other Name Is Just As Confusing," *VARBusiness,* April 13. <www.varbusiness.com/showArticle.jhtml?articleID= 18823038>, accessed October 12, 2004.

Citrix (2001a). "Focusing on Top-Line Growth Through ASP," Enerline Restorations Inc. Customer Profile. <www.citrix.com>, accessed October 12, 2004.

Citrix (2001b). "Moving at the Speed of Business with ASP," Confex ASA Customer Profile. <www.citrix.com>, accessed October 12, 2004.

Clancy, H. (2000). "CRN ASP Roundtable 2000 – Consolidation Is on the Way," *Computer Reseller News,* May 1.

Compaq (2001). Solutions. <h18000.www1.hp.com/>, accessed October 12, 2004.

Corbett, M. F. (2000). "e-Sourcing the Corporation: Harnessing the Power of Web-Based Application Service Providers," *Fortune,* courtesy of Industry Consortium, volume 141, issue 5, March 6. <www.aspindustry.org/fortunesupp.pdf>, accessed October 12, 2004.

Corio (2001a). Products. <www.corio.com>, accessed October 12, 2004.

Corio (2001b). Solutions. <www.corio.com>, accessed October 12, 2004.

Davison, D. (2001). "ASPS: Many Today, Some Tomorrow," *ASPnews,* July 26. <www.aspnews.com/analysis/analyst_cols/article.php/809671>, accessed October 12, 2004.

Dering, B. (2001a). "ASP Veterans Identify Success Factors," *ASPnews,* no date. <www.aspnews.com/analysis/analyst_cols/article.php/376121>, accessed October 12, 2004.

Dering, B. (2001b). "ASPS: Which Will Survive?" *ASPnews,* March 15. <www.aspnews.com/analysis/analyst_cols/article.php/539121>, accessed October 12, 2004.

"Ebusiness: The Analyst's View: Make Sure Your ASP Is the Real Thing" (2001). *Computing,* April 12, p. 17.

Employease.com (2001). Solutions. <www.employease.com>, accessed October 12, 2004.

Euronet (2000). "Application Service Provision: Wonder Drug or Quack Medicine," October. <www.findarticles.com/p/articles/mi_xgo/is_200010/ai_goli020822522 8000000000000>, accessed October 12, 2004.

Exult (2001a). Products and Services. <was4.hewitt.com/hewitt/>, accessed October 12, 2004.

Exult (2001b). Services Overview. <was4.hewitt.com/hewitt/>, accessed October 12, 2004.

eZigma (2001). Services. <www.e-zigma.com>, accessed October 12, 2004.

Flanagan, E.B. (2000a). "ASPs Strive for Acceptance," *VARBusiness,* December 11.

Flanagan, E.B. (2000b). "Today's ASP: Who Are You," *VARBusiness,* September 18.

Flanagan, E.B. (2001). "The Evolving ASP," *VARBusiness,* April 16.

Fonseca, B. and Jones, J. (2001). "Outsourcers Go Big," *Infoworld,* January 29, p. 48.

Foran, T. (2001). "Security Main Fear of ASP Customers: Survey," *CIO Canada,* February, volume 9, issue 2, p. 14.

Forbes.com (2001). "Qwest Cyber.Solutions Offers Industry-Leading Service Levels," *Forbes eBusiness Series,* no date.

Foremski, T. (2000). "Outsourced Hosting Services: Clients Can Focus on Their Core Activities," *Financial Times – ASP Focus Special Report,* May 17, p. 6.

Fortune.com (2001). "E-Health: Building a Virtual Infrastructure for Health Care," no date. <www.fortune.com/site . . . ctions/fortune/science/2001_3ehlth2.htm>, accessed October 12, 2004.

Fujitsu Siemens (2001). Products and Services. <www.fujitsu-siemens.com>, accessed October 12, 2004.

Fullscope (2001). Products and Services. <www.fullscope.com>, accessed October 12, 2004.

FutureLink (2001). Solutions. <www.futurelink.net/default1.asp>, accessed October 12, 2004.

Gartner Group (1999). "Gartner Group's Dataquest Says Application Service Provider Market to Surpass $22 Billion by 2003," October 25. <www3.gartner. com/5_about/press_room/pr19991025.html>, accessed October 12, 2004.

Gartner Group (2001a). "Explore the Digital Future – A Quarterly Report from Infinium," no date. <www.gartner.com/webletter/infinium/index.html>, accessed April 17.

Gartner Group (2001b). "Perspectives for Progress Newsletter," <www.prog-ress.com/aspconnections/news/gartner_newsletter.htm>, accessed September 26.

"Gathering Steam," (2001). *The Economist,* U.S. Edition, April 14.

Gerwig, K. (2001). "Friends in High Places—ASPs Fighting for Survival Are Making Deals with Other Vendors, but to Whose Advantage?" *tele.com,* January 8.

Gibbons, L. (2001). "Picking a Winner," *Network World,* January 22.

Gillan, C., Graham, S., Levitt, M., McArthur, J., Murray, S., Turner, V., Villars, R., and McCarthy Whalen, M. (1999). "The ASP's Impact on the IT Industry: An IDC-Wide Opinion," *International Data Corporation (IDC)*, September. <www.amsys.net/pdf/idpwhitepaper.pdf>, accessed September 23, 2004.

Gilmore, T. (2000a). "ASP Evolution: Enter the Aggregator," *IDC ASP Advisor*, April 12. <www.idc.com/aspadvisor/aa2000-04-12.htm>, accessed October 12, 2004.

Gilmore, T. (2000b). "ASPs: At Home in the UK," *IDC ASP Advisor*, December 20. <www.idc.com/aspadvisor/aa20001220.stm>, accessed October 12, 2004.

Gilmore, T. (2000c). "Is the ASP Sector Collapsing?" *IDC ASP Advisor*, October 18. <www.idc.com:8080/ASPADVISOR/aa20010117.htm>, accessed October 12, 2004.

Gilmore, T. (2000d). "It's All About Choices," *IDC ASP Advisor*, November 8. <www.idc.com/aspadvisor/aa20001108.stm>, accessed October 12, 2004.

Gilmore, T. (2000e). "A Mountain of Windows," *IDC ASP Advisor*, August 9.

Gilmore, T. (2000f). "Personal ASPs: Riding in Microsoft's Slipstream," *ISC ASP Advisor*, September 27. <www.idc.com/aspadvisor/aa20000927.stm>, accessed October 12, 2004.

Gilmore, T. (2000g). "Security: Can Your ASP Hack It?" *IDC ASP Advisor*, November 22. <www.idc.com/aspadvisor/aa20001122.stm>, accessed October 12, 2004.

Gilmore, T. (2001a). "Application Management Companies: Friend or Foe for ASPs?" *IDC ASP Advisor*, March 21. <www.idc.com:8080/ASPADVISOR/aa20010321.htm>, accessed October 12, 2004.

Gilmore, T. (2001b). "IBM Transforms ISVs with ASP Prime," *IDC ASP Advisor*, February 28 and March 15. <www.itaa.org/ASP/idcadvisor/ aa20010228.stm>, accessed October 12, 2004.

Gilmore, T. (2001c). "Top ASPs: What It Takes to Win Today and Tomorrow," *ITAA ASP Resources*, May. <www.itaa.org/ASP/idcadvisormay01.htm>, accessed October 12, 2004.

Gold, S. (2001). "EC Data Protection Laws Not Keeping Up, Says ASP Group," *Newsbytes*, March 6.

Goldman, J. (2000). "TriZetto: The Leading Healthcare ASP," *ASP Island*, May. <www.aspisland.com/focus/trizetto.asp>, accessed September 10, 2004.

Greenemeier, L. and Maselli, J. (2001). "Specialized Service Providers, from ASPs to Z," *Information Week*, February 5. <www.informationweek.com/823/prout.htm>, accessed October 13, 2004.

Gruhn, M. (2001). "New Game, New Rules," *Summit Strategies' Summit Vision*, Volume 3, April. <www.summitstrat.com>, accessed October 13, 2004.

Hall, M. (2000). "ASPs in the Catbird Seat," *Computerworld*, November 13, volume 34, issue 36, p. S14.

Harrington, A. (2001). "IT Decisions; ASPs Future of ASPs Is in Trust," *Financial Director*, April 10, p. 15.

Haskins, M.L. (2000). "Making Sense of the ASP Market," *Billing World*, June. <www.billingworld.com>, accessed October 13, 2004.

Howarth, B. (1999). "Outsourcing: Technology on Tap," *Information Economy*, December 12. <www.brw.com.au/newsadmin/stories/brw/19991203/4335.htm>, accessed October 30, 2000.

Hunter, P. (2001). "Can Enterprise IT Departments Learn from ASPs?" ASP Network World, August 23. <www.aspworldnet.com/Tmpl/print.asp?CID=9&AID=7592&Tcode=FT>, accessed September 25.

iFuel (2001). Products. <www.irevolution.com/>, accessed October 13, 2004.

Imp@ct-it (2001). "ASP Technology Overview," no date. <www.impact-it.net/Pages/tech_asp.html>, accessed October 13, 2004.

Interliant (2001a). Products and Services. <www.navisite.com/messaging-services.cfm>, October 13, 2004.

Interliant (2001b). Solutions. <www. navisite.com/messaging-services.cfm>, October 13, 2004.

Interpath (2001). Products and Services. <www.usi.net/>, accessed October 13, 2004.

Investquest (2000). "Qwest Cyber.Solutions and ADP to Combine Enterprise ASP-Services with Best Practice Payroll Solutions," November 23. <www.investquest.com/iq/a/aud/ne/news/audcombine.htm>, accessed September 28, 2001.

ITAA (Information Technology Association of America) (2000). "The ITAA Customer Demand Survey," May. <www.itaa.org/asp/reportwp/aspwpl.pdf>, accessed October 13, 2004.

ITAA (Information Technology Association of America) (2001a). "ASP Customers: Hear What They Are Saying," September. <www.itaa.org/asp/idcadvisor0901.htm>, accessed October 1.

ITAA (Information Technology Association of America) (2001b). "Interliant Offers Real-Time Performance Monitoring Service for INIT Managed Hosting Solutions," July 25. <www.itaa.org/asp/ASPHeadline.cfm?ReleaseID=84155120>, accessed October 13, 2004.

ITAA (Information Technology Association of America) (2001c). "Interliant's Remote Monitored Firewall Service Gives Customers a Security Safety Net," August 21. <www.itaa.org/asp/ASPHeadline.cfm?ReleaseID=1553093092>, accessed October 13, 2004.

Jamcracker (2001a). Solutions. <www.jamcracker.com>, accessed October 13, 2004.

Jamcracker (2001b). Success Story: B2B Works, Inc. <www.jamcracker.com/customersoverview.htm>, accessed October 13, 2004.

Kersnar, S. (2001). "Which ASP Model Will Work?" *Mortgage Technology*, May, volume 8, number 4, p. 29.

Kerstetter, J. (2001). "Software Shakeout," *Business Week*, March 15, 2001, p. 72.

Kilgore, S. (2000). "Debunking the ASP-Integrator Divide," *Forrester Research*, September 29. <www.applicationplanet.com/facts/DebunkingASP.pdf.>, accessed October 13, 2004.

Knight, A. (2001). "Judgement Day for ASPs Edges Closer," *Computer Weekly*, April 12, p. 24.

Koch, C. (2000). "Boy, That Was Fast!" *CIO Magazine*, November 15.

Komiega, K. (2001). "Storage Decisions 2001 Q&A: The State of SSPS," *searchStorage.com,* September 28. <searchstorage.techtarget.com/qna/0,289202,sid5_gci773039,00.html>, accessed October 13, 2004.

Ladley, E. (2000). "When Should an ASP Outsource?" *ISP Business News,* volume 6, number 40.

Laudon, K.C. and Laudon, J. P. (2001). *Management Information Systems: Managing the Digital Firm,* Seventh Edition. Saddle River, NJ: Prentice-Hall.

LearningStation.com (2001a). Products. <www.learningstation.com>, accessed October 13, 2004.

LearningStation.com (2001b). Services. <www.learningstation.com>, accessed October 13, 2004.

Ledford, J.L. (2000). "With Right Niche and Market, ASPs Can Find Comfort in Aggregation," ASPStreet.com, November 20. <www.aspstreet.com/archive/d.taf/sid,1,11,14,21/id,5043>, accessed October 13, 2004.

Lepeak, S. (2001). "Is Tomorrow Still Hot for the ASP Channel?" *VARBusiness,* February 19.

Lipschultz, D. (2001). "Application Service Providers—Cash-Strapped Companies More Receptive to Industry Survivors," *Internet Week,* July 9. <www.internetweek.com/indepth01/indepth070201.htm>, accessed October 15, 2004.

Luening, E. (2001). "New Report Says ASP Model Isn't So Gloomy After All," <news.zdnet.com/2100-9595_22-528795.html>, accessed October 15, 2004.

Mark, R. (2001). "Outtask Acquires Aspen's ASP Hosting Division." <www.internetnews.com/xSP/article.php/855991>, accessed October 15, 2004.

Marks, R. (2001). "An Analysis of the ASP Delivery Model," <www.aspscope.com/articles/1238.htm>, accessed October 15, 2004.

Maselli, J. (2000a). "ASPs Seek to Hone Vertical Industry Expertise," *Information Week,* December 18, issue 817, p. 30.

Maselli, J. (2000b). "The Great Compromise," *Information Week,* November 27. <www.informationweek.com/814/global.htm>, accessed October 15, 2004.

Maselli, J. (2000c). "Growing Pains," *Information Week,* July 24. <www.informationweek.com/796/asp.htm>, accessed October 15, 2004.

Mateyaschuk, J. (2000). "Biggest Challenge? Find the Right Niche," *Information Week,* March 27. <www.informationweek.com/779/ssvendor.htm>, accessed October 15, 2004.

McCabe, L. (2001). "Microsoft's New Gold Standard: Certified Partners for Hosting, Applications Services," *Summit Strategies' Summit Vision,* Volume 3, April. <www.summitstrat.com>, accessed October 15, 2004.

McCausland, L. (2001). "Application Hosting Prepares for Loft-Off," *Accounting Technology,* March.

Mears, J. (2001a). "ASPs and Multiple Apps: Tying Things Together," *Network World,* March 12. <www.nwfusion.com/news/2001/0312specialfocus.html>, accessed October 14, 2004.

Mears, J. (2001b). "ASPs Get Back to Basics; Trim Staff to Cut Costs," *Network World Fusion,* January 22.

Mears, J. (2001c). "IDC: USi Leads Worldwide ASP Market," *Network World Fusion*, April 18. <www.nwfusion.com/news/2001/0418asplist.html>, accessed October 14, 2004.

Mears, J. (2001d). "IT Department Can Be Hurdle to ASP Acceptance; End Users Get Advice," *Network World Fusion*, January 11. <www.nwfusion.com/news/2001/0111aspit.html>, accessed October 14, 2004.

Mears, J. (2001e). "SLA Picture Clearing Up for ASP Users," *Network World*, January 15. <www.nwfusion.com/archive/2001/00290794.html>, accessed October 14, 2004.

Mears, J. (2001f). "Top ASP Execs Embrace Shakeout, Look to Future," *Network World Fusion*, May 24. <www.nwfusion.com/news/2001/0524topasp.html>, accessed October 14, 2004.

Mi8 (2001). Services. <www.mi8.com>, accessed October 14, 2004.

Microsoft Enterprise Services (2001). Capacity Management for ASPs. Contingency Management for ASPs. Security Management for ASPs. <www.microsoft.com>, accessed October 14, 2004.

Mizoras, A. (2001). "ASPs Are Getting Down to eBusiness," *International Data Corporation*, June. <www.idc.com>, accessed October 14, 2004.

Moran, N. (2000). "Seductive Software Services on Offer," *Financial Times—ASP Focus Special Report*, May 17.

Moran, N. (2001). "After Early Hype, ASP Market Proves Hard to Crack," *Financial Times—Information Technology Special Report*, July 1.

NetLedger (2001). Solutions. <www.netledger.com>, accessed June 1, 2001.

Netsuite (2001). Solutions. <www.netsuite.com>, accessed October 14, 2004.

Newcomb, K. (2001a). "ASP Awareness High, Usage Low," *InternetNews*, June 27. <www.internetnews.com/xSP/article.php/792921>, accessed October 14, 2004.

Newcomb, K. (2001b). "Consortium's ASP Tracking Study Released," *ASPnews*, August 16. <www.aspnews.com/news/weekly/article.php/867291>, accessed October 7, 2004.

Newcomb, K. (2001c). "Enterprise ASP Spending on the Rise," *ASPNews*, July 9. <www.aspnews.com/trends/article.php/797511>, accessed October 14, 2004.

Newcomb, K. (2001d). "Interpath Acquires Interliant's ERP Division," *InternetNews*, July 24. <www.internetnews.com/xSP/article.php/807221>, accessed October 14, 2004.

Newcomb, K. (2001e). "Jamcracker: More Than an Aggregator," *ASPNews*, July 24. <www.aspnews.com/strategies/companies/article.php/806731>, accessed October 14, 2004.

Newing, R. (2001a). "How 'Pay As You Go' Systems Cuts IT Costs," *Financial Times—ASP Focus Special Report*, May 17.

Newing, R. (2001b). "Plain Vanilla Solutions Are No Longer Enough," *Financial Times*, July 4.

Newing, R. (2001c). "Wednesday Survey—FT Telecoms," *Financial Times*, March 21.

Newswire (2001). "ASPs Hit by Job Insecurity," May 3. <www.Web.lexis=nexis.com/universe>, accessed May 15, 2001.

Nicolle, L. (2000). "ASP, the IT Messiah?" *Computer Weekly,* December 7. <www.computerweekly.com/articles/article.asp?liArticleID=21674>, accessed October 14, 2004.

Oracle (2001). Solutions. <www.oracle.com>, accessed October 14, 2004.

Outtask (2001). Products. <www.outtask.com>, accessed October 14, 2004.

Ovum (2000). "Huge Opportunities for Service Providers, Telecos and ISPs." February 2. <www.ovum.com/press/pressreleases/defaultasp?wp=ASP.htm>, accessed October 14, 2004.

Panker, J. (2001). "New Healthcare Regulations: Are ASPs Just What the Doctor Ordered?", *SearchCIO.com,* July 26. <searchcio.techtarget.com/qna/0,289202, sid19_gci819288,00.html>, accessed October 14, 2004.

Parizo, E. (2001a). "Analyst Gives Survival Edge to Vertical ASPs," *SearchxSP.com,* February 2. <searchserviceprovide . . . com/qna/0,289202,sid28 _gci519264,00.html>, accessed October 13, 2004.

Parizo, E. (2001b). "Microsoft Demystifies Its ASP Plans," *searchCIO.com,* October 17, 2004. <searchcio.techtarget.com/newsItem/0,289139,gci763884,00. html>, accessed October 13, 2004.

Parizo, E. (2001c). "USi's Stern: ASP Size Matters," *searchCIO.com,* May 30. <searchserviceprovide . . . com/qna/0,289202,sid28_gci555912,00.html>, accessed October 17, 2004.

Pastore, M. (2000). "ASP Gaining Awareness, Following Dot-Com Path," *Clickz.com,* November 9. <www.clickz.com/stats/big_picture/applications/article. php/507791>, accessed September 23, 2004.

Paul, L. (2001a). "ASP Success Stories—Rochester Institute of Technology," *ASPIsland.com,* no date. <www.aspisland.com/success/rit1.asp>, accessed October 13, 2004.

Paul, L. (2001b). "The State of the ASP Market," *ASPNews,* April 11. <www. aspnews.com/strategies/industries/article.php/740821>, accessed July 22.

PC Dealer (2001). "ASP is Dead, Long Live ASP," May 2.

Peitsch, C. (2001). "ASP Consortium Chair Shares Insight on ASP Market," *ASPconnection.com,* May 2001, Special Report. <www.aspconnection.com/ SRPrint.asp. . . 5&type=A&folder=SR0501&SRdATE=05/01/2000.htm>, accessed September 5.

"Play the ASP Survivor Games to Win with the Newly Released Survival Guide from Zanthus" (2001). *Business Wire,* June 12, p. 1.

Portera (2001). Solutions. <www.portera.com>, accessed October 13, 2004.

Pring, B. (2000). "ASP-Quicksilver Rather Than Gold?" *ASPnews.com,* no date. <www.aspnews.com/analysis/analyst_cols/article.php/375951>, accessed October 13, 2004.

PR Newswire (2000). "Study Says Larger Companies Will Account for Majority of ASP Market," September 12.

PR Newswire (2001). "Fullscope Redefines ASP Market with Niche Offering for Engineering Services," May 7.

Qwest Communications (2001). Resources. <www.qwest.com>, accessed October 13, 2004.

Qwest Cyber.Solutions (2001a). Press Room. <www.qwestcybersolutions.com/qwest_home.htm>, accessed October 13, 2004.

Qwest Cyber.Solutions (2001b). Products. <www.qwestcybersolutions.com/qwest_home.htm>, accessed October 13, 2004.

"Reshaping IT" (2001). *VARBusiness,* January 22, p. 5.

Rosenthal, B.E. (2001). "Revenues Determine Rating," *Outsourcing-journal.com,* June. <www.outsourcing-journal.com/issues/jun2001/asp-2.html>, accessed October 13, 2004.

Rubens, P. (2001). "The One True ASP?" *ASPnews.com,* August 23. <www.aspnews.com/strategies/companies/print.php/871891>, accessed October 13, 2004.

Ruber, P. (2000). "Keep the Knowledge You're Paying For," *Information Week,* October 30.

Rudy, J. and Corridore, J. (2001). "Computers: Commercial Services," Standard and Poor's Industry Surveys, June 28. <www.netadvantage.standardandpoors.com/docs/indsur/pdf/ccs_0601.pdf>, accessed October 13, 2004.

Russell, J. (2001). "Surviving in the Sea of ASPs," *VARBusiness,* April 13. <www.varbusiness.com/sections/research/research.asp?ArticleID=25753>, accessed October 13, 2004.

Rutherford, E. (2000). "ABC of ASP's," *CIO.com,* June 26. <www.cio.com/forums/asp/edit/062600_abc_content.html>, accessed October 13, 2004.

Salesforce.com (2001a). News & Events. <www.salesforce.com>, accessed October 8, 2004.

Salesforce.com (2001b). Solution Showcase. <www.salesforce.com/partners/solutions.jsp>, accessed October 8, 2004.

Shand, D. (2001). "Service-Level Agreements," *Computerworld,* January 22.

Sound Consulting (2000). "Understanding the ASP Market," June. <www.siia.net/software/pubs/GASP-00.pdf>, accessed October 8, 2004.

Sovie, D. (2000). "Mercer Viewpoint: Telecoms Search for New Life in the Emerging ASP Market," *Business Wire,* October 17.

Sovie, D. and Hanson, J. (2000). "Application Service Providers: Where Are the Real Profit Zones?" Mercer Management Consulting. <www.aspindustry.org/MercerASP.pdf>, accessed March 15, 2001.

Sperling, E. (2001). "Editor's Note," *ZDNet,* June 4. <www.zdnet.com>, accessed September 5.

Stanco, T. (2000). "Application Service Providers," *Boardwatch Magazine,* October.

Stobie, I. (2000). "Management: Surviving the ASP Minefield," *Computing,* November 23.

Sun Microsystems (2001a). Sun Solutions. <www.sun.com/solutions/gateway/gateway.xml>, accessed October 8, 2004.

Sun Microsystems (2001b). SunTone Initiative. <www.suntone.org>, accessed October 8, 2004.

Surebridge (2001a). "Achieving Success in Customer Relationship Management Through the ASP Model," <www.surebridge.com/pdf/surebridge_CRM_Whitep.pdf>, accessed October 6, 2004.

Surebridge (2001b). Business Solutions.<www.surebridge.com>, accessed October 6, 2004.

Surebridge (2001c). Customers. <www.surebridge.com>, accessed October 8, 2004.

Surebridge (2001d). Robinson Nugent, Inc. Customer Profile. <www.surebridge. com>, accessed June 26.

"Surebridge Ranked Among Top 10 ASP's by International Data Corporation" (2001). *Business Wire,* May 9, p. 1.

Swoyer, S. and Maselli, J. (2000). "Application Service Providers Get Down to Business," *Information Week,* October 23.

Tally, G. (2001). "Customer Systems Integration Key to ASP Success," *ISP World,* February 22.

"Techniques: ASP Infrastructure: What Really Goes on Inside an ASP" (2000). *Computing,* October 26. <www.Web.lexis-nexis.com/universe>, accessed September 3, 2004.

TeleComputing (2001a). News. <www.TeleComputing.com>, accessed October 6, 2004.

TeleComputing (2001b). Products. <www.TeleComputing.com>, accessed October 6, 2004.

TeleComputing (2001c). Resources. <www.TeleComputing.com>, accessed September 19, 2004.

TeleComputing (2001d). "Telecomputing Announces Strategic Alliance with Safeguard to Help Customers Deploy and Manage the Microsoft .NET Framework with Speed and Ease," August 21, 2004.

Thompson A.A. and Strickland, A.J. (1999). *Strategic Management: Concept and Cases.* Boston, MA: Irwin McGraw Hill.

Toigo, J.W. (2001). "ASPs Hit the Mainstream," *Network Computing,* May 28.

Torode, C. (2000a). "ASP Pulse: Order Please! Defining the ASP Space," CRN, May 15. <www.crn.com/components/search/Article.asp?ArticleID=16670>, accessed October 5, 2004.

Torode, C. (2000b). "Will the Real ASP Please Stand Up?" *CRN,* February 15.

Torode, C. (2001). "Rising Above the ASP Shakeout," *CRN,* March 26.

Torode, C. and Hagendorf, J. (2000). "Slowdown No Sweat for ASPs—Sector Confident About Prospects," *CRN,* November 27.

Total Telecom (2001). "The European ASP Market," March 20, <itpapers.zdnet. com/abstract.aspx?&scid=90&sortby=compd&docid=12994>, accessed October 7, 2004.

TriZetto Group (2001a). Products. <www.trizetto.com>, accessed October 5, 2004.

TriZetto Group (2001b). Solutions. <www.trizetto.com>, accessed October 5, 2004.

United Messaging (2001a). Customer Case Studies. <www.unitedmessaging.com>, accessed July 31, 2001.

United Messaging (2001b). Press Room. <www.unitedmessaging.com>, accessed September 26, 2001.

United Messaging (2001c). Solutions. <www.unitedmessaging.com>, accessed July 27, 2001.

USi (2001). Solutions. <www.usi.net>, accessed October 5, 2004.

"USinternetworking Expands Data Center Capacity in Europe" (2001). *Business Wire,* April 2, p. 1.

"Vertical Service Providers to Boost Internet-Hosting Adoption Rates" (2001). *Business Wire,* April 16, p. 1.

W3Health (2001). Products. <www.w3health.com/index.html>, accessed October 5, 2004.

Wainewright, P. (2000a). "ASPire Winners Show How It's Done," InternetNews, November 15. <www.internetnews.com/xSP/print.php/3411_512631>, accessed October 5, 2004.

Wainewright, P. (2000b). "Packaged Software Rental: The Net's Killer App," *ASPnews.com,* January 30, <www.aspnews.com/analysis/article.php/375651>, accessed September 29, 2004.

Wainewright, P. (2001a). "ASPs—Masters of the Internet," *ASPnews,* May 21. <www.aspnews.com/analysis/analyst_cols/article.php/770741>, accessed October 5, 2004.

Wainewright, P. (2001b). "The ASP Value Chain," *ASPnews.com,* February 21. <www.aspnews.com/analysis/analyst_cols/article.php/584731>, accessed October 5, 2004.

Wainewright, P. (2001c). "Don't Worry, Be Happy," *ASPnews,* July 27. <www.aspnews.com/analysis/analyst_cols/article.php/855861>, accessed October 5, 2004.

Wainewright, P. (2001d). "Industry Basics: Application Service Providers," *ASPnews.com,* May 18. <www.aspnews.com/strategies/asp_basics/article.php/769151>, accessed October 5, 2004.

Whalen, M., Mizoras A., Goepfert, J., Moser, K., and Graham, S. (2001). "Worldwide ASP Forecast and Analysis 2000-2005," *IDC,* June <www.gii.co.jp/english/id7526_world_wide.html>, accessed September 29, 2004.

Whittle, S. (2001). "Management; ASPs Are Under Attack from the CyberCarriers," *Computing,* March 15.

Willan, P. (2001). "ASP Conference Stressed Need for Customer Education," *InfoWorld Daily News,* March 7.

Wohl, A. (2001). "Picking the Right ASP," *VARBusiness,* April 13. <www.varbusiness.com/article/showArticle.jhtml?articleId=18835718&_requestid=107075>, accessed October 4, 2004.

Wright, R. (2001). "ASP Pioneer Hribar Holds onto the Reins of a Runaway Market," *VARBusiness,* March 22. <www.varbusiness.com/showArticle.jhtml?articleID=18835583>, accessed October 4, 2004.

Yankee Group (2000). "Executive Summary of Applications Service Providers: Evaluating Strategies for Success." <www.yankeegroup.com>, accessed October 4, 2004.

Index

Page numbers followed by the letter "f" indicate figures; those followed by the letter "b" indicate boxed text; and those followed by the "t" indicate tables.

Order a copy of this book with this form or online at:
http://www.haworthpress.com/store/product.asp?sku=5182

APPLICATION SERVICE PROVIDERS IN BUSINESS

_____in hardbound at $39.95 (ISBN: 0-7890-2480-2)

_____in softbound at $29.95 (ISBN: 0-7890-2481-0)

Or order online and use special offer code HEC25 in the shopping cart.

COST OF BOOKS_____

☐ **BILL ME LATER:** (Bill-me option is good on US/Canada/Mexico orders only; not good to jobbers, wholesalers, or subscription agencies.)

☐ Check here if billing address is different from shipping address and attach purchase order and billing address information.

POSTAGE & HANDLING_____
(US: $4.00 for first book & $1.50 for each additional book)
(Outside US: $5.00 for first book & $2.00 for each additional book)

Signature_____

SUBTOTAL_____

☐ **PAYMENT ENCLOSED: $**_____

IN CANADA: ADD 7% GST_____

☐ **PLEASE CHARGE TO MY CREDIT CARD.**

STATE TAX_____
(NJ, NY, OH, MN, CA, IL, IN, PA, & SD residents, add appropriate local sales tax)

☐ Visa ☐ MasterCard ☐ AmEx ☐ Discover
☐ Diner's Club ☐ Eurocard ☐ JCB

Account # _____

FINAL TOTAL_____
(If paying in Canadian funds, convert using the current exchange rate, UNESCO coupons welcome)

Exp. Date_____

Signature_____

Prices in US dollars and subject to change without notice.

NAME_____

INSTITUTION_____

ADDRESS_____

CITY_____

STATE/ZIP_____

COUNTRY_____ COUNTY (NY residents only)_____

TEL_____ FAX_____

E-MAIL_____

May we use your e-mail address for confirmations and other types of information? ☐ Yes ☐ No We appreciate receiving your e-mail address and fax number. Haworth would like to e-mail or fax special discount offers to you, as a preferred customer. **We will never share, rent, or exchange your e-mail address or fax number.** We regard such actions as an invasion of your privacy.

Order From Your Local Bookstore or Directly From
The Haworth Press, Inc.
10 Alice Street, Binghamton, New York 13904-1580 • USA
TELEPHONE: 1-800-HAWORTH (1-800-429-6784) / Outside US/Canada: (607) 722-5857
FAX: 1-800-895-0582 / Outside US/Canada: (607) 771-0012
E-mailto: orders@haworthpress.com

For orders outside US and Canada, you may wish to order through your local sales representative, distributor, or bookseller.
For information, see http://haworthpress.com/distributors

(Discounts are available for individual orders in US and Canada only, not booksellers/distributors.)

PLEASE PHOTOCOPY THIS FORM FOR YOUR PERSONAL USE.
http://www.HaworthPress.com   BOF04